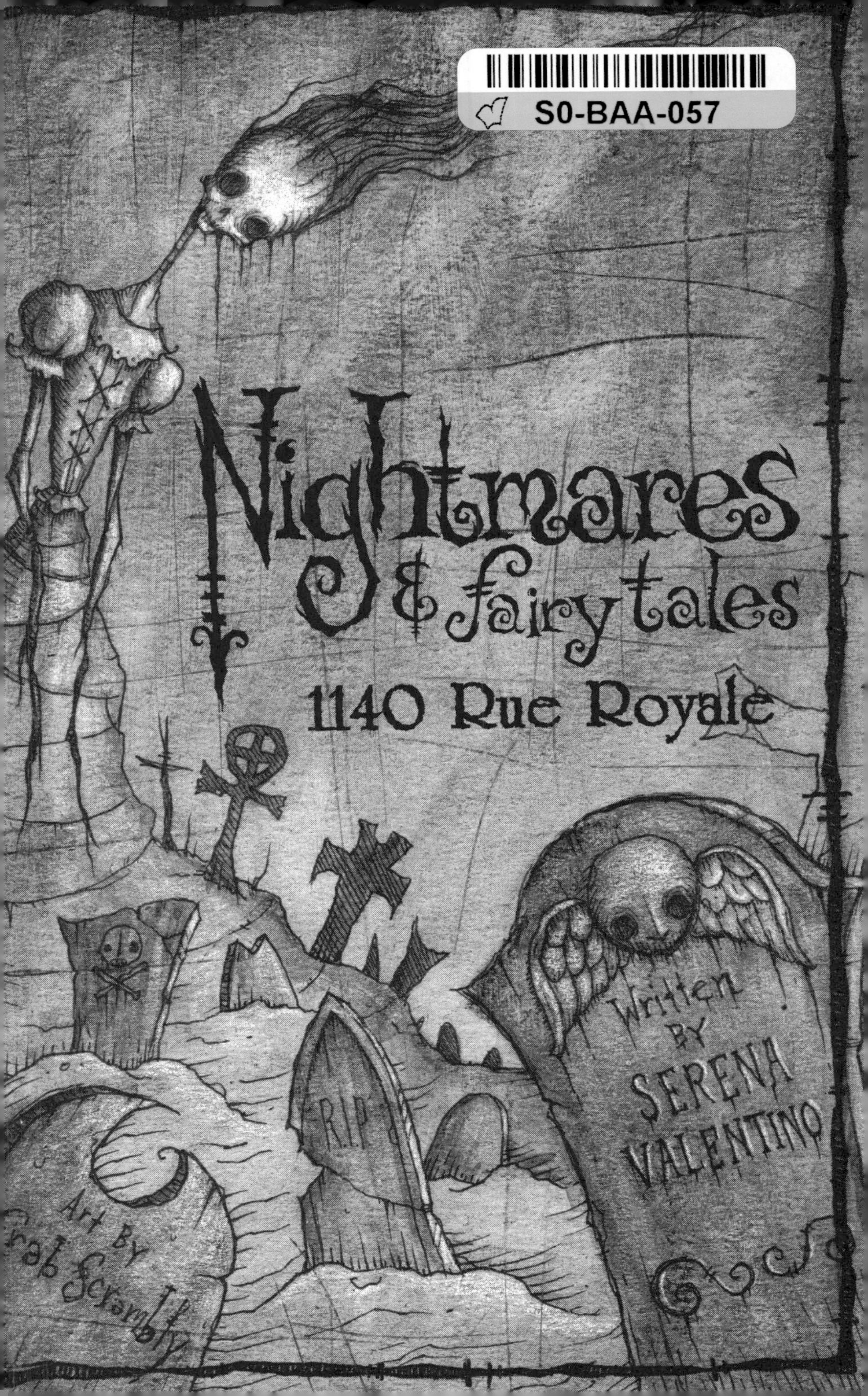
Nightmares & fairy tales
1140 Rue Royale
Written By SERENA VALENTINO
Art By Crab Scrambly
R.I.P

Nightmares & Fairy Tales

Volume Three: 1140 Rue Royale

*This tale belongs to the dead
and the house they dwell in...*

Written by
Serena Valentino

Art by
Crab Scrambly

Published by SLG Publishing

President & Publisher
Dan Vado

Editrix-in-Chief
Jennifer de Guzman

Director of Art
Scott Saavedra

SLG Publishing • P.O. Box 26427 • San Jose, CA 95159

Nightmares and Fairy Tales Volume
Three: 1140 Rue Royale reprints issues
#13 - 18 of the SLG series Nightmares
and Fairy Tales.
www.slgcomic.com

First Printing: April 2007
ISBN 978-1-59362-065-3

"Little white flowers will never awaken you,
Not where the black coach of sorrow has taken you."
—Billie Holiday, "Gloomy Sunday"

Dedicated to my sister Jesse.

And to this beautiful and frightening new universe and all that it brings.

-Serena

Crab Scrambly would like to dedicate this book to Ish, who always believed in him.

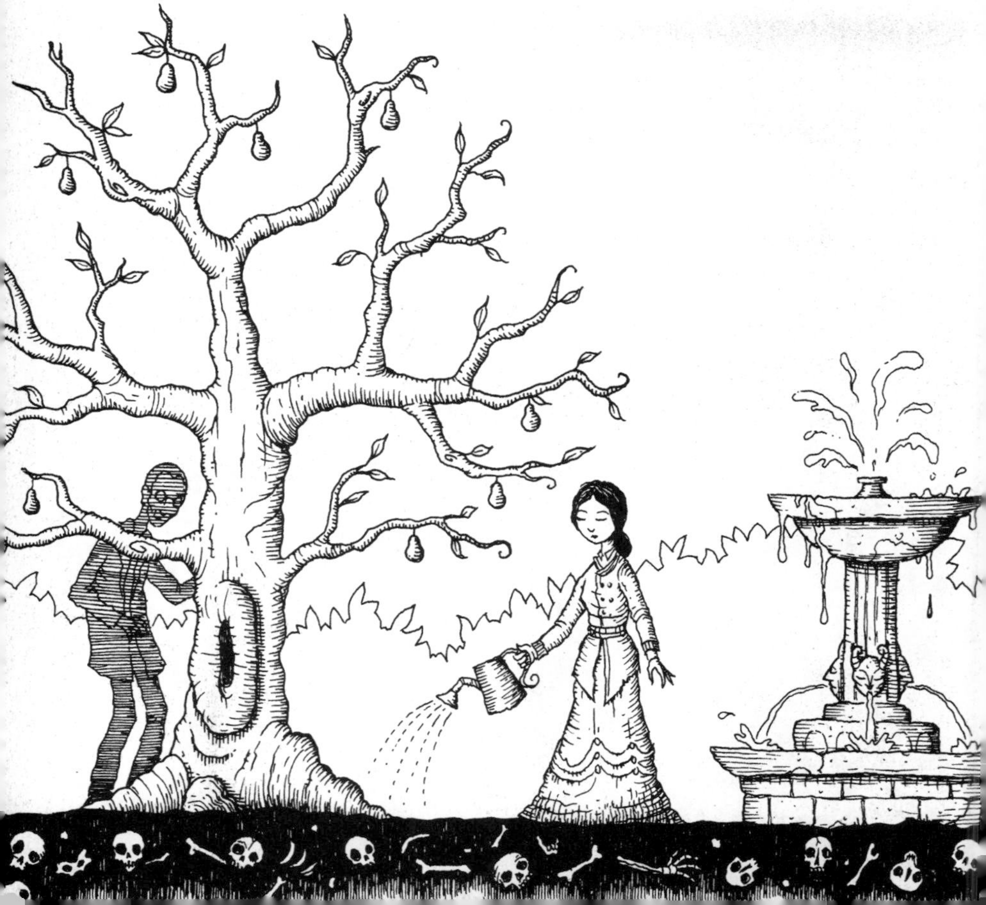

A Word
from the Author

There is a truth embedded within the layers of fiction that fill this volume. There is a lesson to be learned and a horror to be revealed, lurking there in the shadows of our darkest times in history.

Nightmares & Fairy Tales: 1140 Rue Royale is a work of fiction inspired by historical events. It was not written to exploit or trivialize this manner of human suffering and atrocities — rather, I am rewriting history in an attempt at giving the victims a voice, a means for revenge and serenity.

Serena Valentino

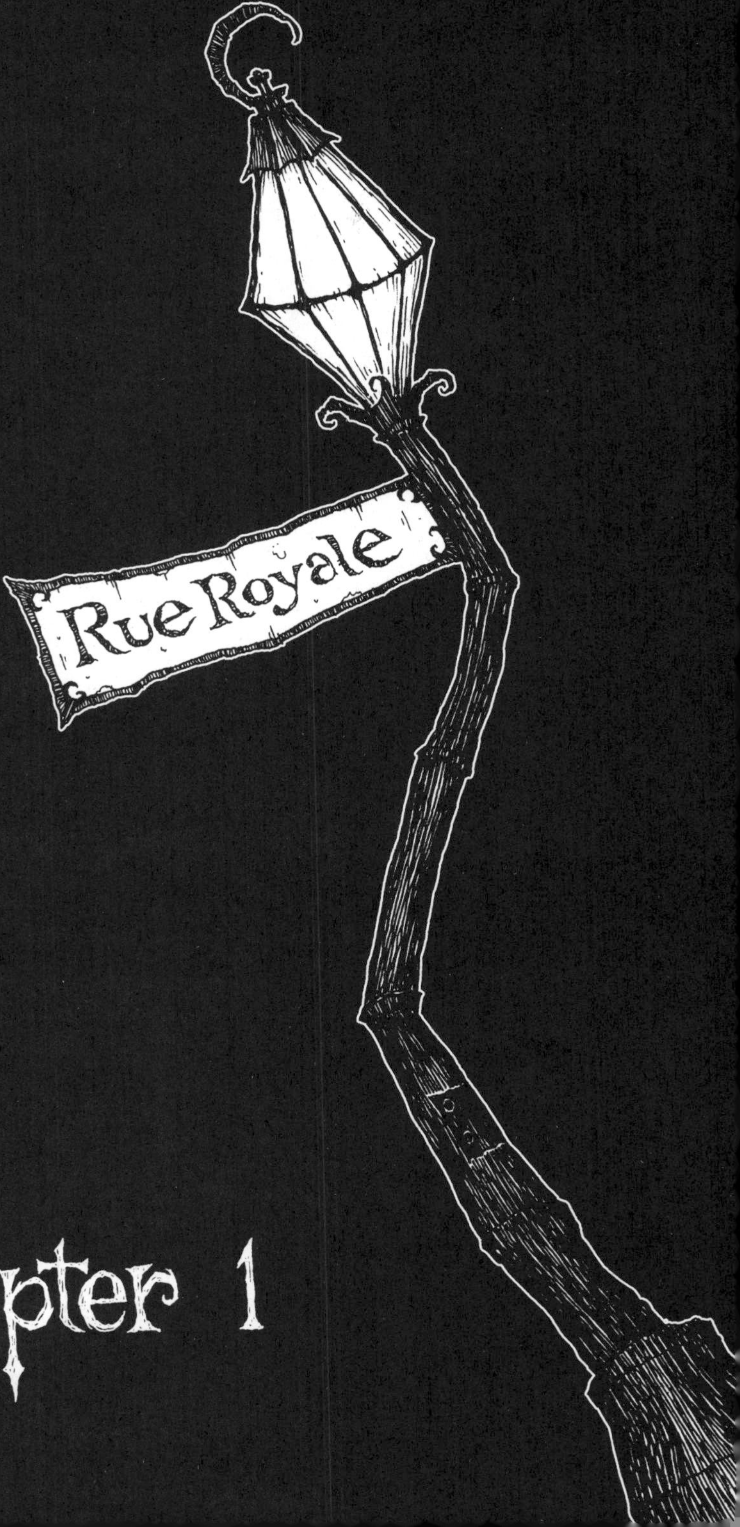
Rue Royale

Chapter 1

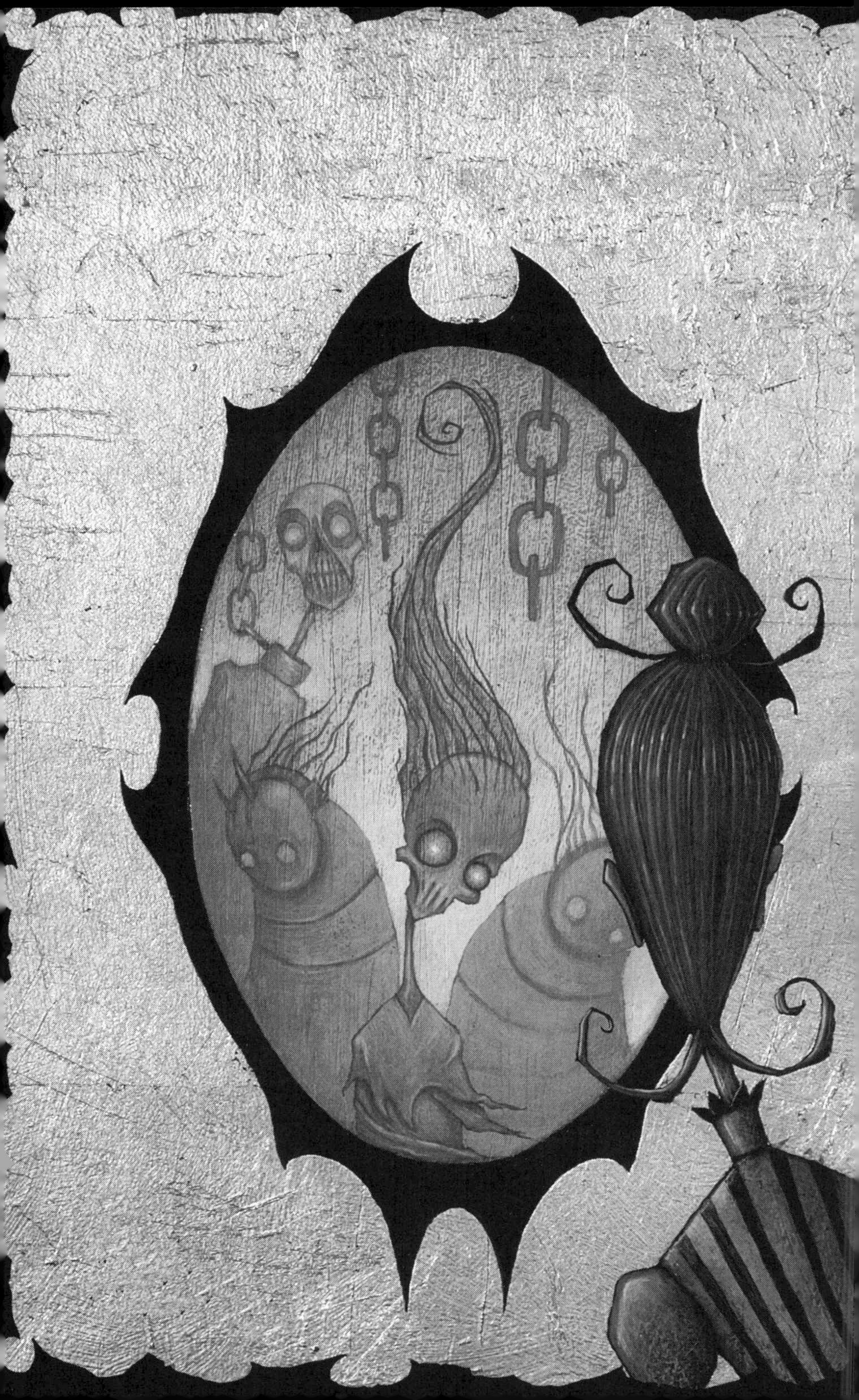

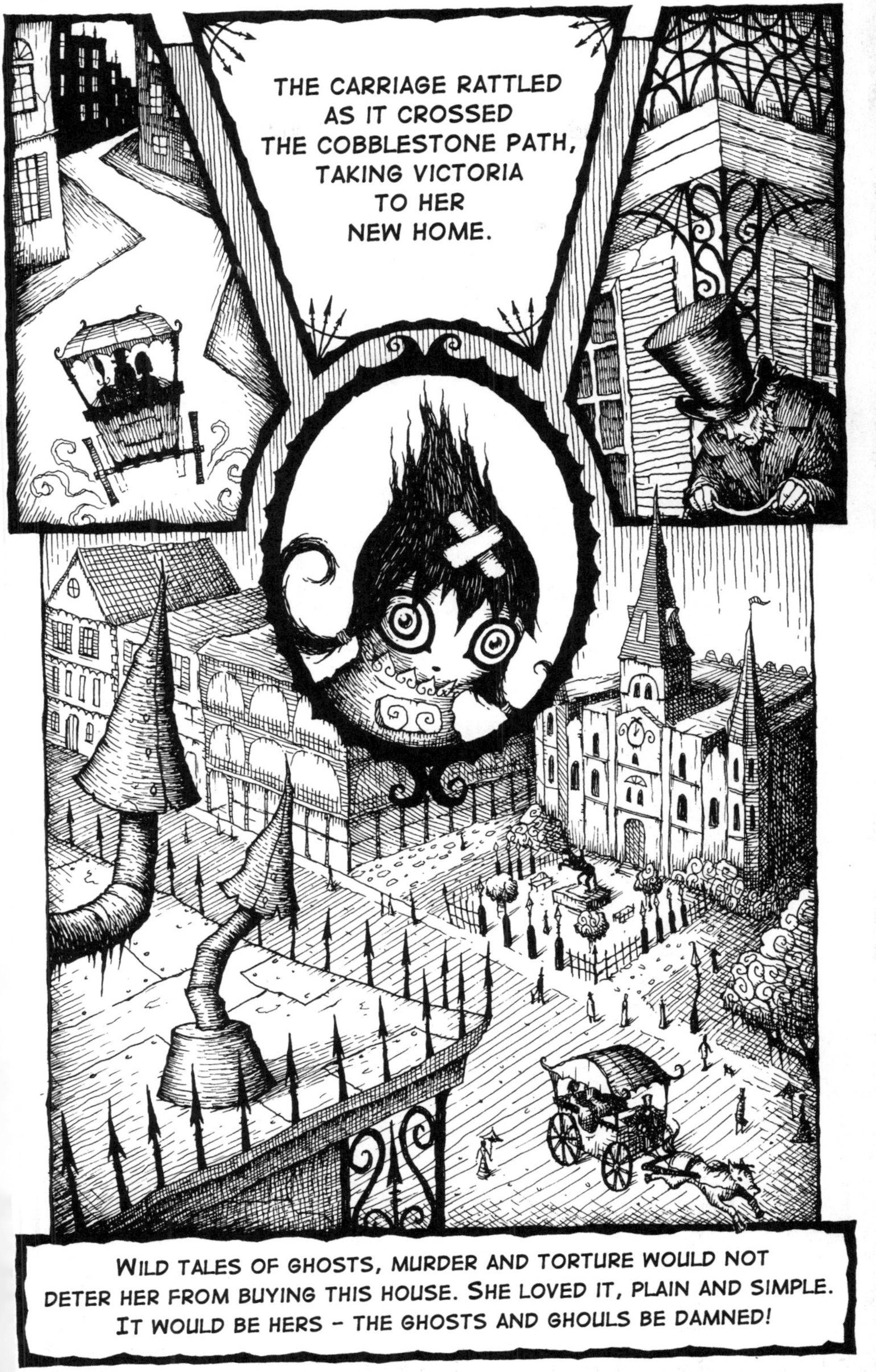
THE CARRIAGE RATTLED AS IT CROSSED THE COBBLESTONE PATH, TAKING VICTORIA TO HER NEW HOME.
WILD TALES OF GHOSTS, MURDER AND TORTURE WOULD NOT DETER HER FROM BUYING THIS HOUSE. SHE LOVED IT, PLAIN AND SIMPLE. IT WOULD BE HERS - THE GHOSTS AND GHOULS BE DAMNED!

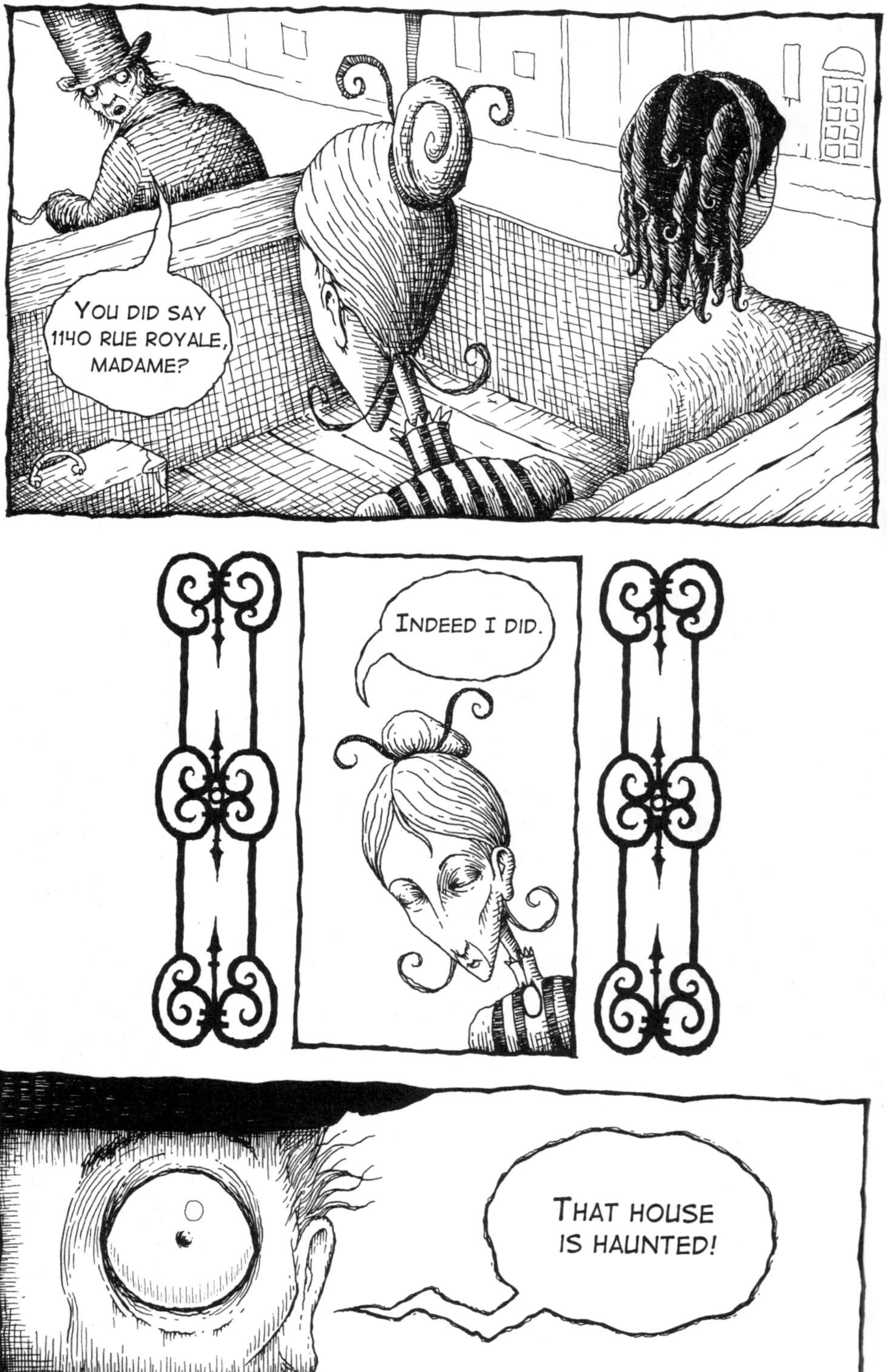
YOU DID SAY 1140 RUE ROYALE, MADAME?
INDEED I DID.
THAT HOUSE IS HAUNTED!

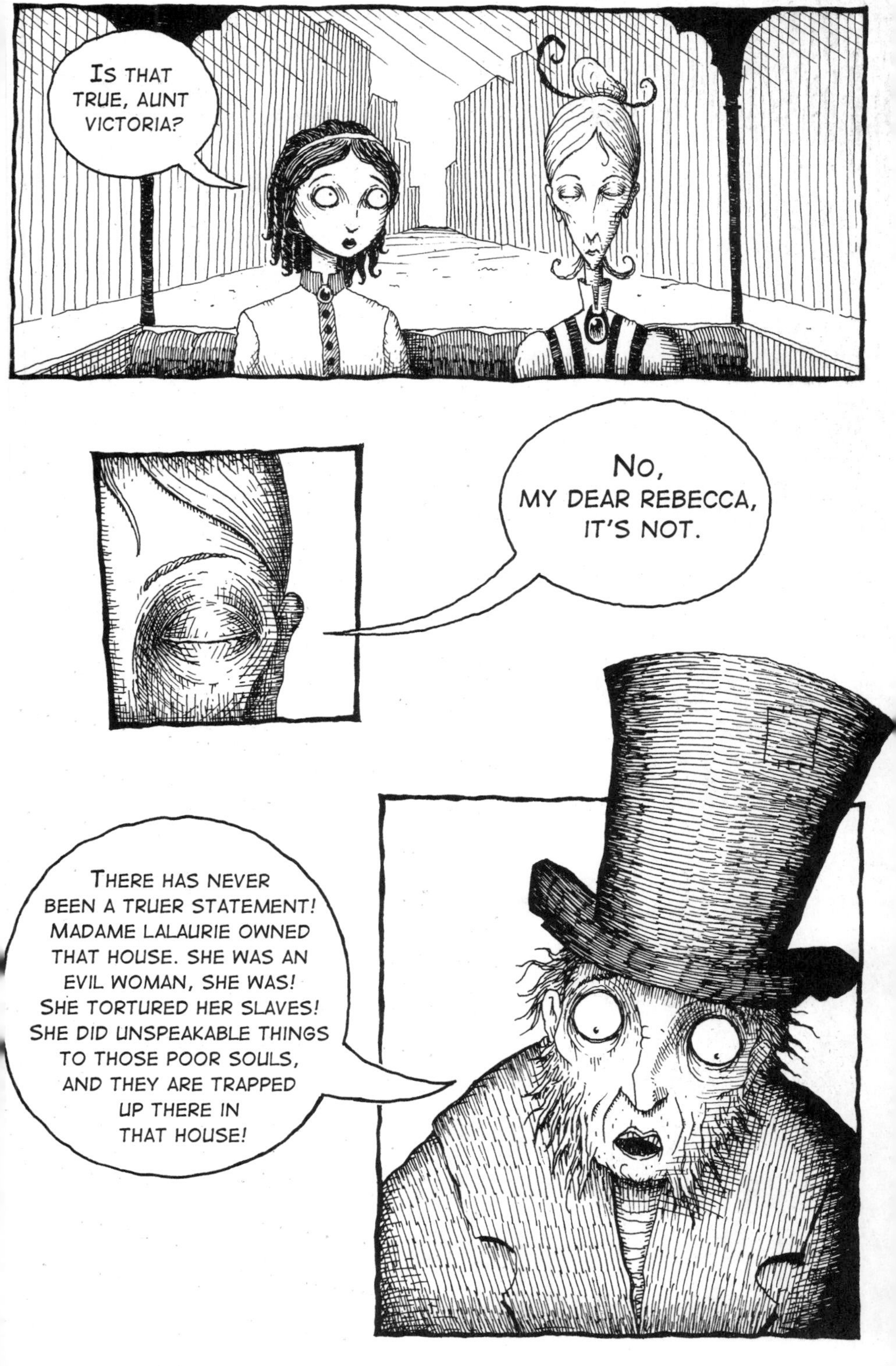
IS THAT TRUE, AUNT VICTORIA?
NO, MY DEAR REBECCA, IT'S NOT.
THERE HAS NEVER BEEN A TRUER STATEMENT! MADAME LALAURIE OWNED THAT HOUSE. SHE WAS AN EVIL WOMAN, SHE WAS! SHE TORTURED HER SLAVES! SHE DID UNSPEAKABLE THINGS TO THOSE POOR SOULS, AND THEY ARE TRAPPED UP THERE IN THAT HOUSE!

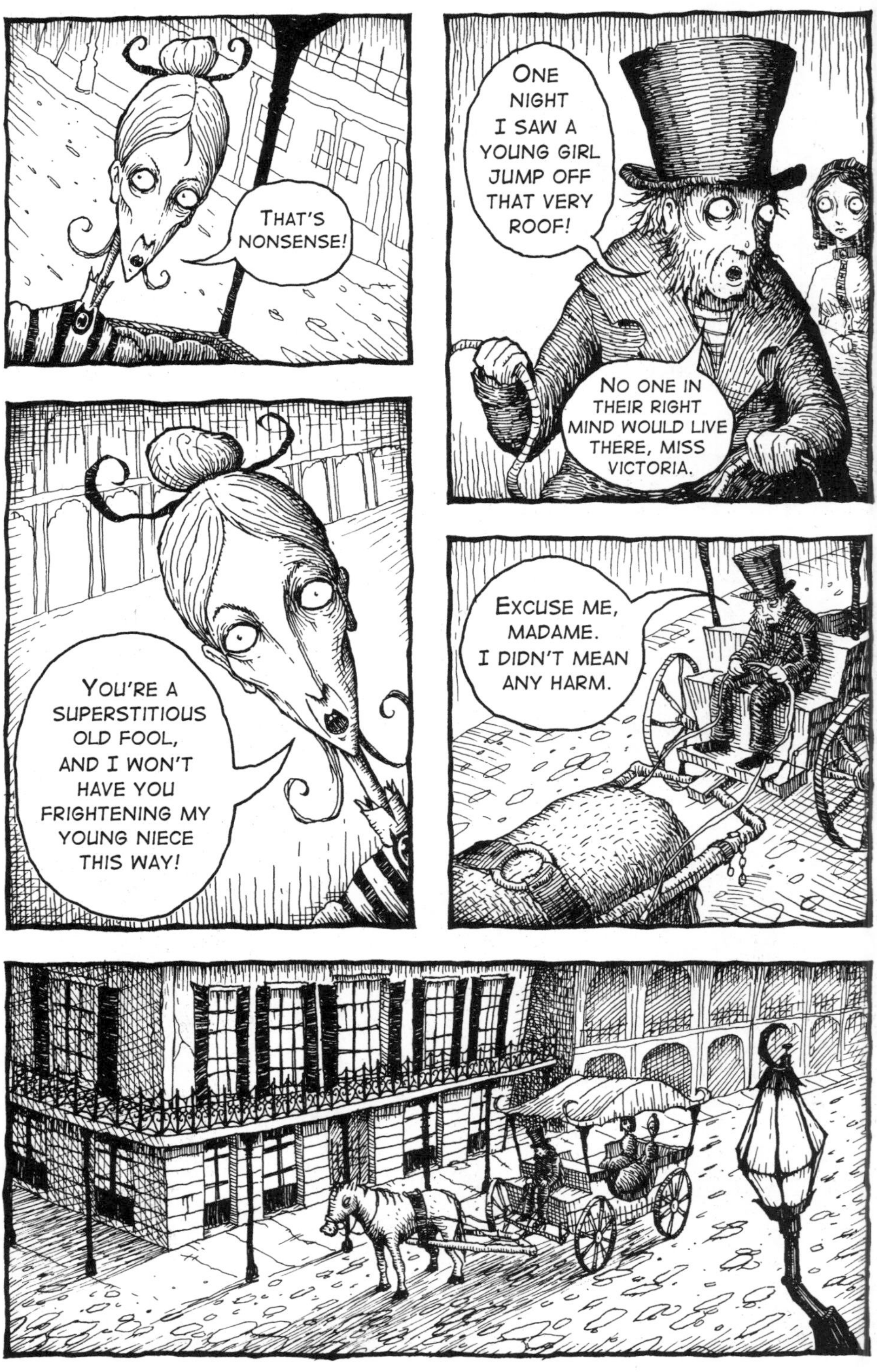
THAT'S NONSENSE!
ONE NIGHT I SAW A YOUNG GIRL JUMP OFF THAT VERY ROOF!
NO ONE IN THEIR RIGHT MIND WOULD LIVE THERE, MISS VICTORIA.
YOU'RE A SUPERSTITIOUS OLD FOOL, AND I WON'T HAVE YOU FRIGHTENING MY YOUNG NIECE THIS WAY!
EXCUSE ME, MADAME. I DIDN'T MEAN ANY HARM.

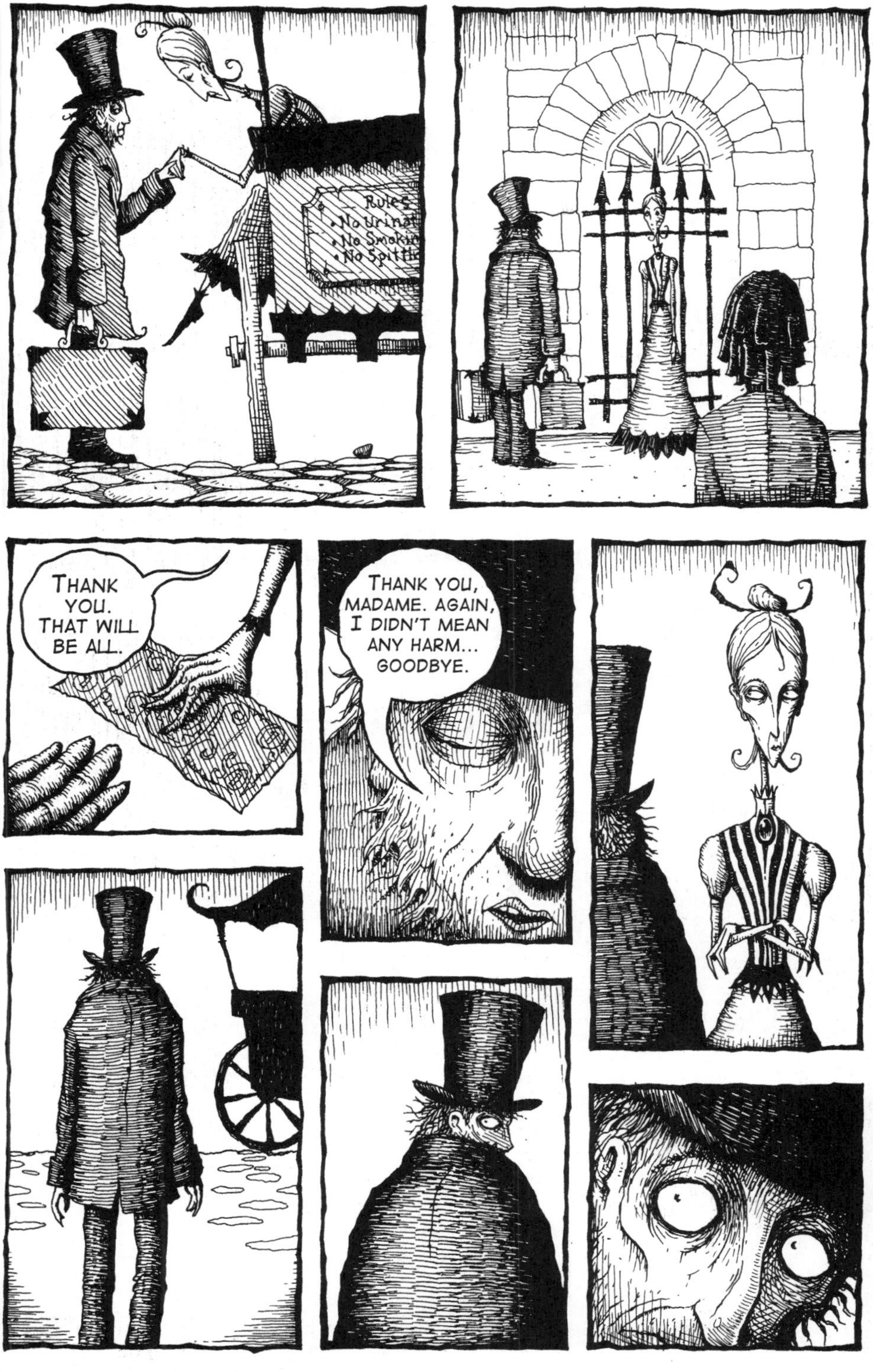
Rules
• No Urinat
• No Smokin
• No Spittin
THANK YOU. THAT WILL BE ALL.
THANK YOU, MADAME. AGAIN, I DIDN'T MEAN ANY HARM... GOODBYE.

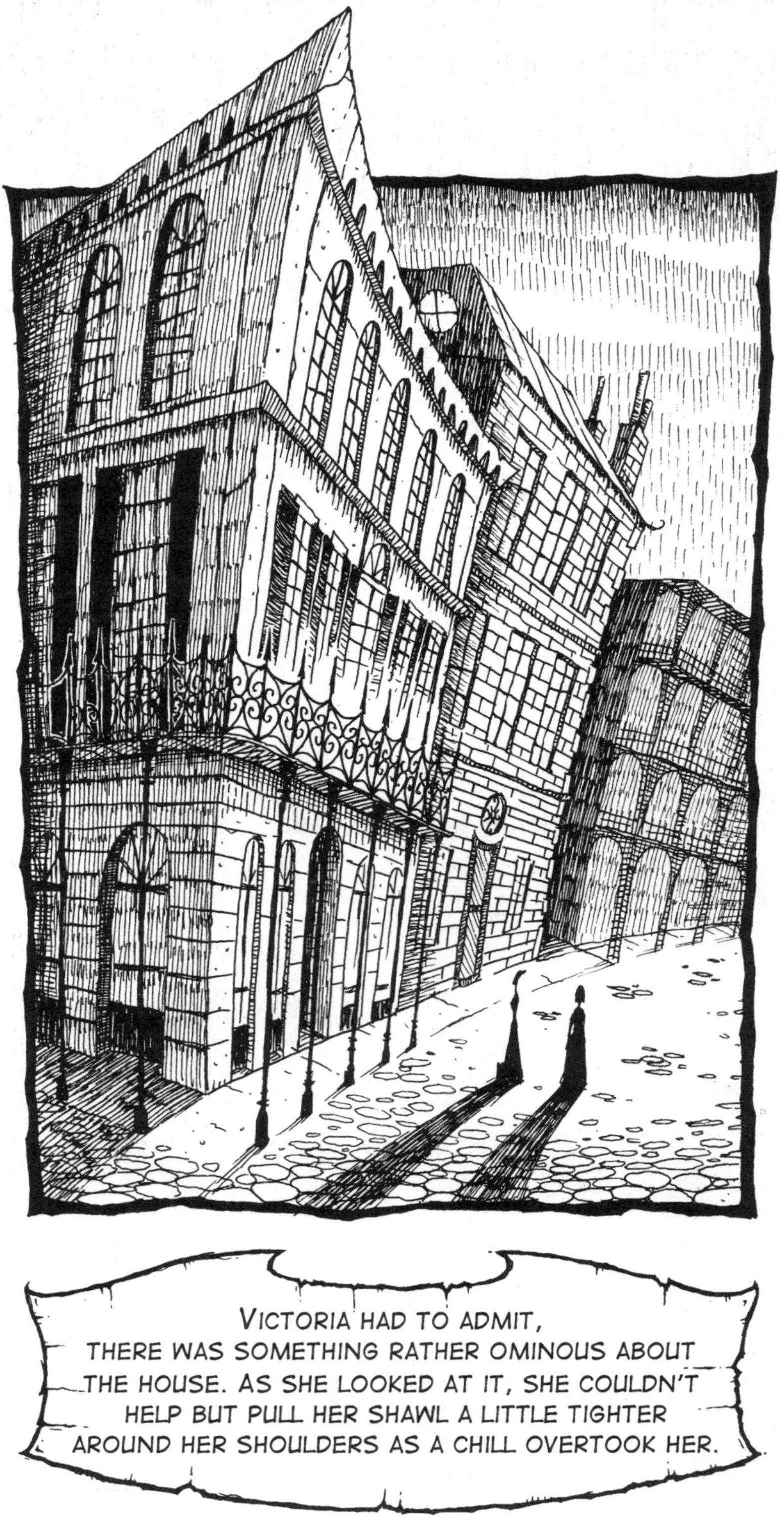
VICTORIA HAD TO ADMIT,
THERE WAS SOMETHING RATHER OMINOUS ABOUT
THE HOUSE. AS SHE LOOKED AT IT, SHE COULDN'T
HELP BUT PULL HER SHAWL A LITTLE TIGHTER
AROUND HER SHOULDERS AS A CHILL OVERTOOK HER.

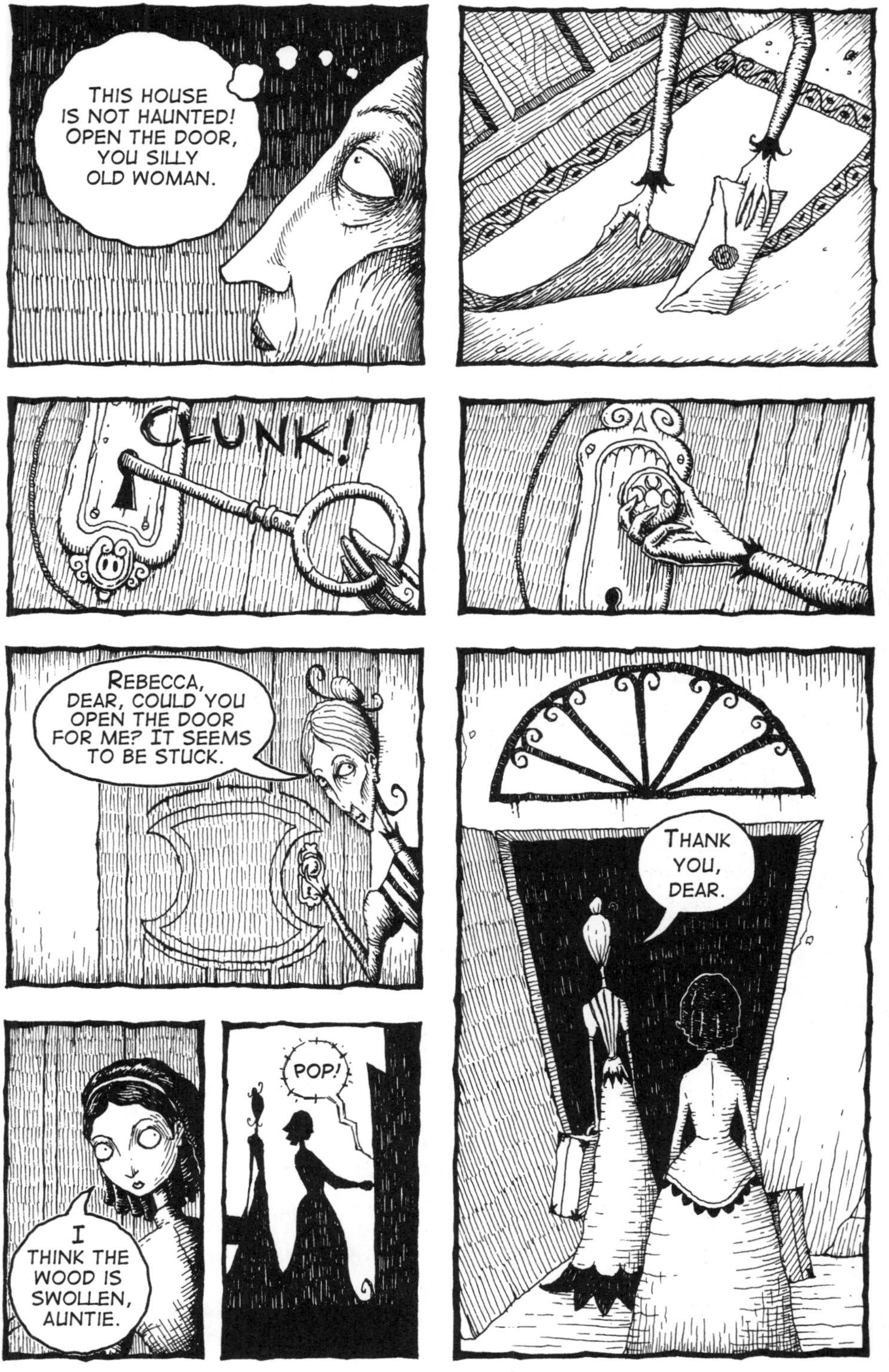
THIS HOUSE IS NOT HAUNTED! OPEN THE DOOR, YOU SILLY OLD WOMAN.
CLUNK!
REBECCA, DEAR, COULD YOU OPEN THE DOOR FOR ME? IT SEEMS TO BE STUCK.
I THINK THE WOOD IS SWOLLEN, AUNTIE.
POP!
THANK YOU, DEAR.

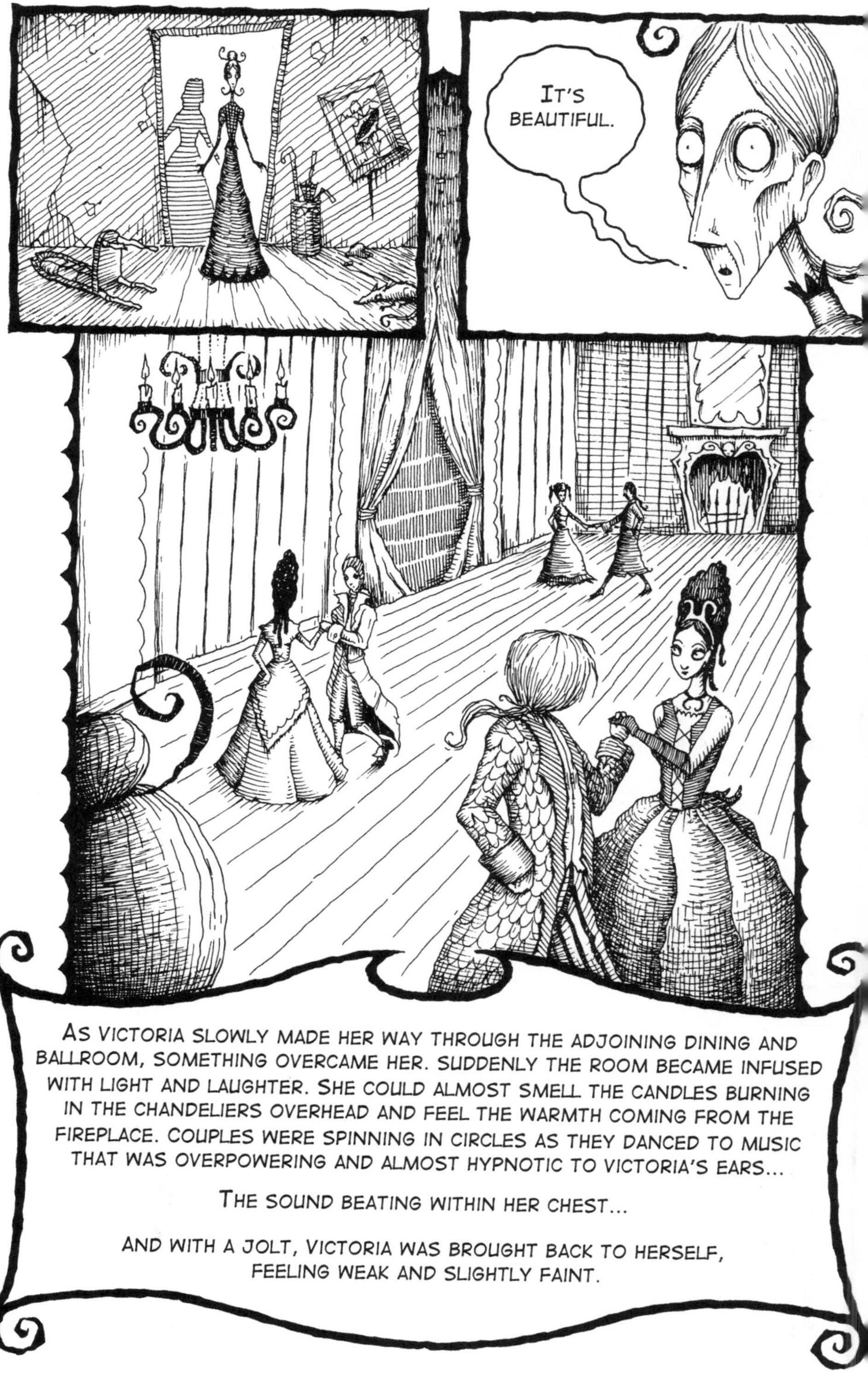
IT'S BEAUTIFUL.
AS VICTORIA SLOWLY MADE HER WAY THROUGH THE ADJOINING DINING AND BALLROOM, SOMETHING OVERCAME HER. SUDDENLY THE ROOM BECAME INFUSED WITH LIGHT AND LAUGHTER. SHE COULD ALMOST SMELL THE CANDLES BURNING IN THE CHANDELIERS OVERHEAD AND FEEL THE WARMTH COMING FROM THE FIREPLACE. COUPLES WERE SPINNING IN CIRCLES AS THEY DANCED TO MUSIC THAT WAS OVERPOWERING AND ALMOST HYPNOTIC TO VICTORIA'S EARS...
THE SOUND BEATING WITHIN HER CHEST...
AND WITH A JOLT, VICTORIA WAS BROUGHT BACK TO HERSELF, FEELING WEAK AND SLIGHTLY FAINT.

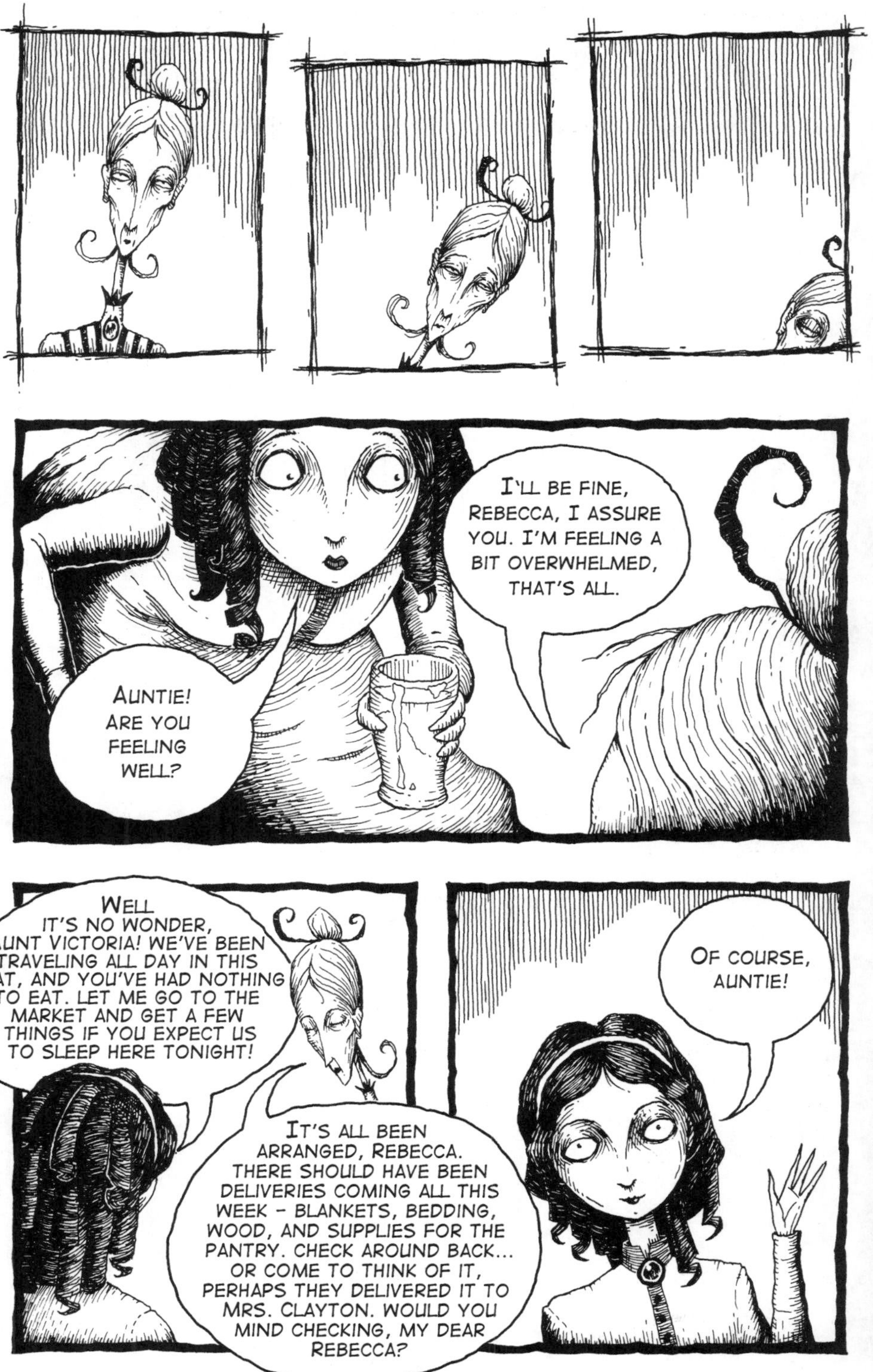
AUNTIE! ARE YOU FEELING WELL?
I'LL BE FINE, REBECCA, I ASSURE YOU. I'M FEELING A BIT OVERWHELMED, THAT'S ALL.
WELL IT'S NO WONDER, AUNT VICTORIA! WE'VE BEEN TRAVELING ALL DAY IN THIS HEAT, AND YOU'VE HAD NOTHING TO EAT. LET ME GO TO THE MARKET AND GET A FEW THINGS IF YOU EXPECT US TO SLEEP HERE TONIGHT!
IT'S ALL BEEN ARRANGED, REBECCA. THERE SHOULD HAVE BEEN DELIVERIES COMING ALL THIS WEEK - BLANKETS, BEDDING, WOOD, AND SUPPLIES FOR THE PANTRY. CHECK AROUND BACK... OR COME TO THINK OF IT, PERHAPS THEY DELIVERED IT TO MRS. CLAYTON. WOULD YOU MIND CHECKING, MY DEAR REBECCA?
OF COURSE, AUNTIE!

I'M BEING FOOLISH... WE JUST NEED TO OPEN SOME WINDOWS, AIR IT OUT AND BRING IN THE LIGHT!

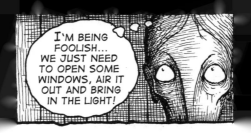

MELLED MUSTY, LIKE OLD WET WOOD, AND
E A LAYER OF DUST UPON IT. IT SEEMED S
LIKE THE HOUSE DIDN'T WANT HER THERE.

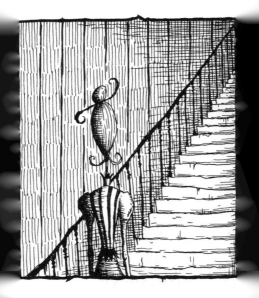

HER ALONE AND A LITTLE FRIGHTENED, VIC
UP THE STAIRS TO SEE THE BEDROOMS. S
TO SEE THAT IT WAS MUCH LESS GLOOMY
R ROOMS, ALMOST AS IF SOMEONE HAD B
HER ROOM, IN PARTICULAR, READY FOR H

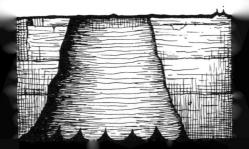

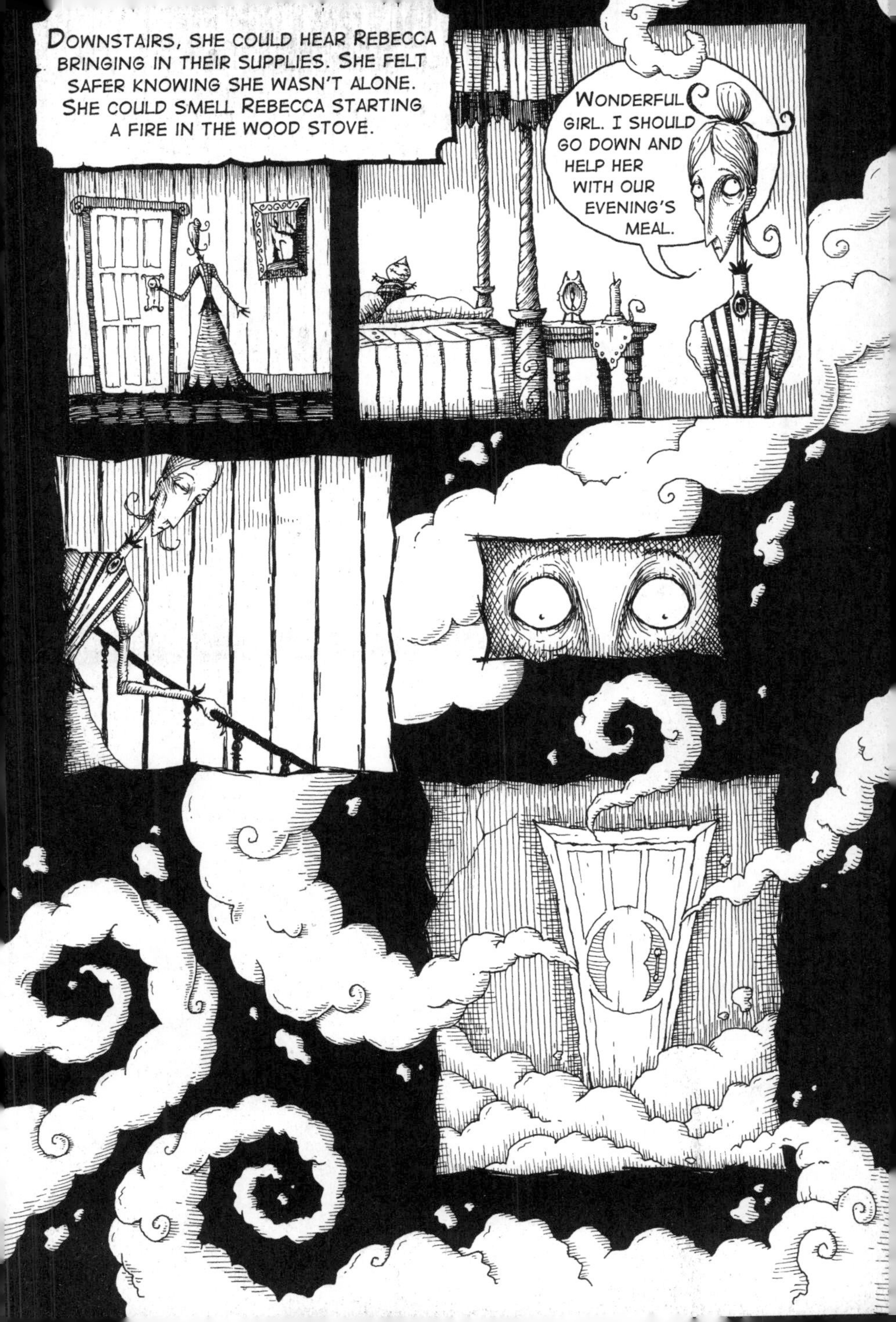
DOWNSTAIRS, SHE COULD HEAR REBECCA BRINGING IN THEIR SUPPLIES. SHE FELT SAFER KNOWING SHE WASN'T ALONE. SHE COULD SMELL REBECCA STARTING A FIRE IN THE WOOD STOVE.
WONDERFUL GIRL. I SHOULD GO DOWN AND HELP HER WITH OUR EVENING'S MEAL.

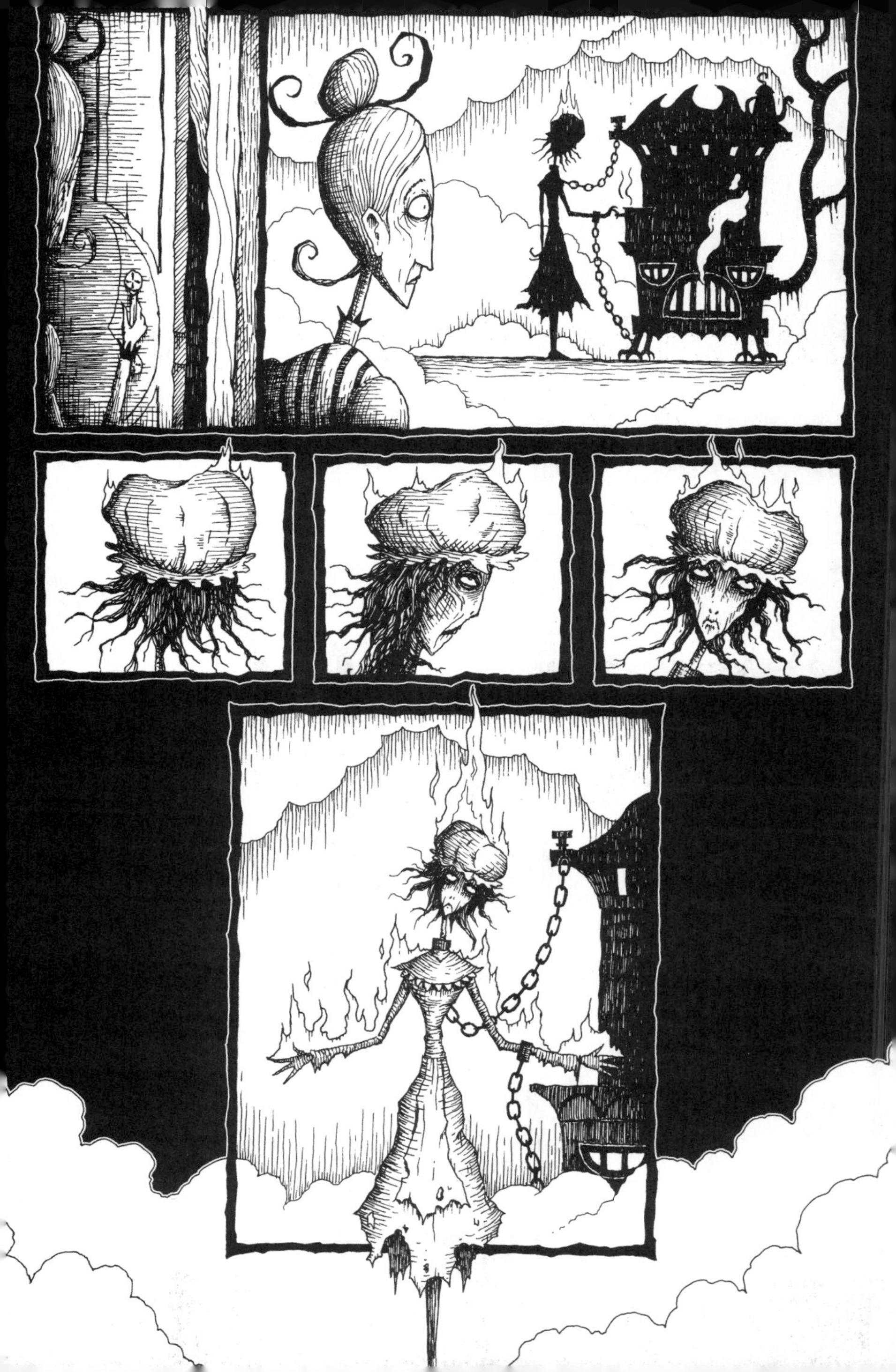

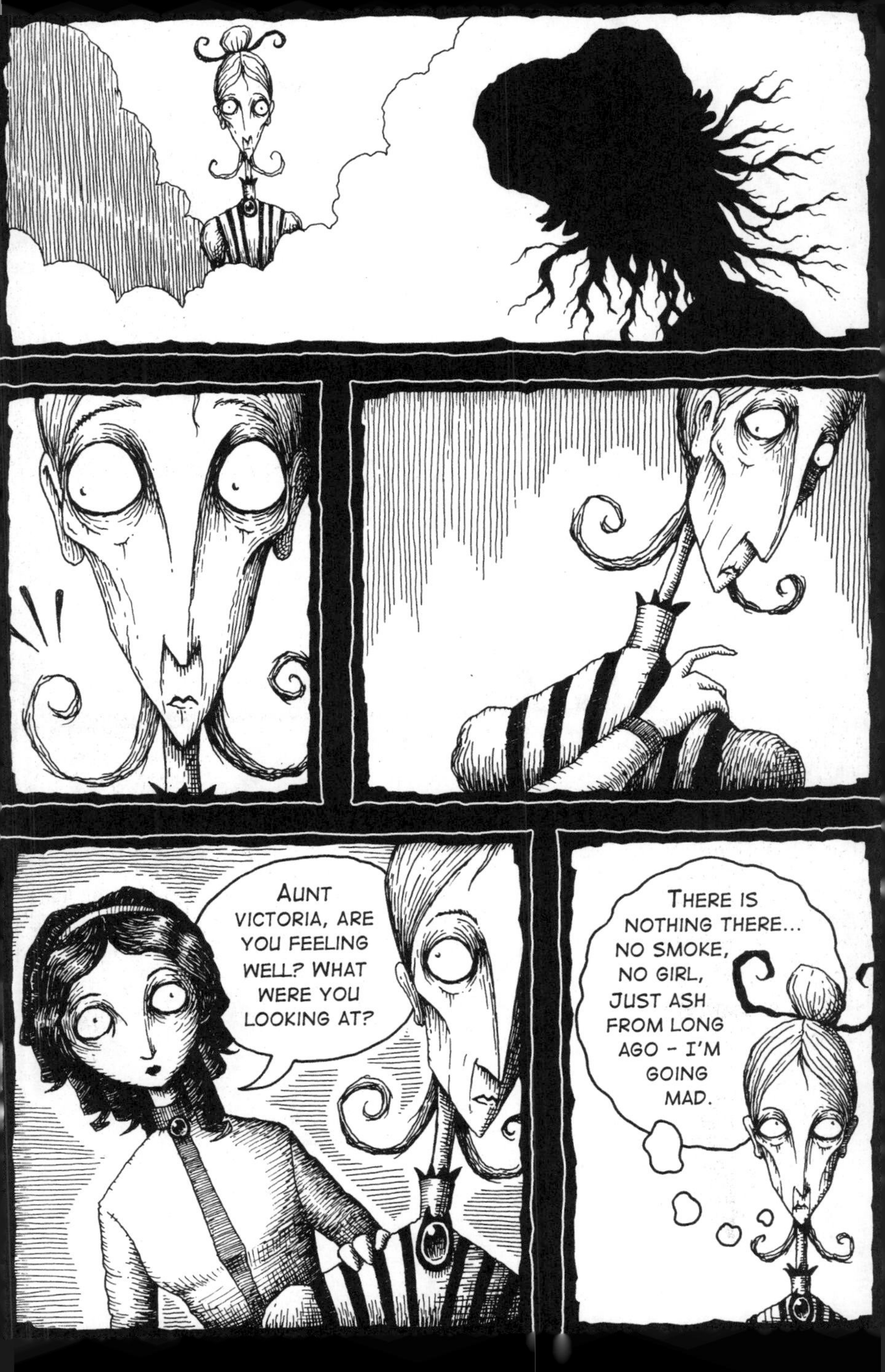
AUNT VICTORIA, ARE YOU FEELING WELL? WHAT WERE YOU LOOKING AT?
THERE IS NOTHING THERE... NO SMOKE, NO GIRL, JUST ASH FROM LONG AGO - I'M GOING MAD.

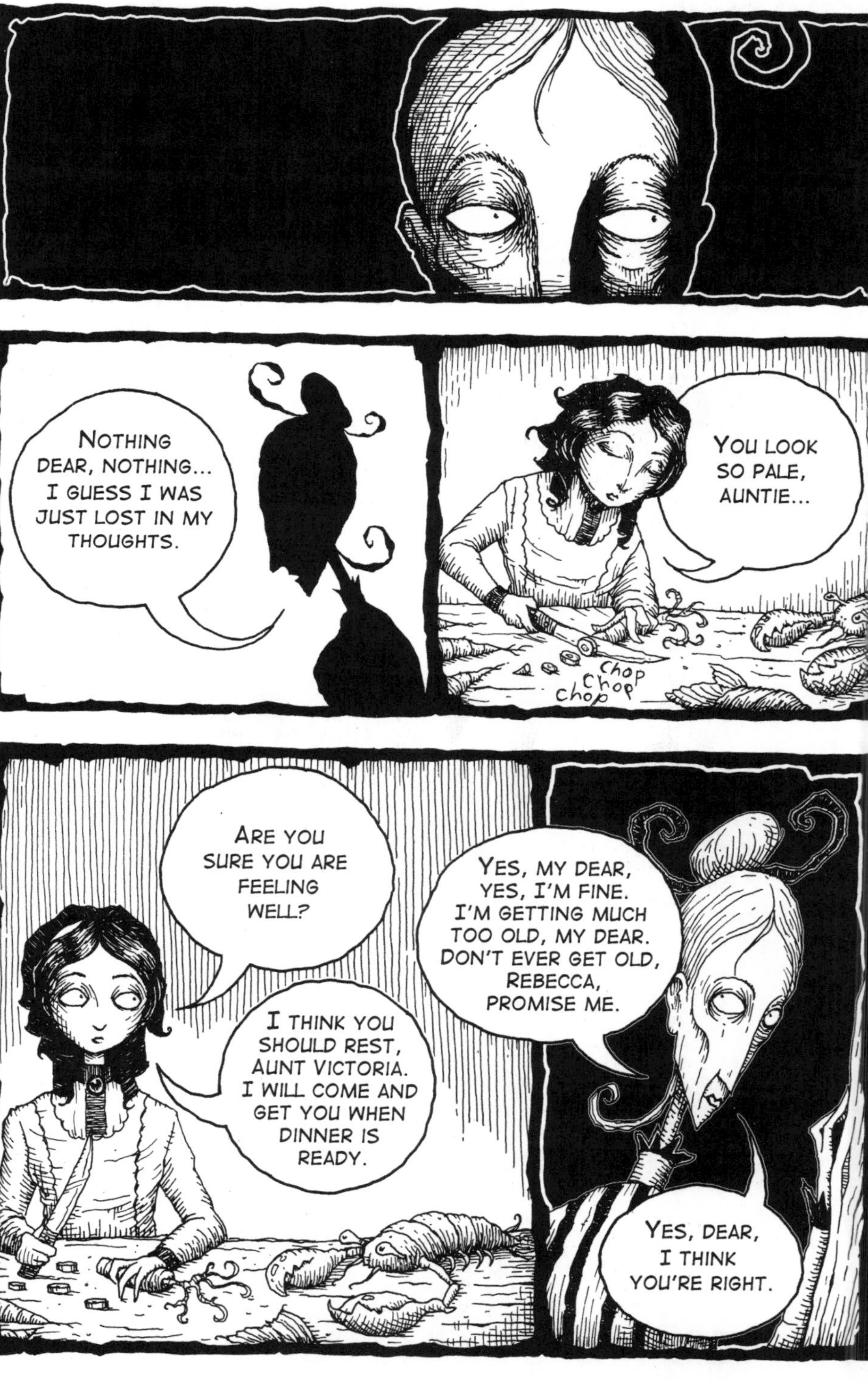
NOTHING DEAR, NOTHING... I GUESS I WAS JUST LOST IN MY THOUGHTS.
YOU LOOK SO PALE, AUNTIE...
CHOP CHOP CHOP
ARE YOU SURE YOU ARE FEELING WELL?
I THINK YOU SHOULD REST, AUNT VICTORIA. I WILL COME AND GET YOU WHEN DINNER IS READY.
YES, MY DEAR, YES, I'M FINE. I'M GETTING MUCH TOO OLD, MY DEAR. DON'T EVER GET OLD, REBECCA, PROMISE ME.
YES, DEAR, I THINK YOU'RE RIGHT.

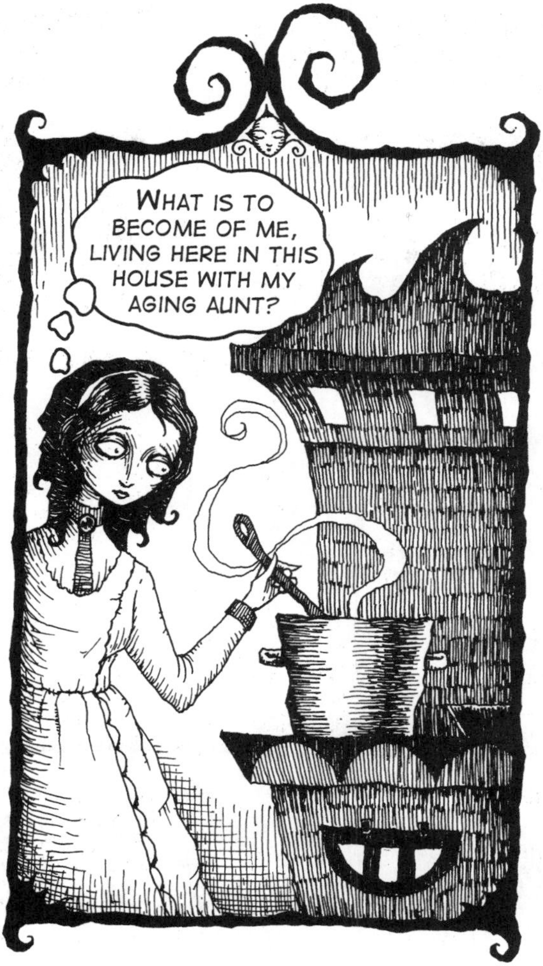
WHAT IS TO BECOME OF ME, LIVING HERE IN THIS HOUSE WITH MY AGING AUNT?

REBECCA STOOD THERE FOR A FEW MOMENTS STARING AT THE ASH AND BLACK SMUDGE AROUND THE STOVE, THINKING ABOUT THE STORY HER NEIGHBOR HAD JUST TOLD HER....

HAD A WOMAN REALLY DIED HERE, CHAINED TO THAT STOVE? OR WAS MRS. CLAYTON JUST RELAYING OLD MYTHS?

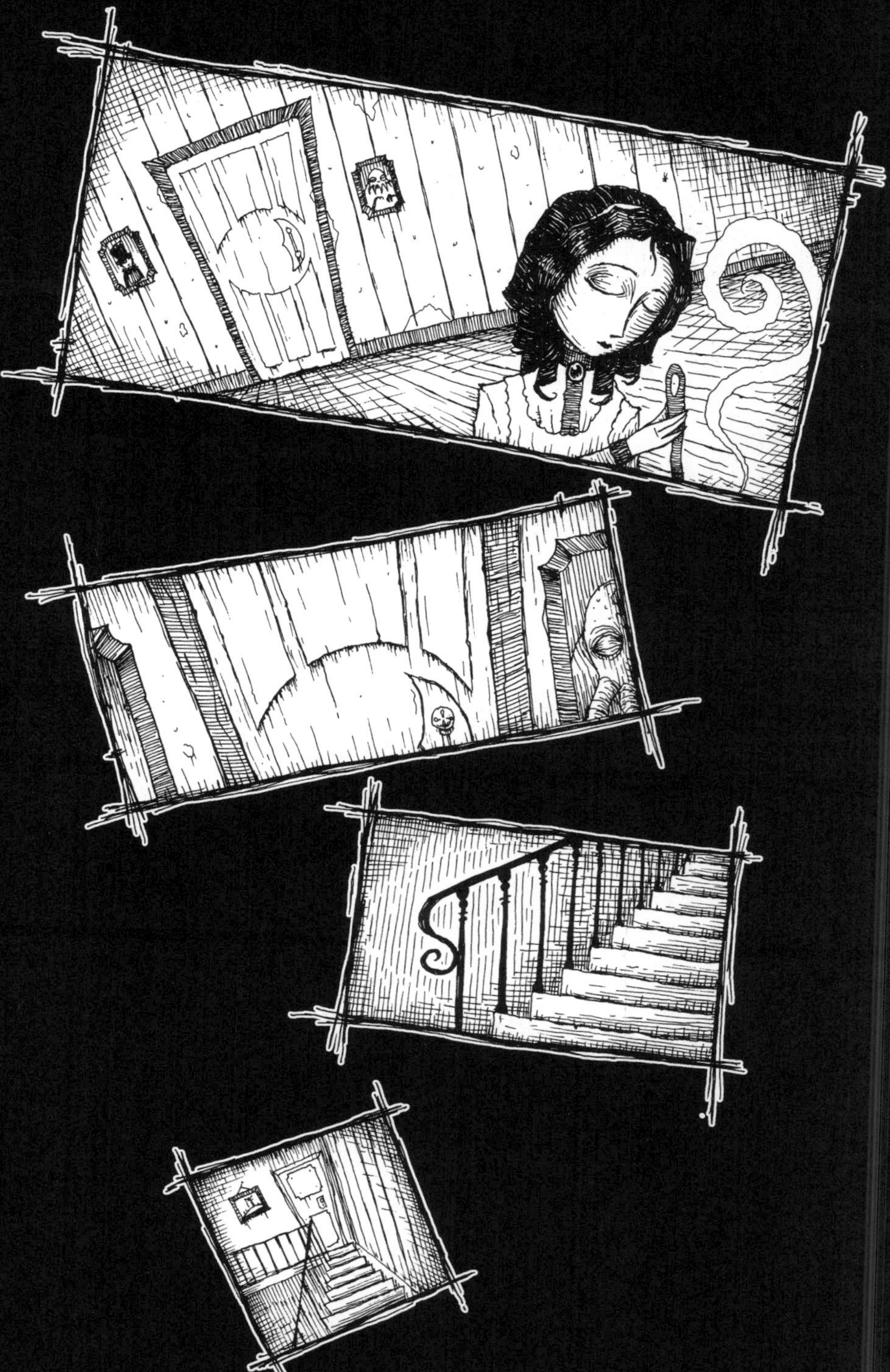

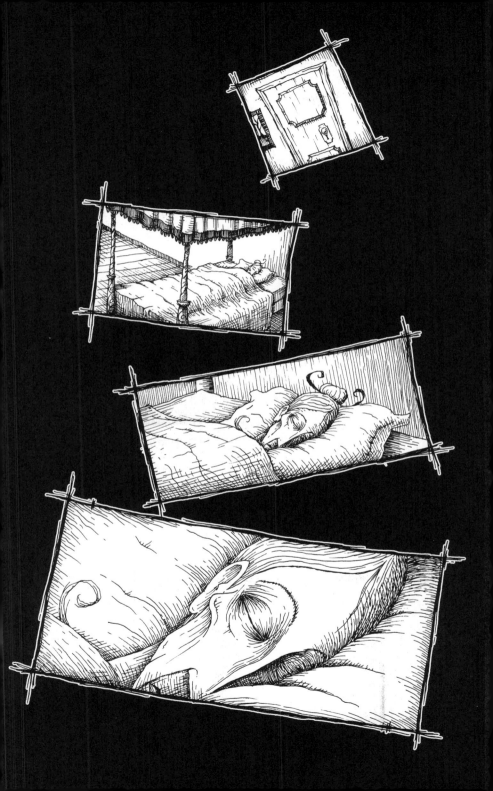

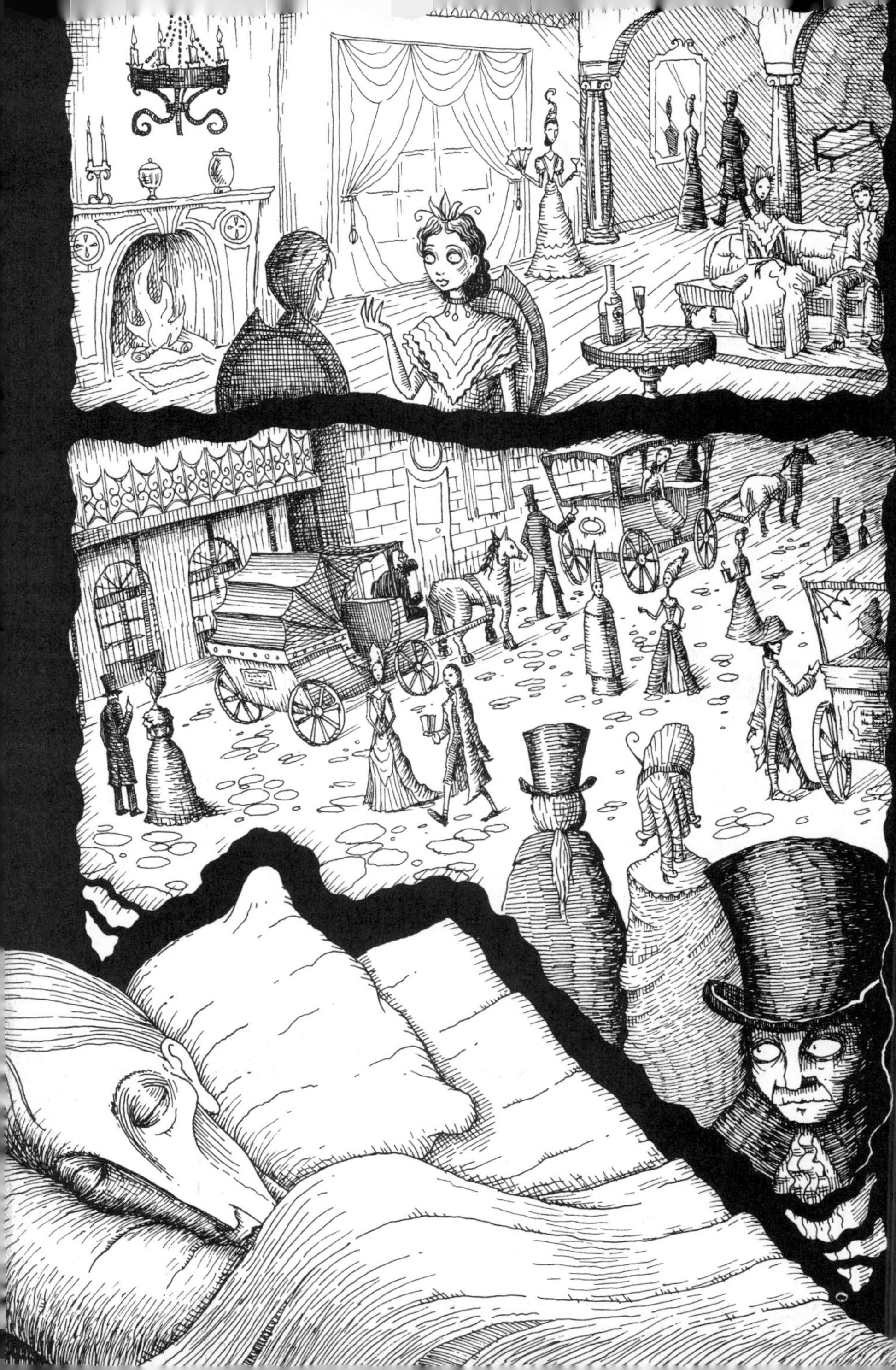

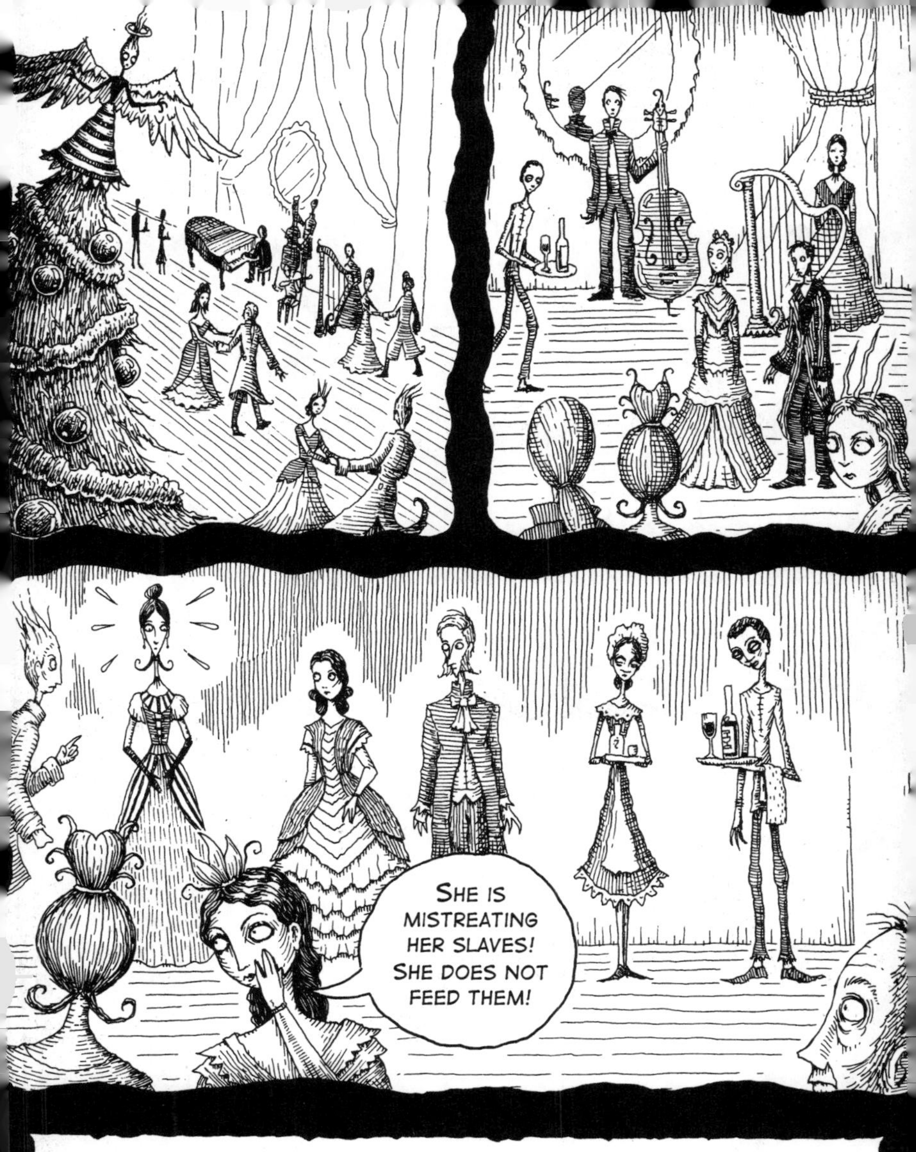
SHE IS MISTREATING HER SLAVES! SHE DOES NOT FEED THEM!

VICTORIA'S HEART WAS RACING AGAIN. SHE KNEW SHE WAS DREAMING, BUT SHE COULD NOT WAKE...THE MUSIC WAS LULLING HER INTO PARALYSIS, HER HEART POUNDING TO THE RHYTHM, SENDING HER DEEPER WITHIN THE DREAM... OVERCOME WITH VIBRATION, UNABLE TO MOVE OR WAKE - SURELY HER HEART WOULD BURST!

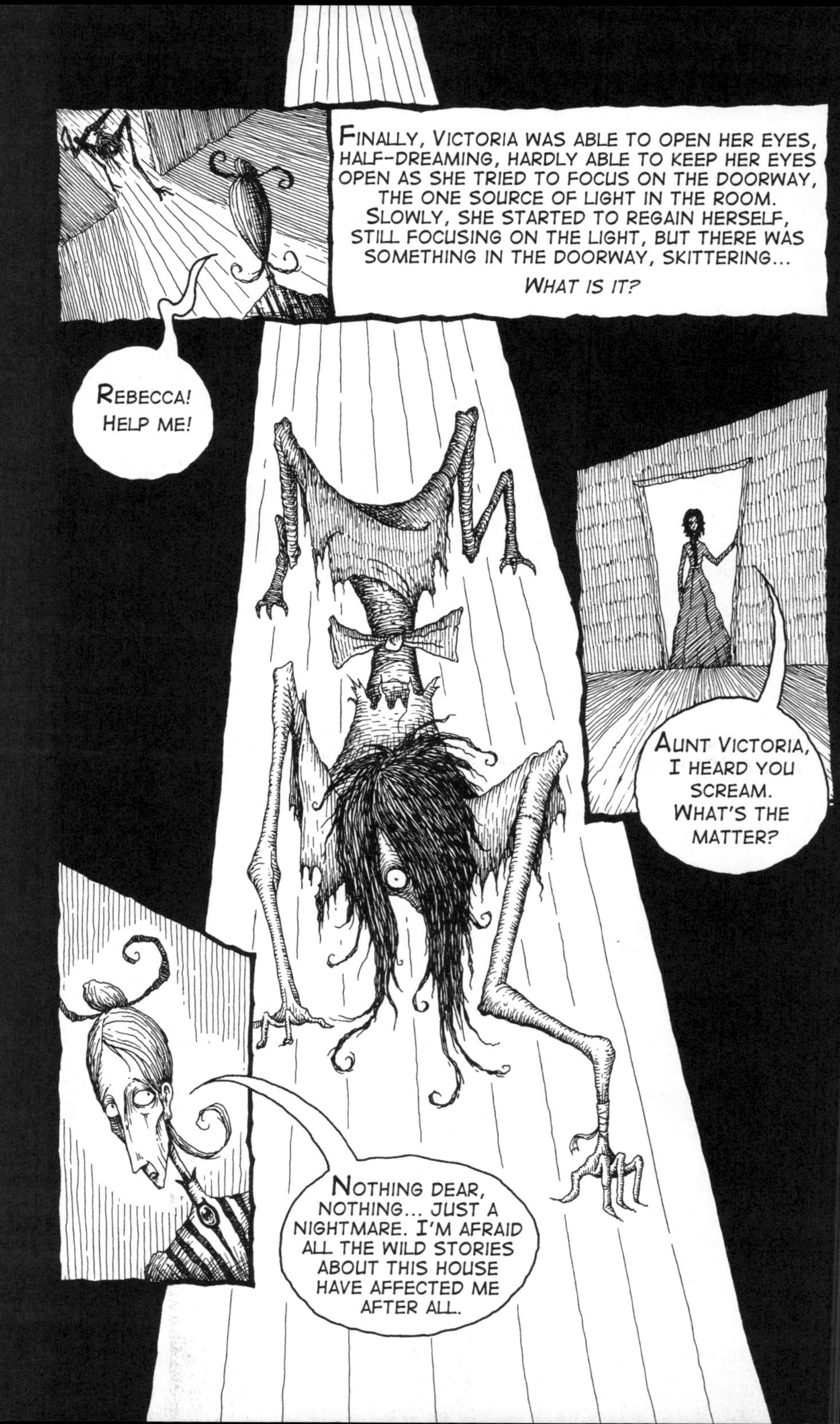
FINALLY, VICTORIA WAS ABLE TO OPEN HER EYES, HALF-DREAMING, HARDLY ABLE TO KEEP HER EYES OPEN AS SHE TRIED TO FOCUS ON THE DOORWAY, THE ONE SOURCE OF LIGHT IN THE ROOM. SLOWLY, SHE STARTED TO REGAIN HERSELF, STILL FOCUSING ON THE LIGHT, BUT THERE WAS SOMETHING IN THE DOORWAY, SKITTERING...
WHAT IS IT?
REBECCA! HELP ME!
AUNT VICTORIA, I HEARD YOU SCREAM. WHAT'S THE MATTER?
NOTHING DEAR, NOTHING... JUST A NIGHTMARE. I'M AFRAID ALL THE WILD STORIES ABOUT THIS HOUSE HAVE AFFECTED ME AFTER ALL.

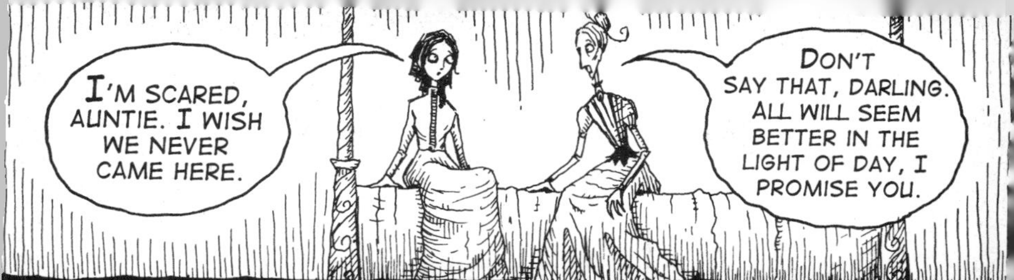
I'M SCARED, AUNTIE. I WISH WE NEVER CAME HERE.
DON'T SAY THAT, DARLING. ALL WILL SEEM BETTER IN THE LIGHT OF DAY, I PROMISE YOU.

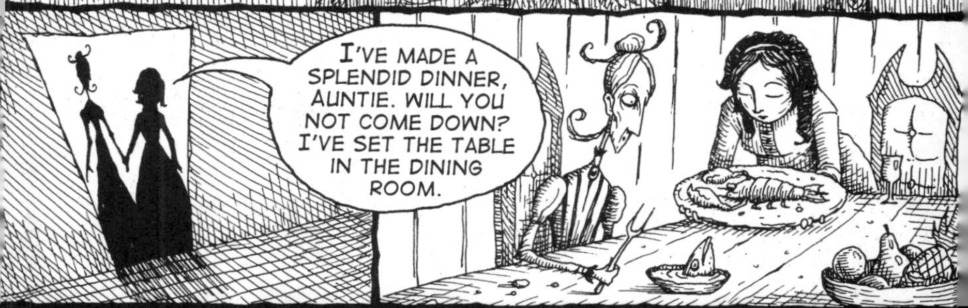
I'VE MADE A SPLENDID DINNER, AUNTIE. WILL YOU NOT COME DOWN? I'VE SET THE TABLE IN THE DINING ROOM.

THE ROOM WAS WONDROUS, WARM AND INVITING.
VICTORIA ALMOST FORGOT HOW FRIGHTENED SHE REALLY WAS.

AFTER DINNER THE TWO OF THEM SLIPPED IN TO BED TOGETHER.
THEY BOTH SLEPT DREAMLESSLY... DEEP, MARVELOUS SLEEP.

THEY WOKE THE NEXT DAY
TO SUN STREAMING THROUGH THE MOTH-EATEN CURTAINS.

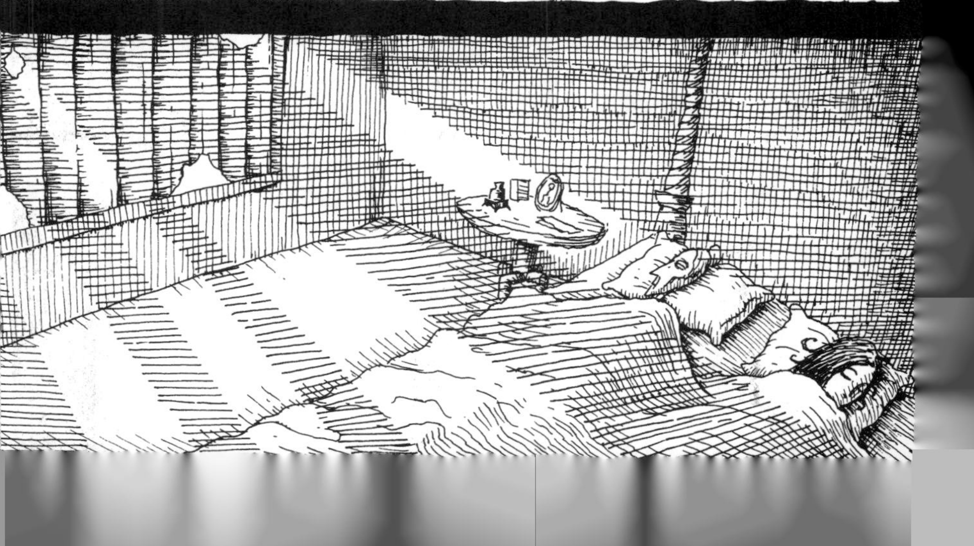

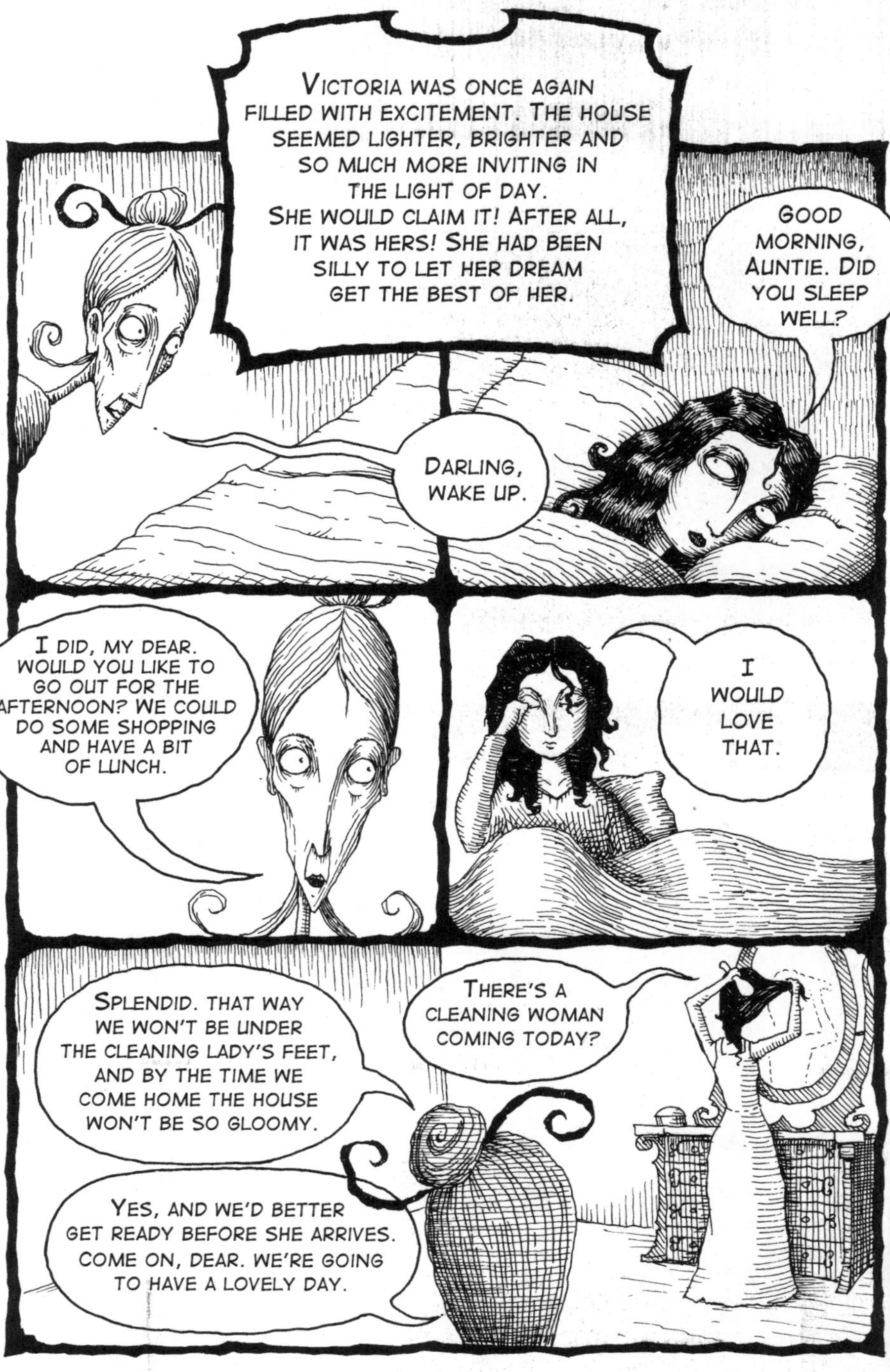
Victoria was once again filled with excitement. The house seemed lighter, brighter and so much more inviting in the light of day. She would claim it! After all, it was hers! She had been silly to let her dream get the best of her.
Darling, wake up.
Good morning, Auntie. Did you sleep well?
I did, my dear. Would you like to go out for the afternoon? We could do some shopping and have a bit of lunch.
I would love that.
Splendid. That way we won't be under the cleaning lady's feet, and by the time we come home the house won't be so gloomy.
There's a cleaning woman coming today?
Yes, and we'd better get ready before she arrives. Come on, dear. We're going to have a lovely day.

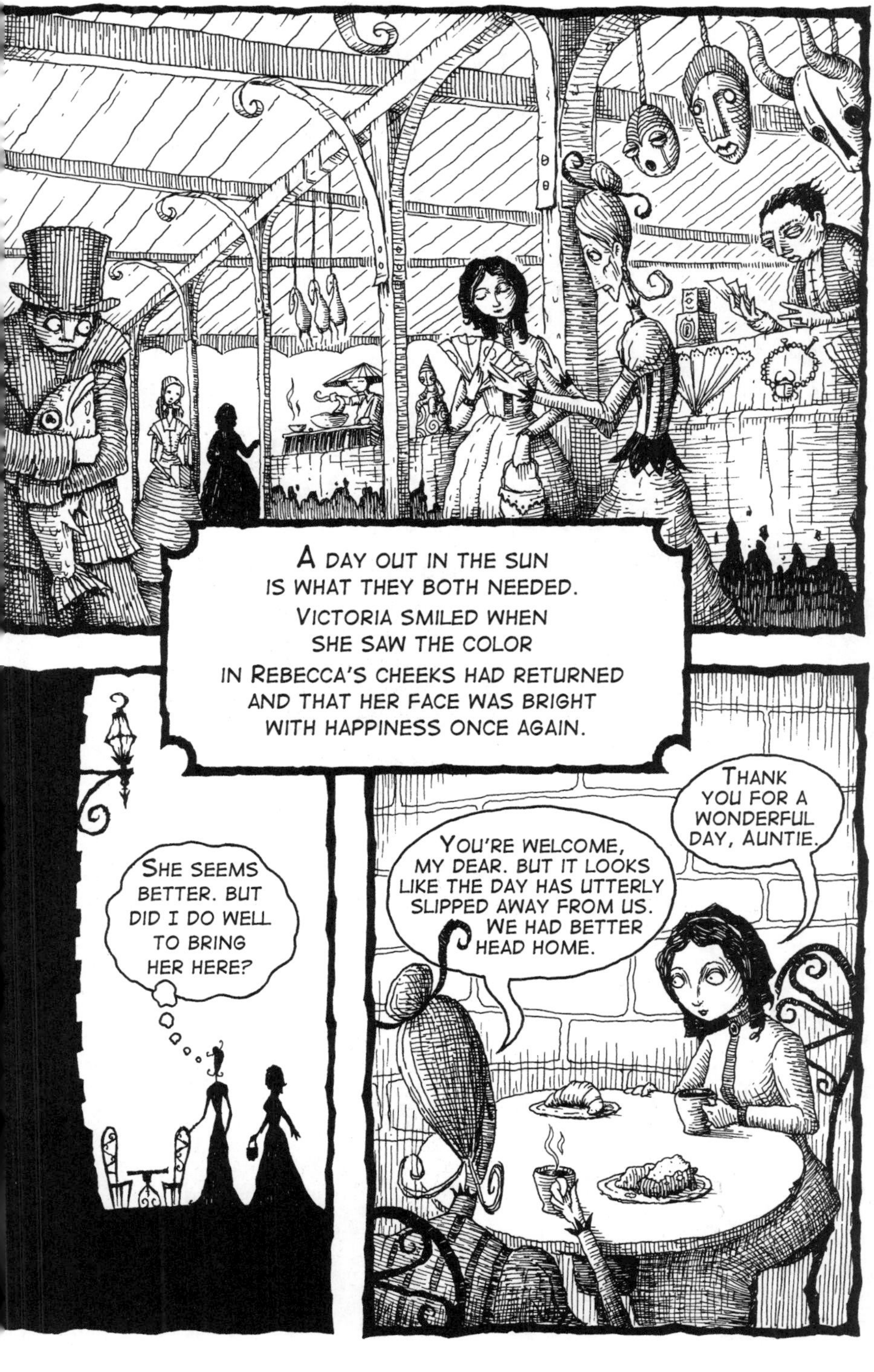
A DAY OUT IN THE SUN IS WHAT THEY BOTH NEEDED. VICTORIA SMILED WHEN SHE SAW THE COLOR IN REBECCA'S CHEEKS HAD RETURNED AND THAT HER FACE WAS BRIGHT WITH HAPPINESS ONCE AGAIN.
SHE SEEMS BETTER. BUT DID I DO WELL TO BRING HER HERE?
THANK YOU FOR A WONDERFUL DAY, AUNTIE.
YOU'RE WELCOME, MY DEAR. BUT IT LOOKS LIKE THE DAY HAS UTTERLY SLIPPED AWAY FROM US. WE HAD BETTER HEAD HOME.

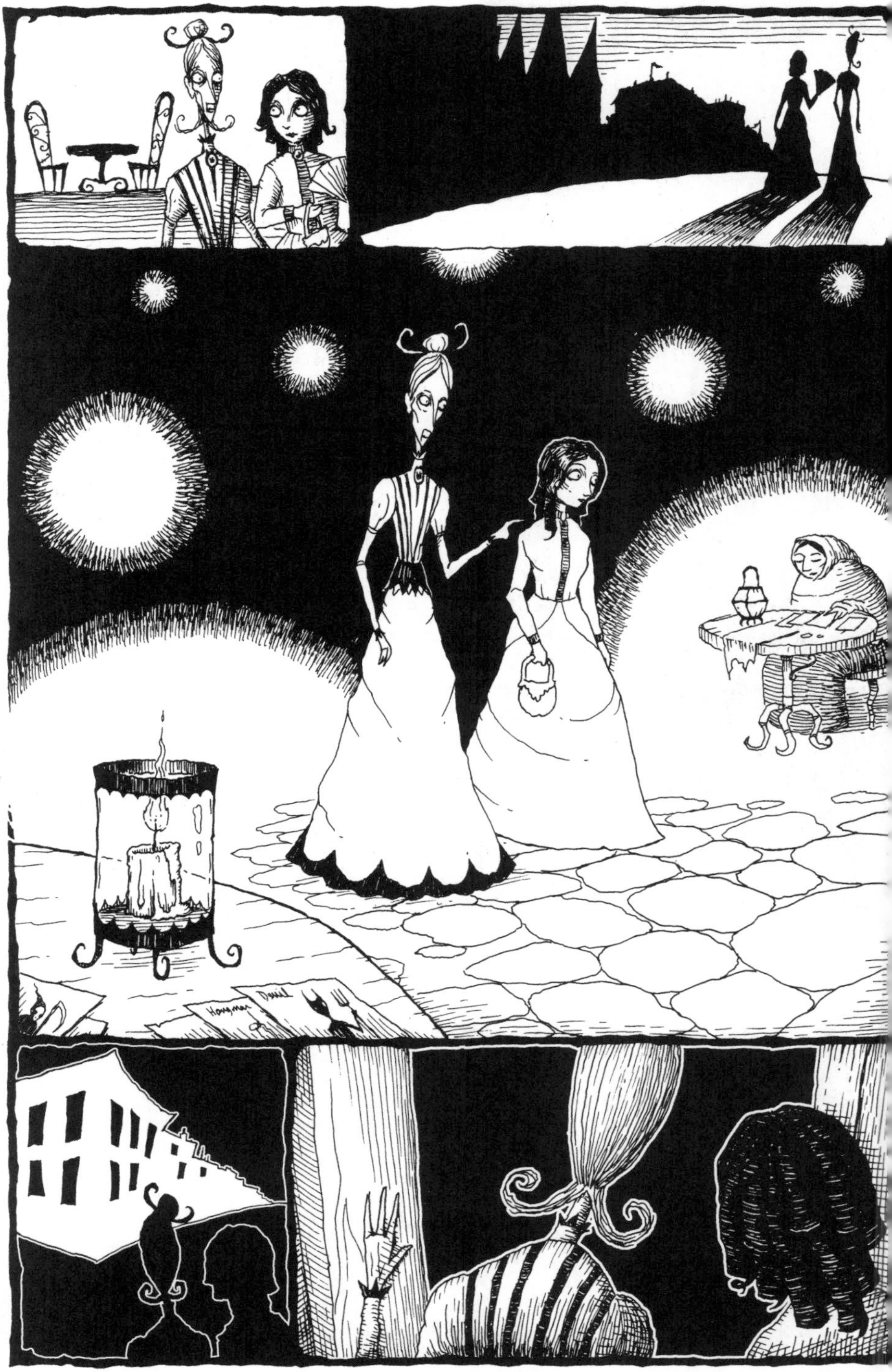
Hangman
Devil

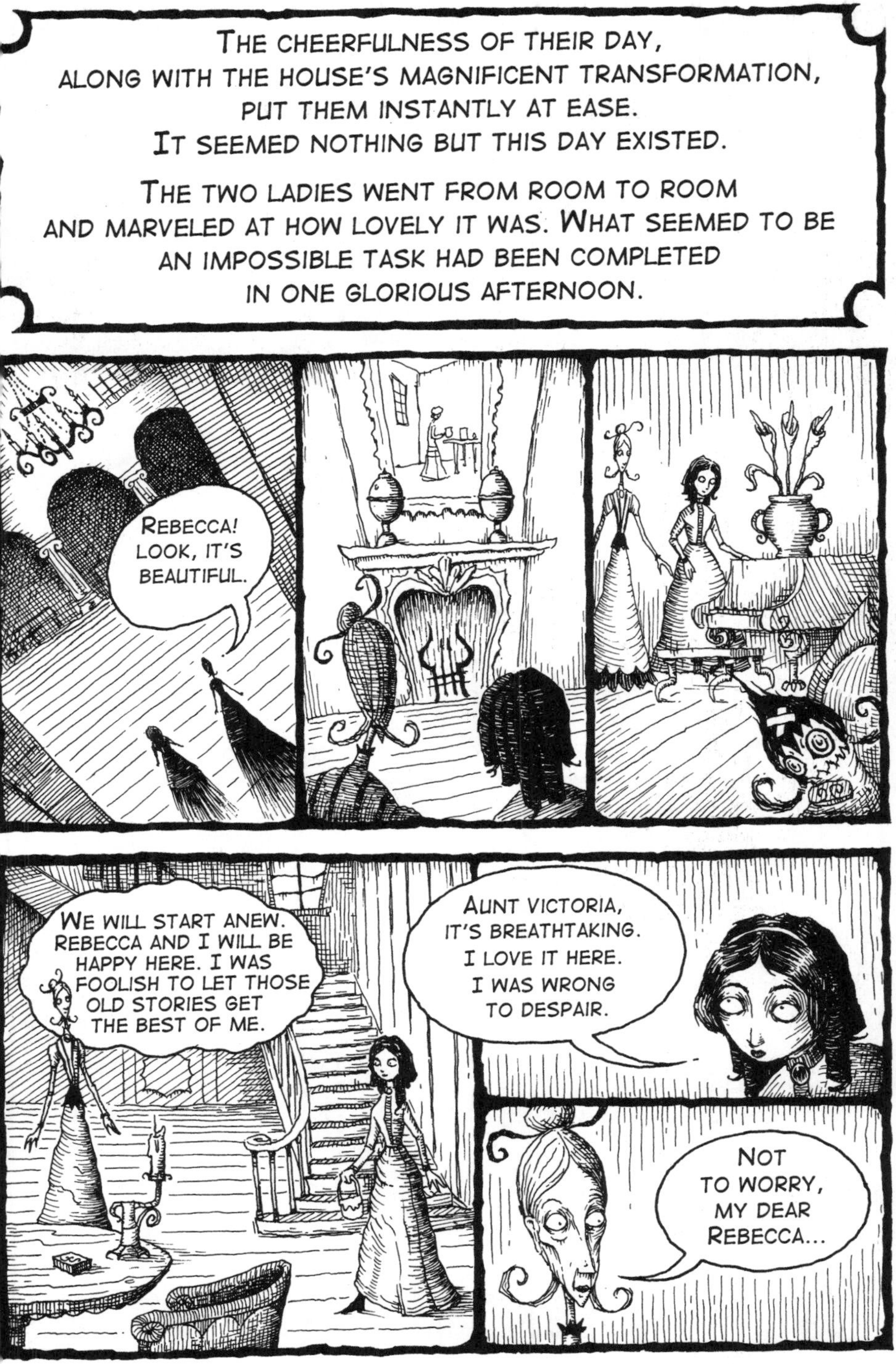
THE CHEERFULNESS OF THEIR DAY, ALONG WITH THE HOUSE'S MAGNIFICENT TRANSFORMATION, PUT THEM INSTANTLY AT EASE. IT SEEMED NOTHING BUT THIS DAY EXISTED.
THE TWO LADIES WENT FROM ROOM TO ROOM AND MARVELED AT HOW LOVELY IT WAS. WHAT SEEMED TO BE AN IMPOSSIBLE TASK HAD BEEN COMPLETED IN ONE GLORIOUS AFTERNOON.
REBECCA! LOOK, IT'S BEAUTIFUL.
WE WILL START ANEW. REBECCA AND I WILL BE HAPPY HERE. I WAS FOOLISH TO LET THOSE OLD STORIES GET THE BEST OF ME.
AUNT VICTORIA, IT'S BREATHTAKING. I LOVE IT HERE. I WAS WRONG TO DESPAIR.
NOT TO WORRY, MY DEAR REBECCA...

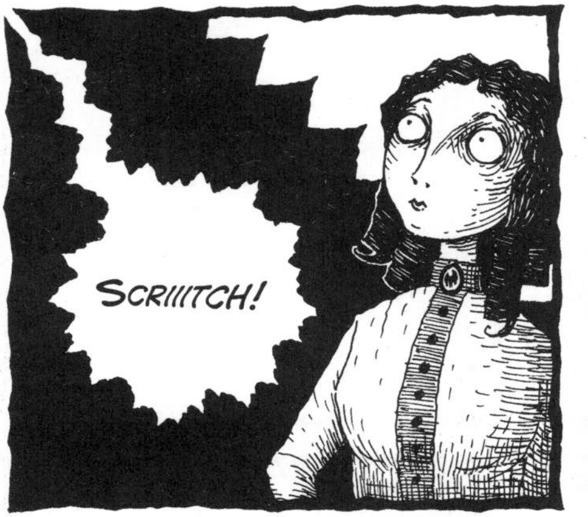
SCRIIITCH!

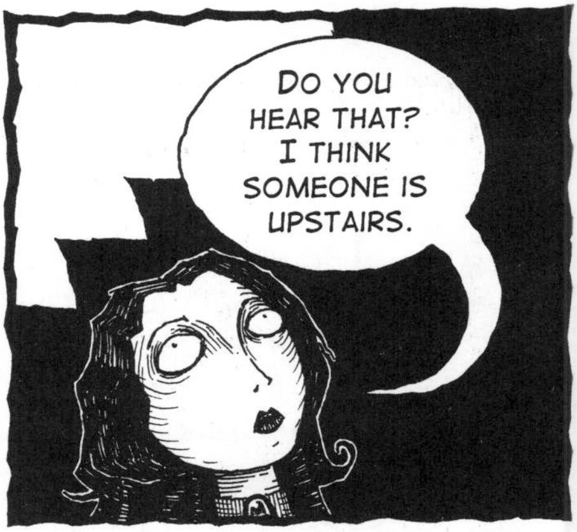
DO YOU HEAR THAT? I THINK SOMEONE IS UPSTAIRS.

VICTORIA RAN HER HAND ALONG THE RAILING AS SHE ASCENDED THE STAIRS. THE WOOD FELT FRESHLY POLISHED, AND THE HOUSE SMELLED OF JASMINE.

DID I TELL THE CLEANING GIRL THAT IS MY FAVORITE SCENT?

THE UPPER ROOMS WERE AS BEAUTIFUL AS THE LOWER ONES, EVERY VASE FILLED WITH FRESH FLOWERS; THE ROOMS WERE WARM AND FILLED WITH THE GLOW OF CANDLES.

HOW IN HEAVEN'S NAME DID SHE DO ALL OF THIS IN ONE AFTERNOON?

VICTORIA'S ROOM WAS STUNNING, BUT THERE WAS NO CLEANING GIRL IN SIGHT.

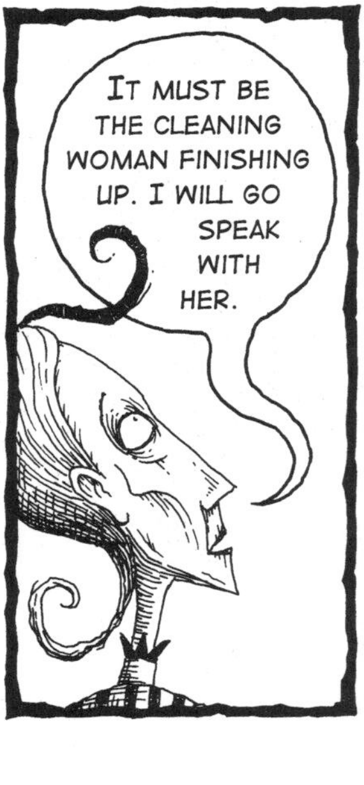
IT MUST BE THE CLEANING WOMAN FINISHING UP. I WILL GO SPEAK WITH HER.

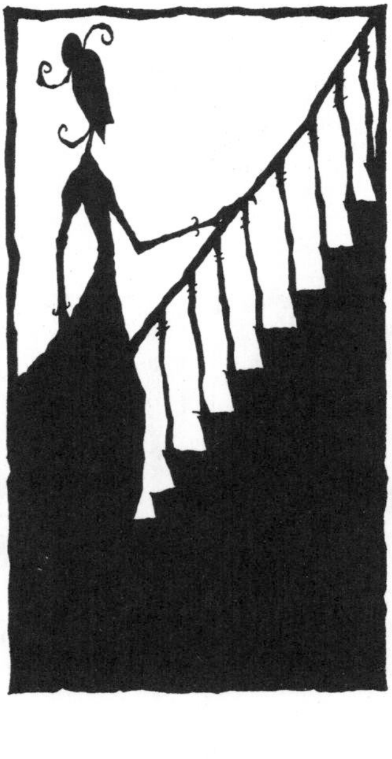

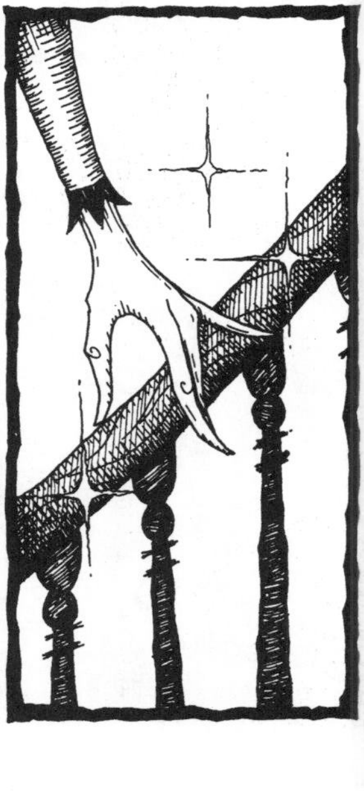

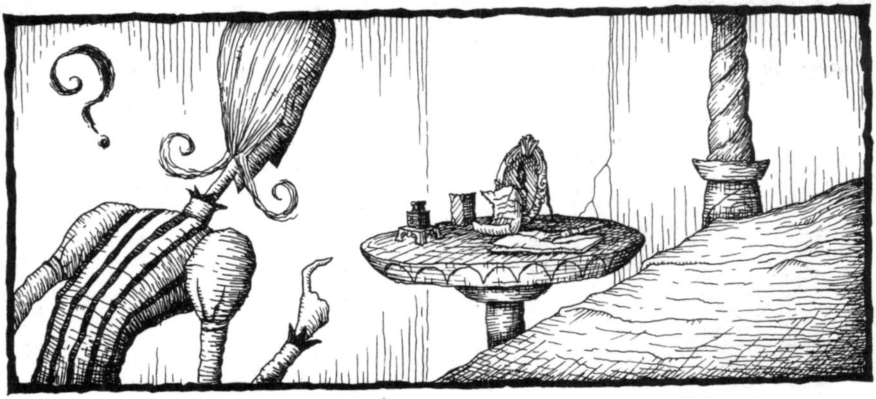

Madame Victoria,

It grieves me to inform you I was unable to clean your house as promised. You will find that I have returned the payment you sent me in full. You may think me ignorant and foolish for being frightened of this house, but the fact remains that it does terrify me. You would do well to find another home, Madame Victoria. I wish you all the best - you are in my prayers,

Molly O'Brien

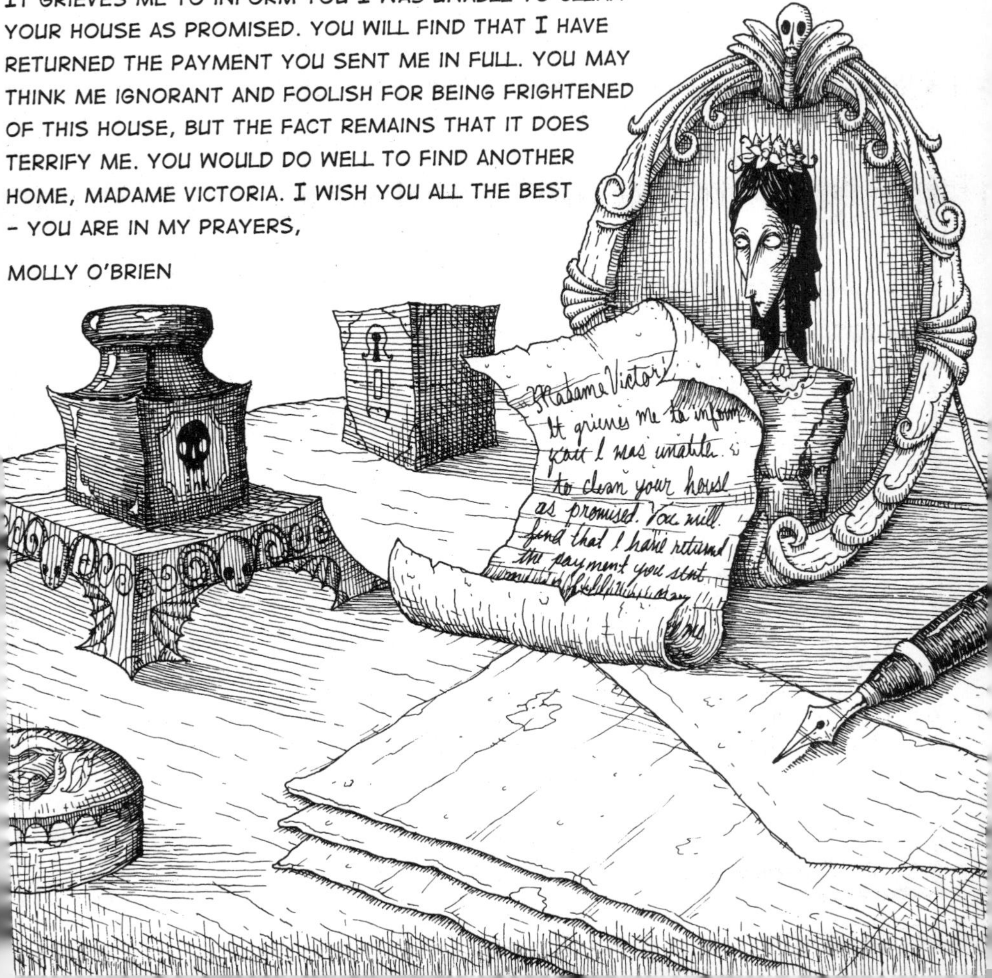
Madame Victor
It grieves me to inform
you I was unable
to clean your house
as promised. You will
find that I have returned
the payment you sent

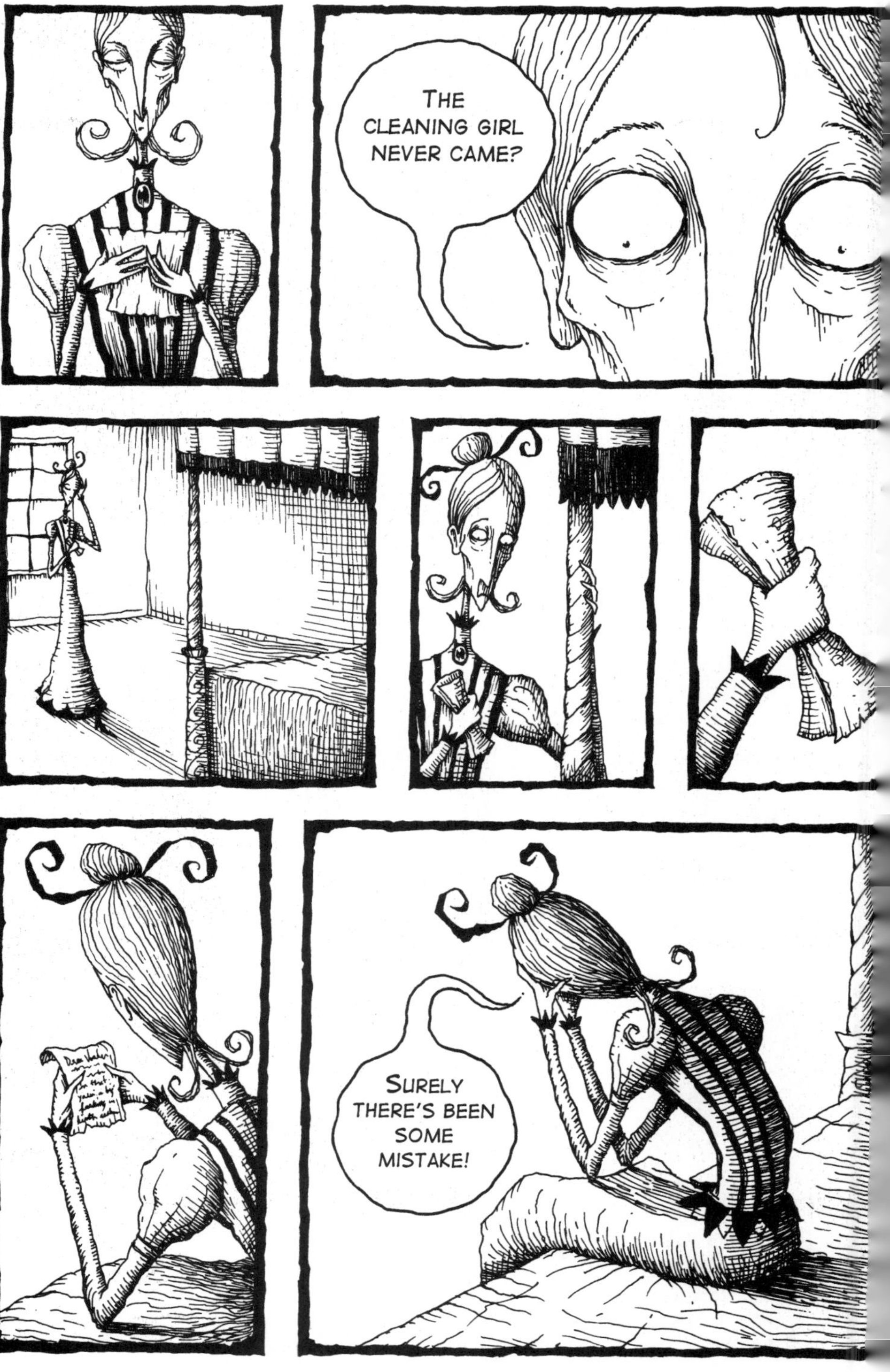
THE CLEANING GIRL NEVER CAME?
SURELY THERE'S BEEN SOME MISTAKE!

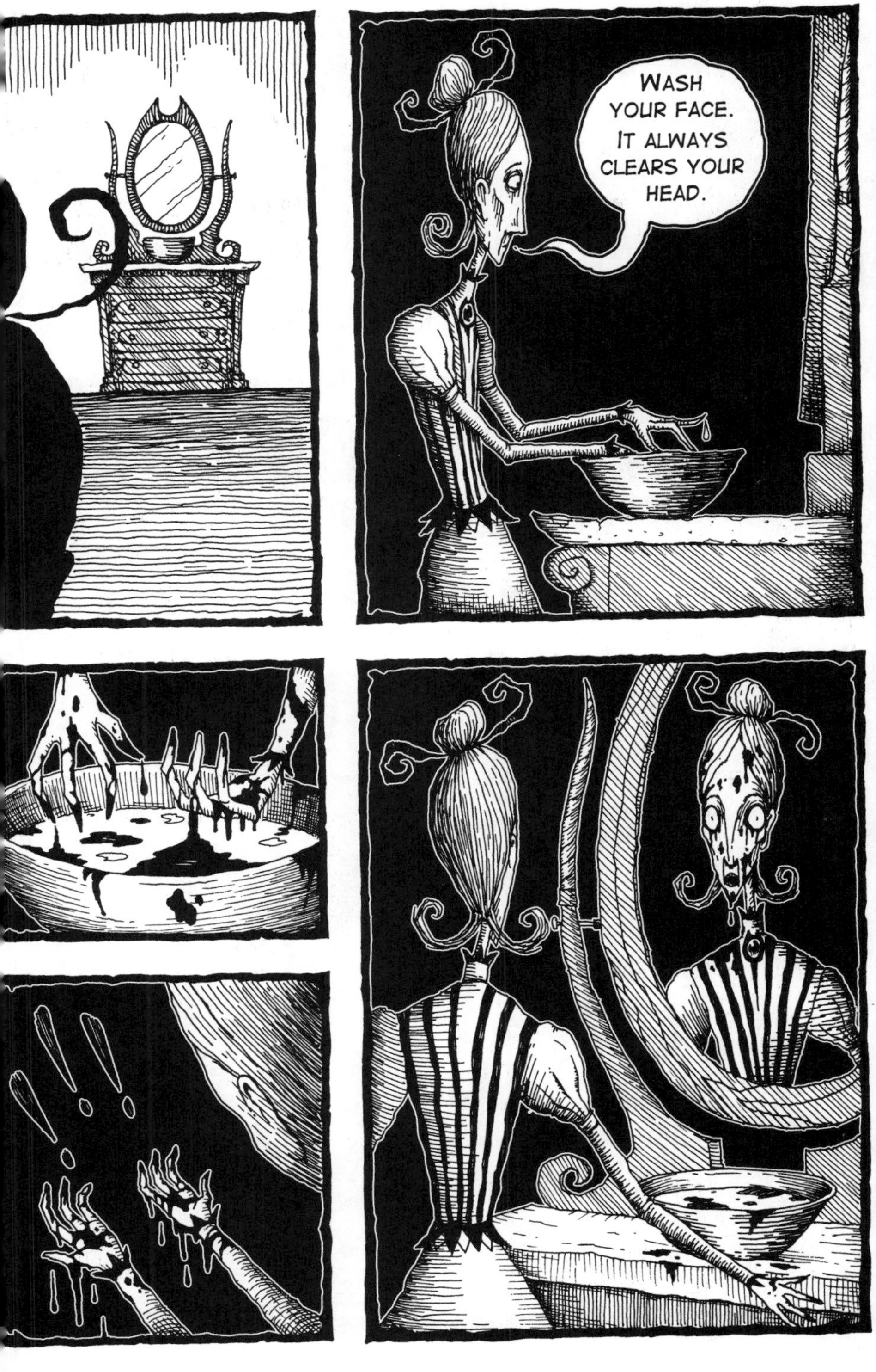
WASH YOUR FACE. IT ALWAYS CLEARS YOUR HEAD.

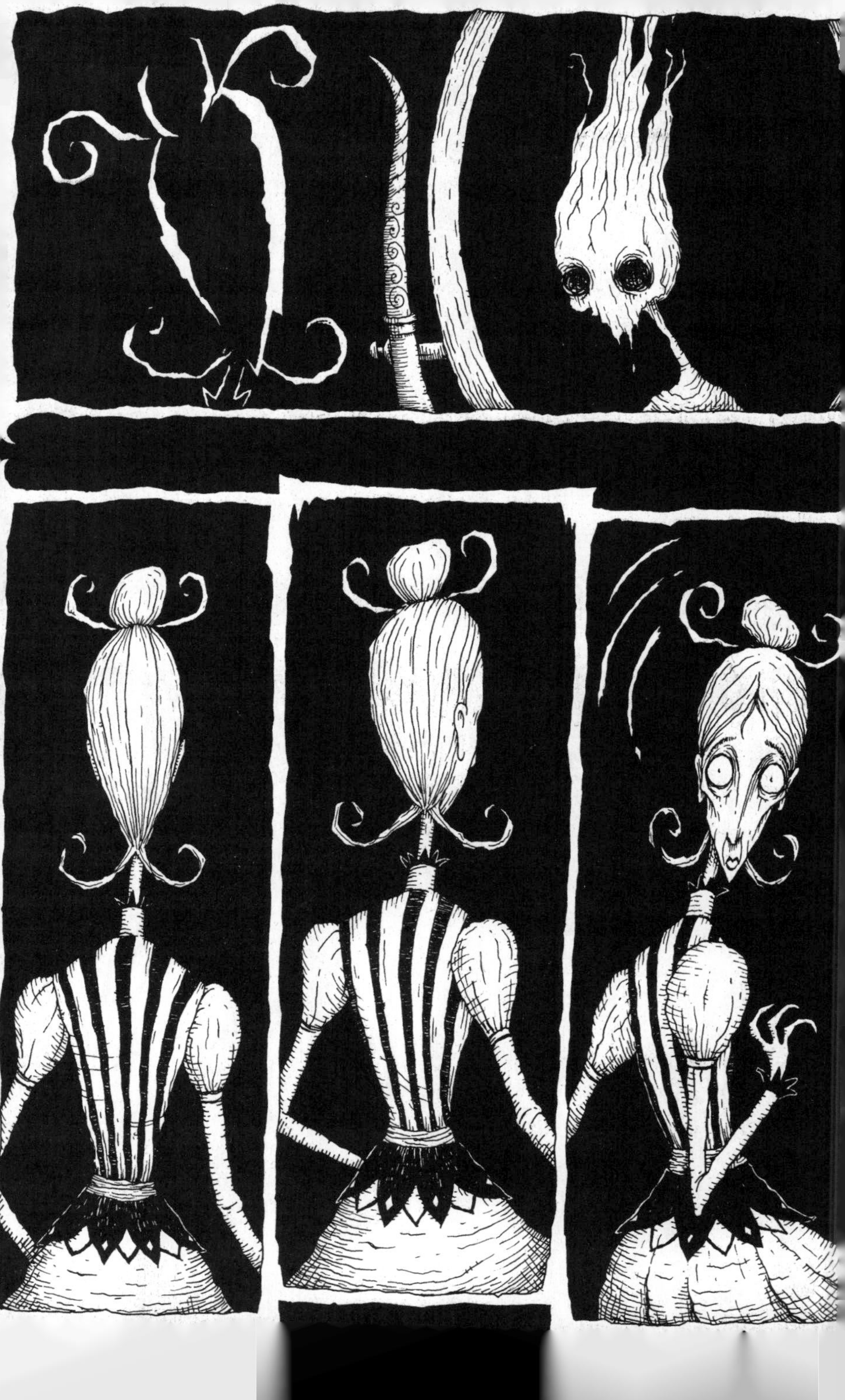

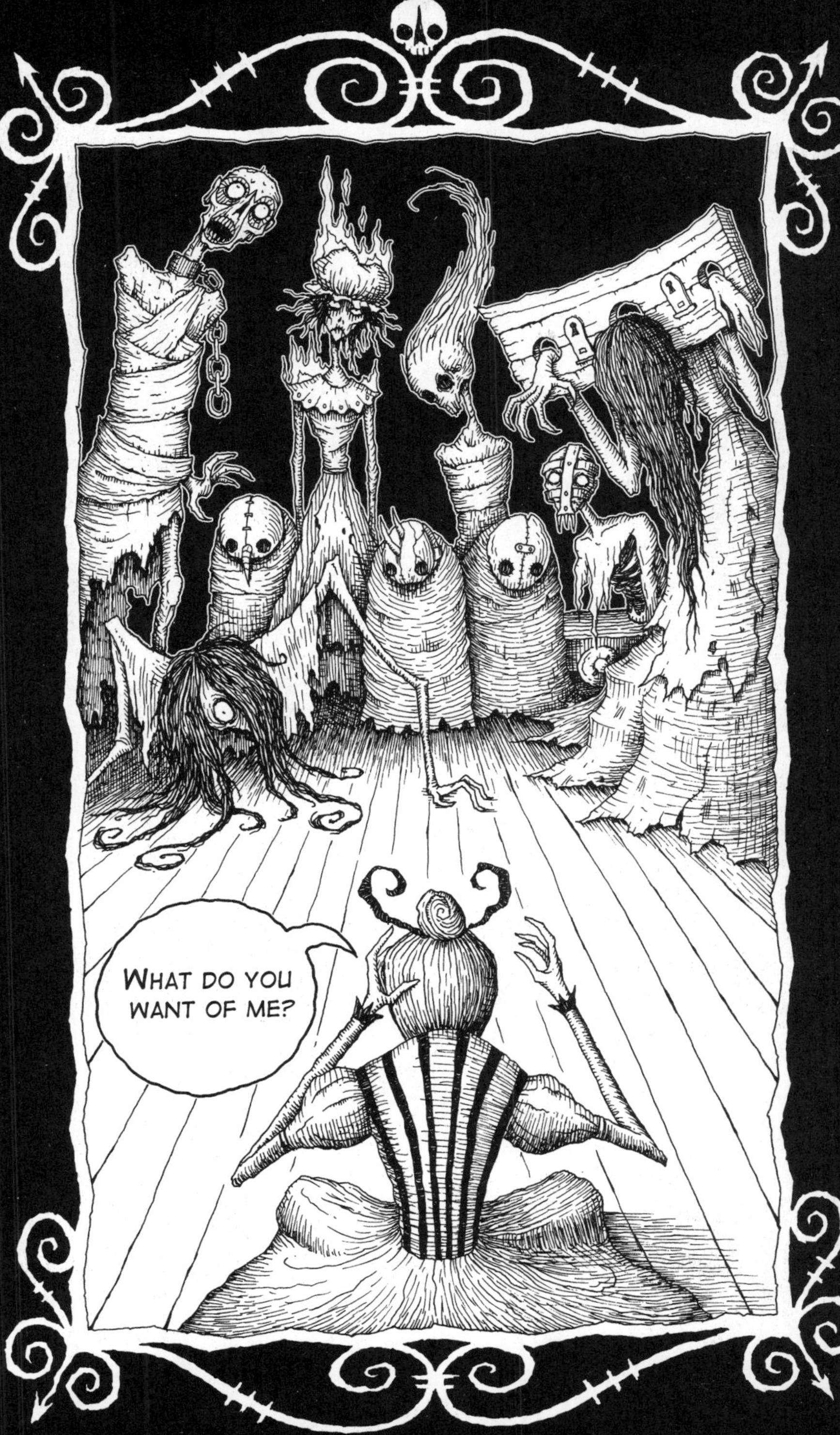
WHAT DO YOU WANT OF ME?

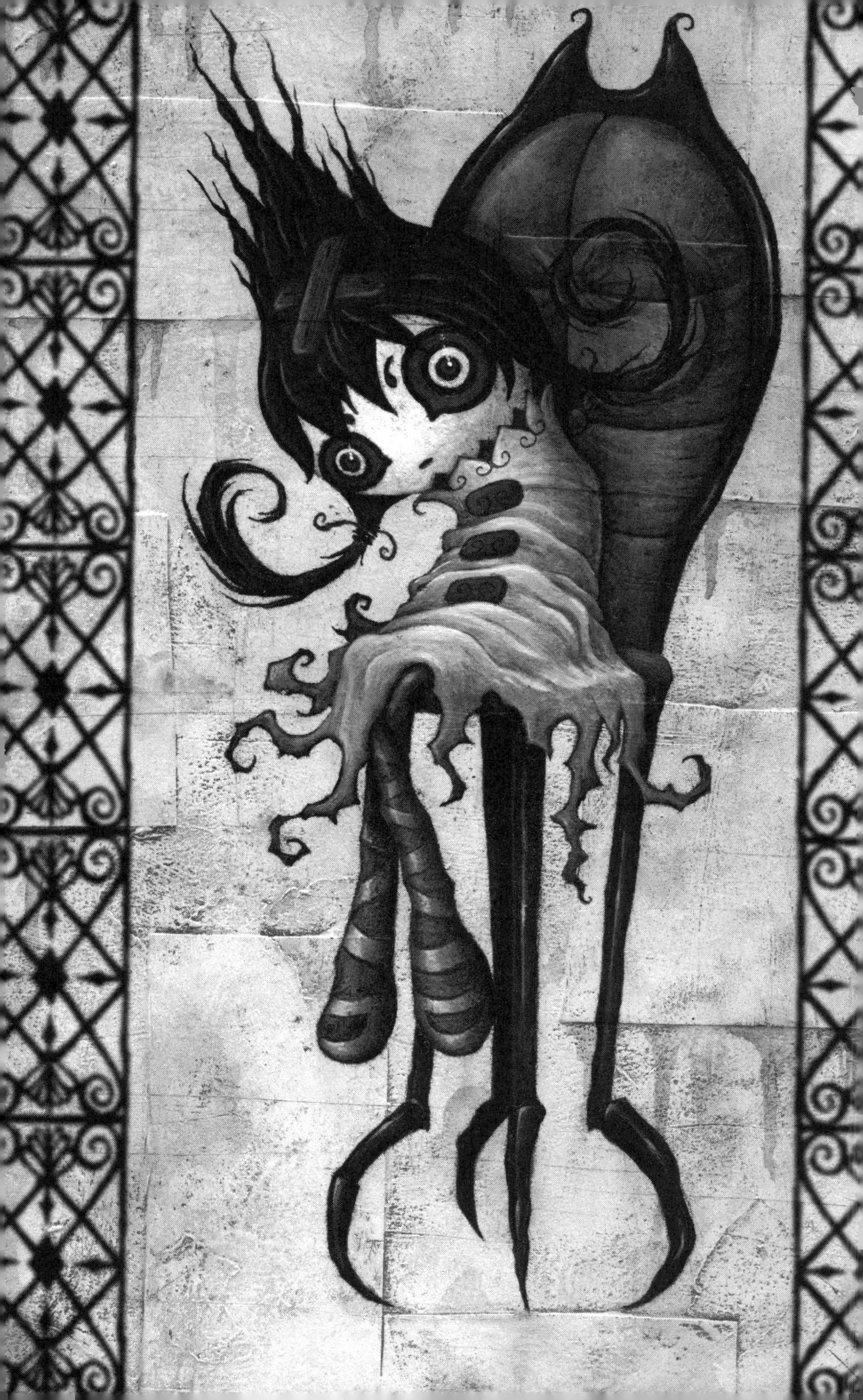

Chapter 2

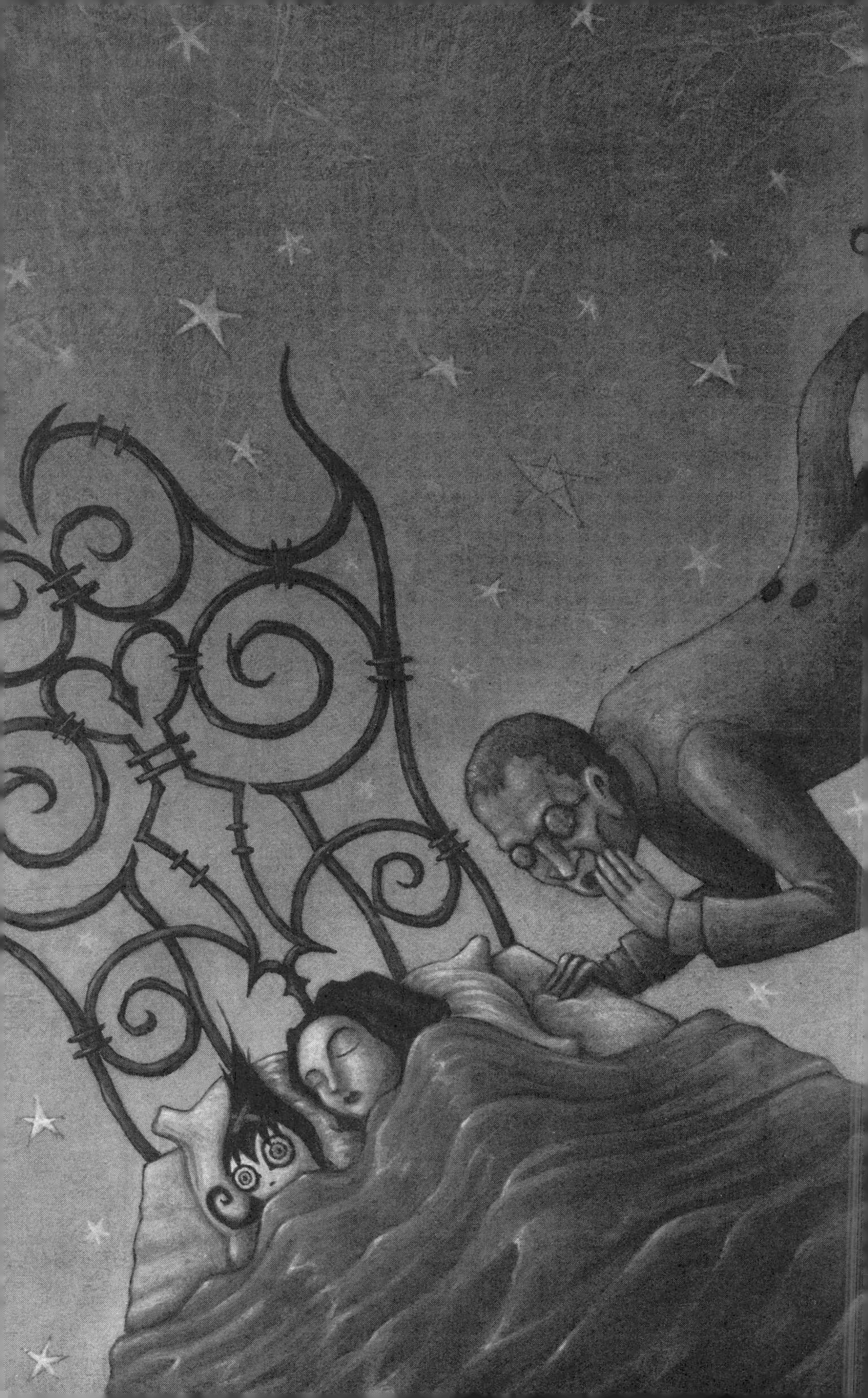

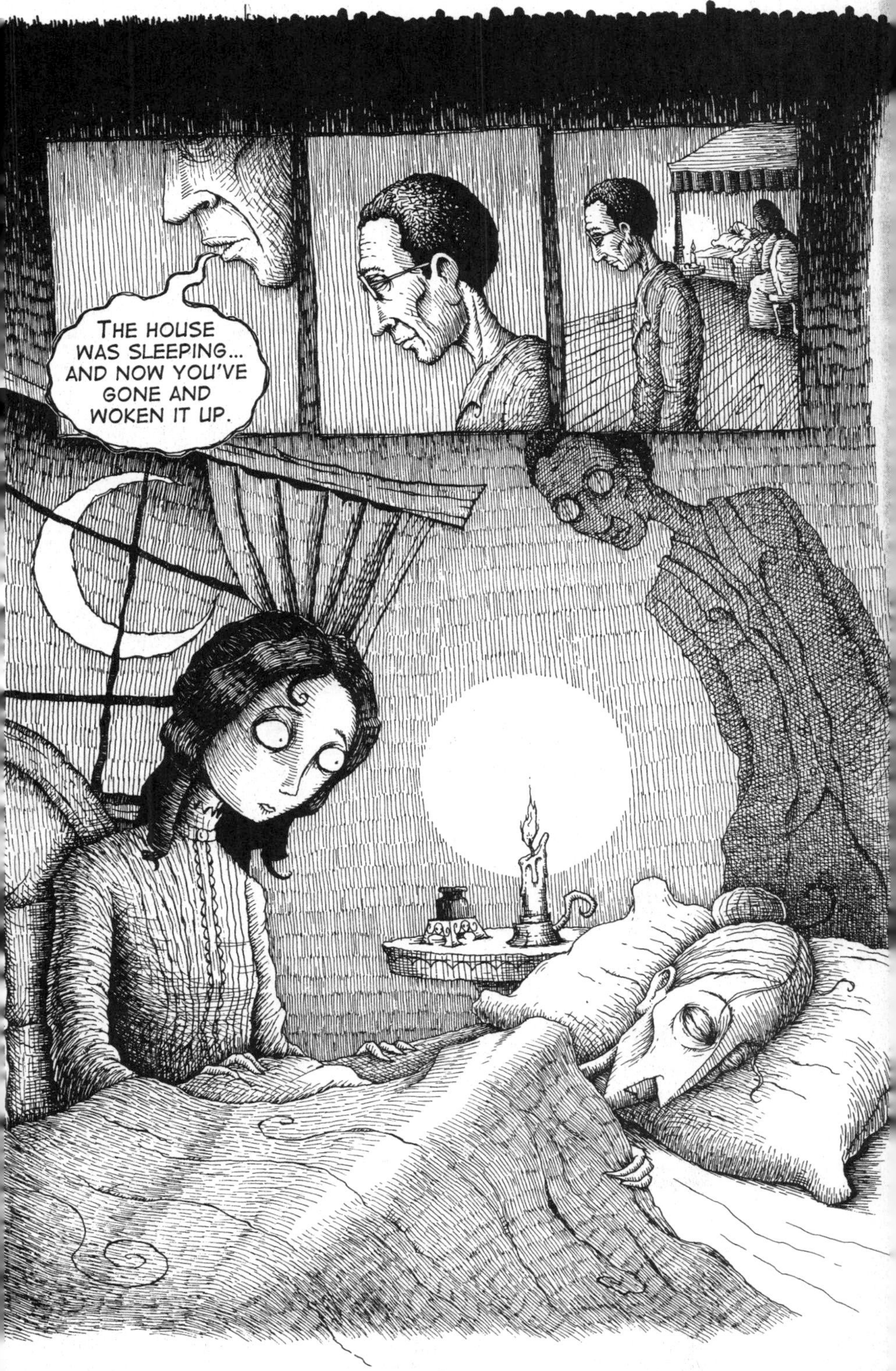
THE HOUSE WAS SLEEPING... AND NOW YOU'VE GONE AND WOKEN IT UP.

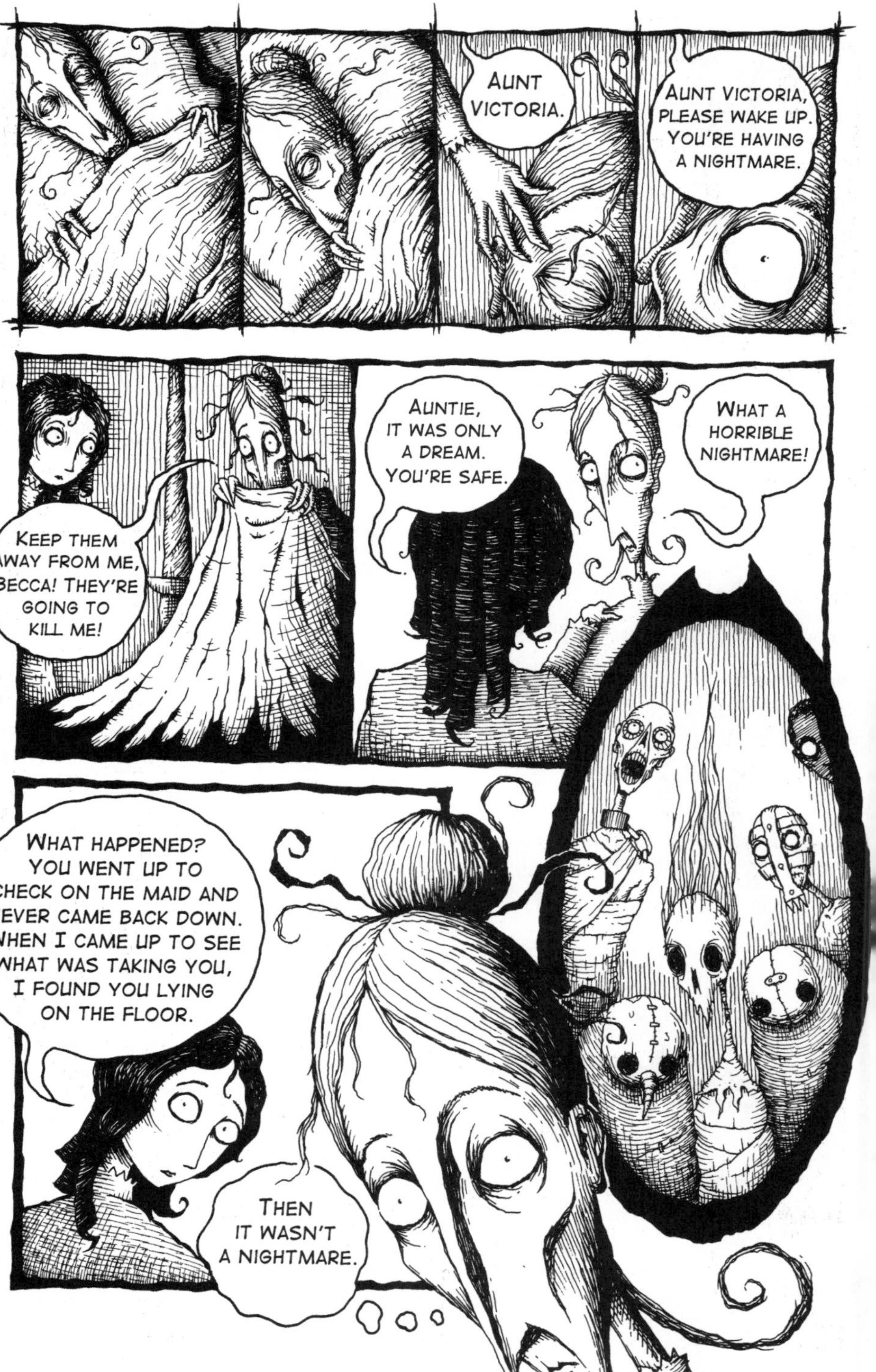
Aunt Victoria.
Aunt Victoria, please wake up. You're having a nightmare.
Keep them away from me, Becca! They're going to kill me!
Auntie, it was only a dream. You're safe.
What a horrible nightmare!
What happened? You went up to check on the maid and never came back down. When I came up to see what was taking you, I found you lying on the floor.
Then it wasn't a nightmare.

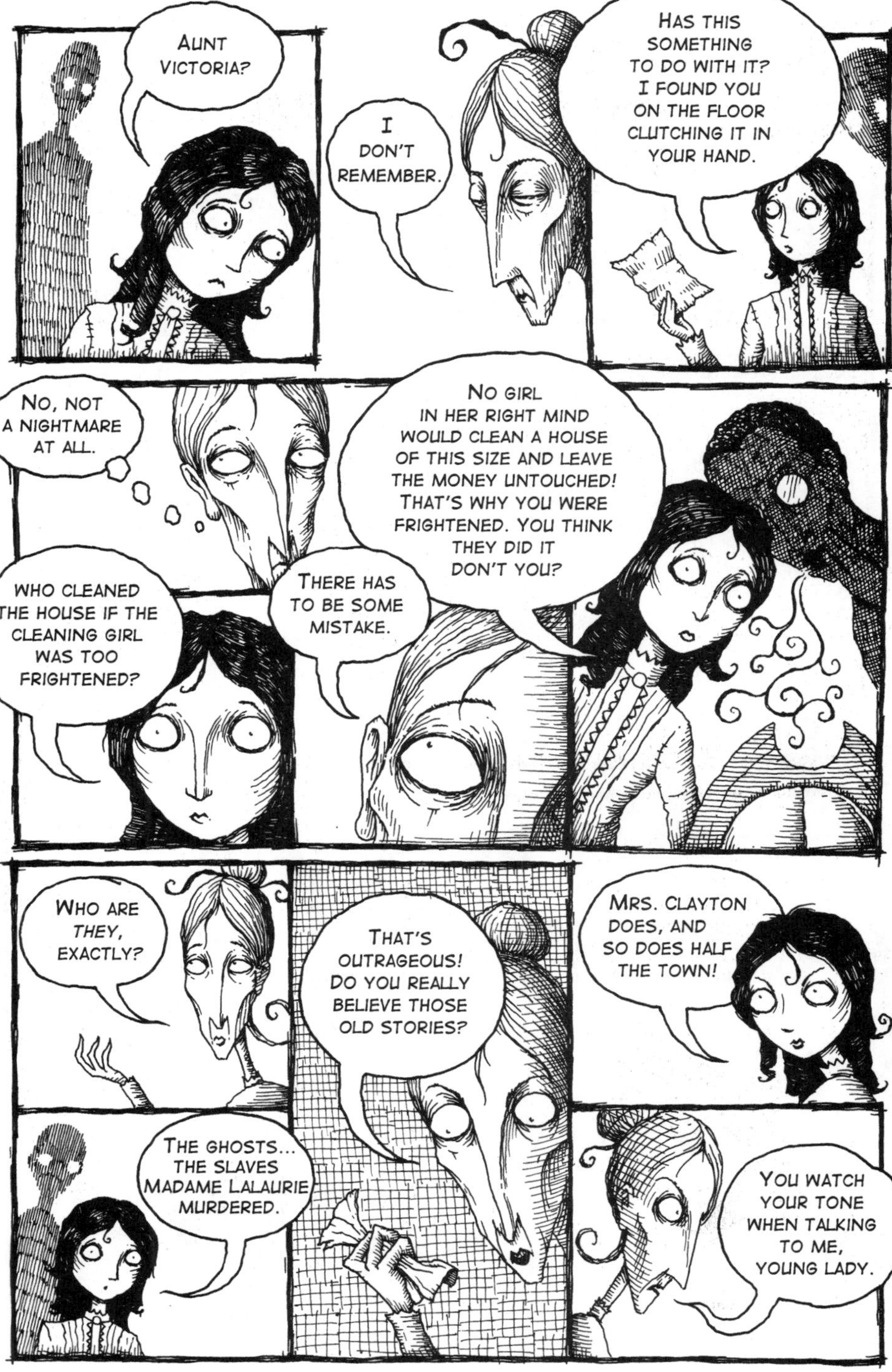
Aunt Victoria?
I don't remember.
Has this something to do with it? I found you on the floor clutching it in your hand.
No, not a nightmare at all.
No girl in her right mind would clean a house of this size and leave the money untouched! That's why you were frightened. You think they did it don't you?
Who cleaned the house if the cleaning girl was too frightened?
There has to be some mistake.
Who are *they*, exactly?
The ghosts... the slaves Madame Lalaurie murdered.
That's outrageous! Do you really believe those old stories?
Mrs. Clayton does, and so does half the town!
You watch your tone when talking to me, young lady.

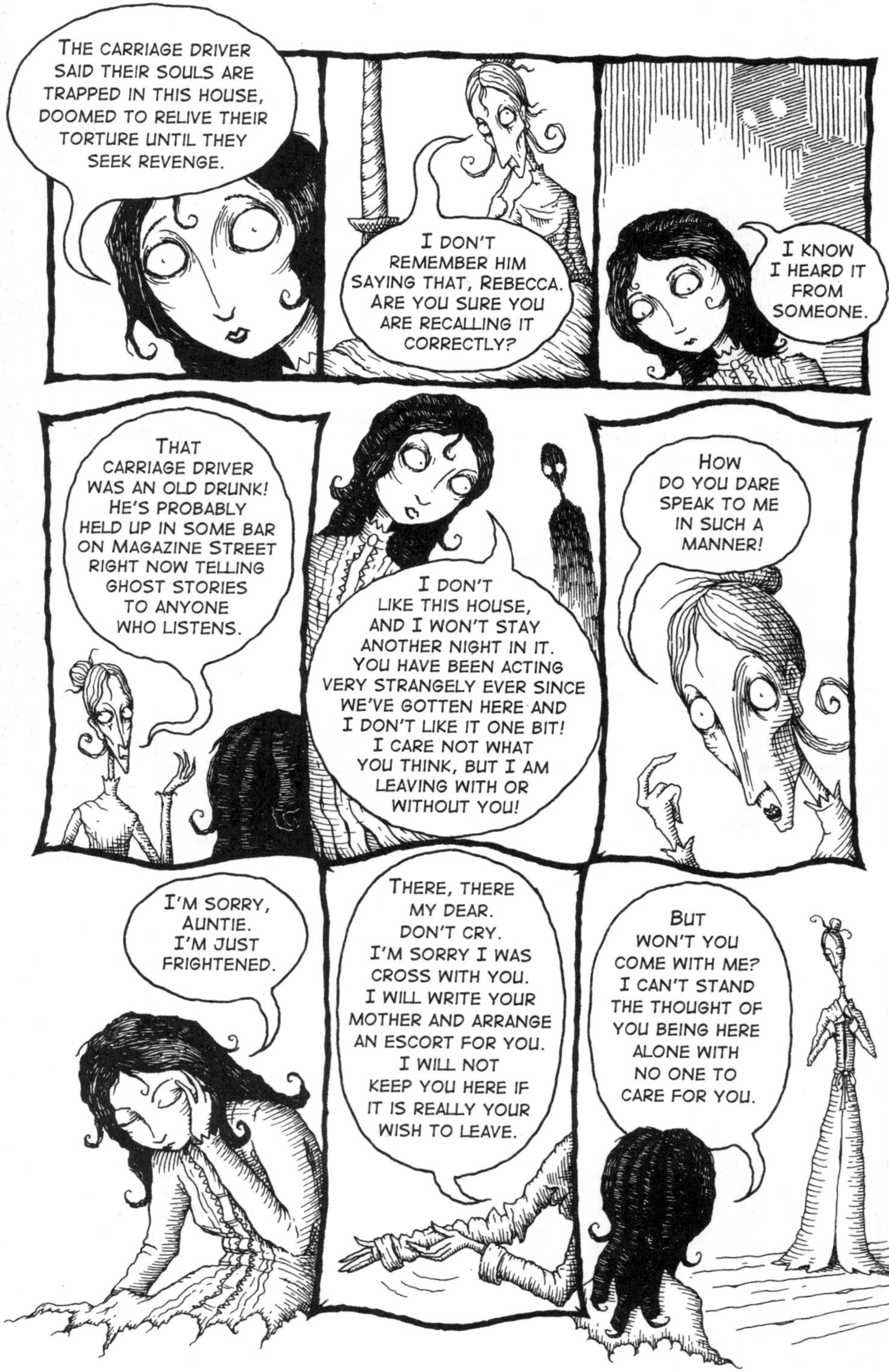
THE CARRIAGE DRIVER SAID THEIR SOULS ARE TRAPPED IN THIS HOUSE, DOOMED TO RELIVE THEIR TORTURE UNTIL THEY SEEK REVENGE.
I DON'T REMEMBER HIM SAYING THAT, REBECCA. ARE YOU SURE YOU ARE RECALLING IT CORRECTLY?
I KNOW I HEARD IT FROM SOMEONE.
THAT CARRIAGE DRIVER WAS AN OLD DRUNK! HE'S PROBABLY HELD UP IN SOME BAR ON MAGAZINE STREET RIGHT NOW TELLING GHOST STORIES TO ANYONE WHO LISTENS.
I DON'T LIKE THIS HOUSE, AND I WON'T STAY ANOTHER NIGHT IN IT. YOU HAVE BEEN ACTING VERY STRANGELY EVER SINCE WE'VE GOTTEN HERE AND I DON'T LIKE IT ONE BIT! I CARE NOT WHAT YOU THINK, BUT I AM LEAVING WITH OR WITHOUT YOU!
HOW DO YOU DARE SPEAK TO ME IN SUCH A MANNER!
I'M SORRY, AUNTIE. I'M JUST FRIGHTENED.
THERE, THERE MY DEAR. DON'T CRY. I'M SORRY I WAS CROSS WITH YOU. I WILL WRITE YOUR MOTHER AND ARRANGE AN ESCORT FOR YOU. I WILL NOT KEEP YOU HERE IF IT IS REALLY YOUR WISH TO LEAVE.
BUT WON'T YOU COME WITH ME? I CAN'T STAND THE THOUGHT OF YOU BEING HERE ALONE WITH NO ONE TO CARE FOR YOU.

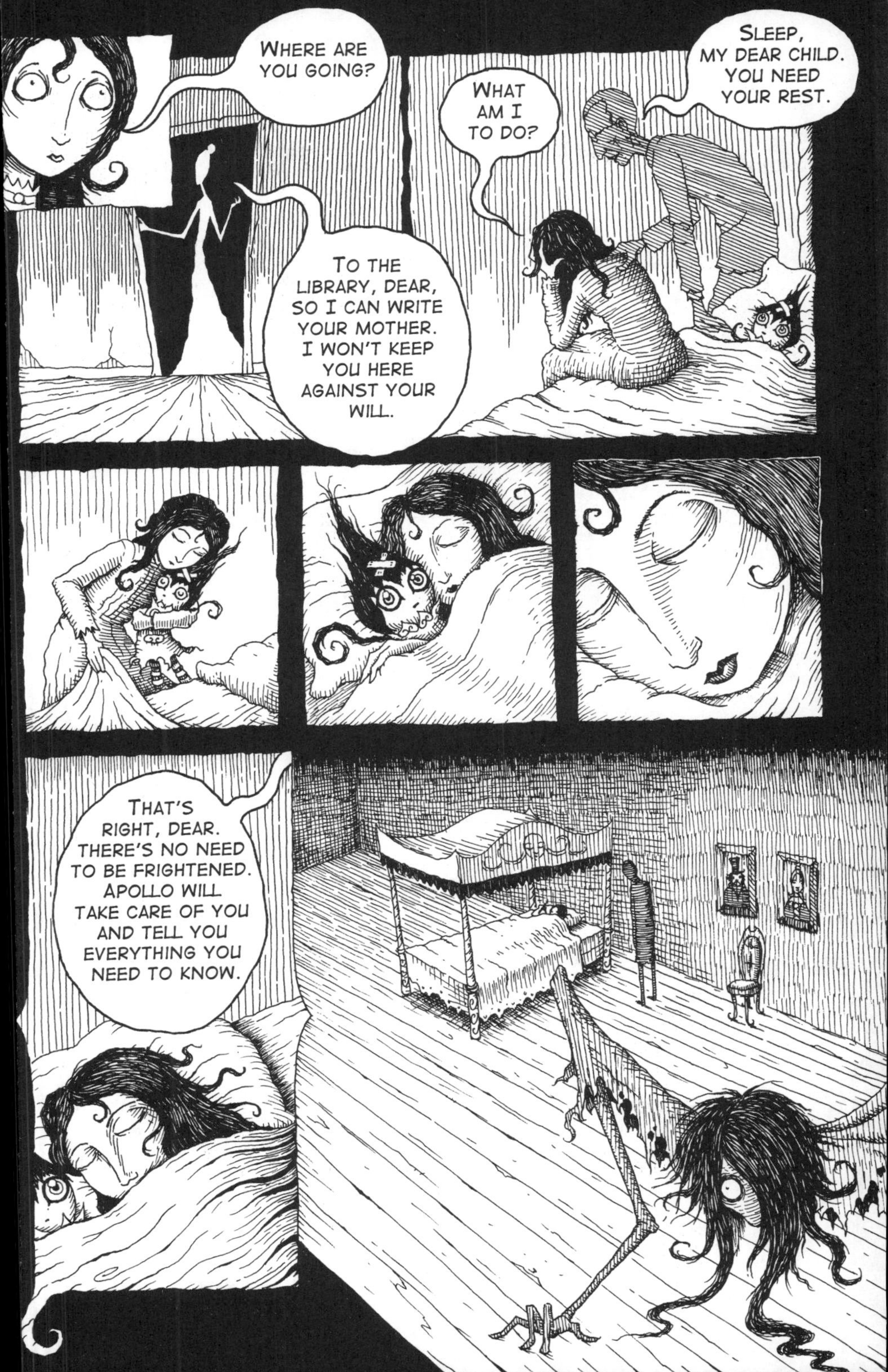
WHERE ARE YOU GOING?
TO THE LIBRARY, DEAR, SO I CAN WRITE YOUR MOTHER. I WON'T KEEP YOU HERE AGAINST YOUR WILL.
WHAT AM I TO DO?
SLEEP, MY DEAR CHILD. YOU NEED YOUR REST.
THAT'S RIGHT, DEAR. THERE'S NO NEED TO BE FRIGHTENED. APOLLO WILL TAKE CARE OF YOU AND TELL YOU EVERYTHING YOU NEED TO KNOW.

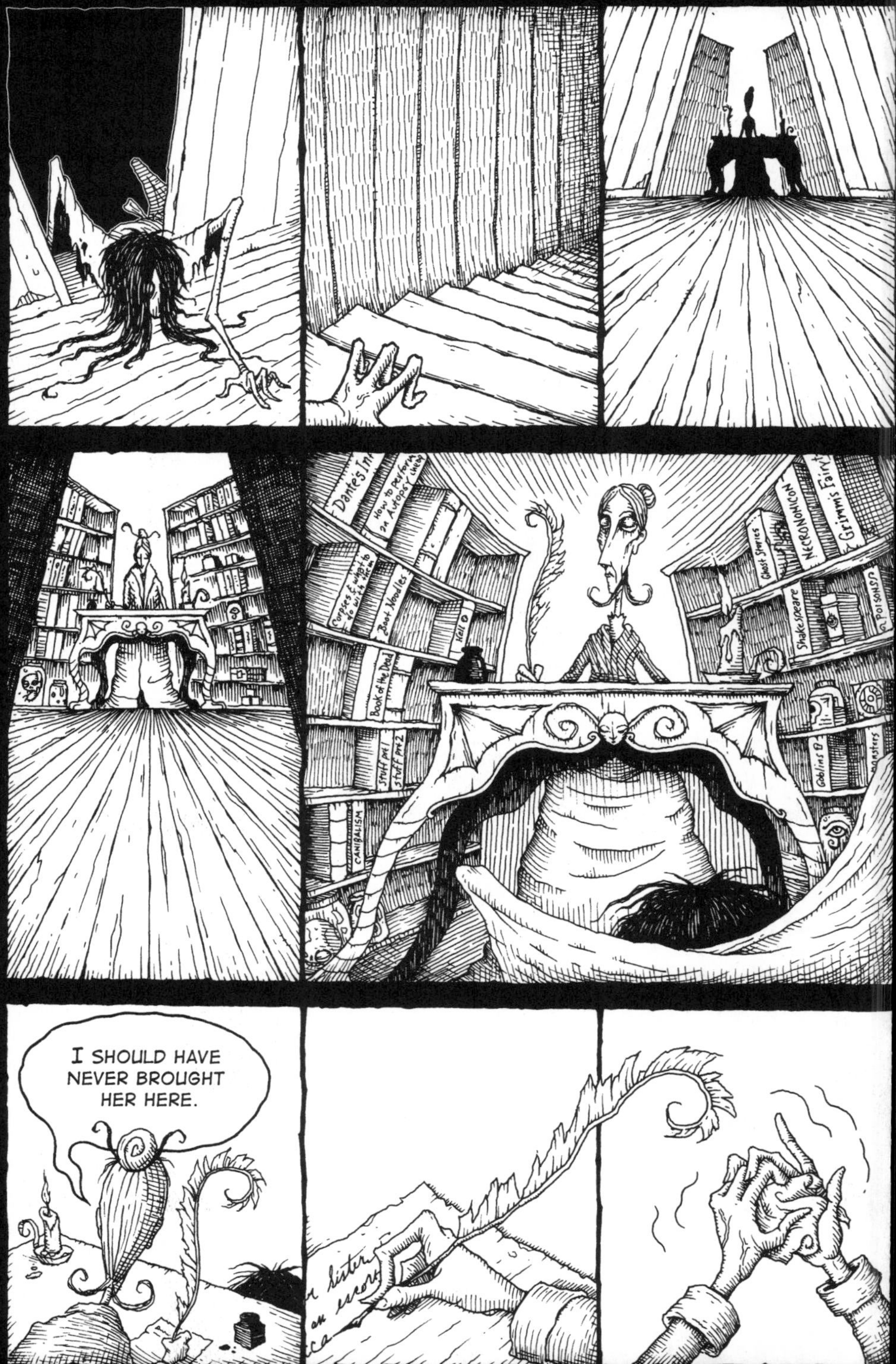

How to perform an Autopsy cheap
Corpses & what to do with them
Boot Noodles
Kell
Book of the Dead
stuff prt 1
stuff prt 2
CANIBALISM
Ghost Stories
NECRONOMICON
Shakespeare
POISONS
I SHOULD HAVE NEVER BROUGHT HER HERE.

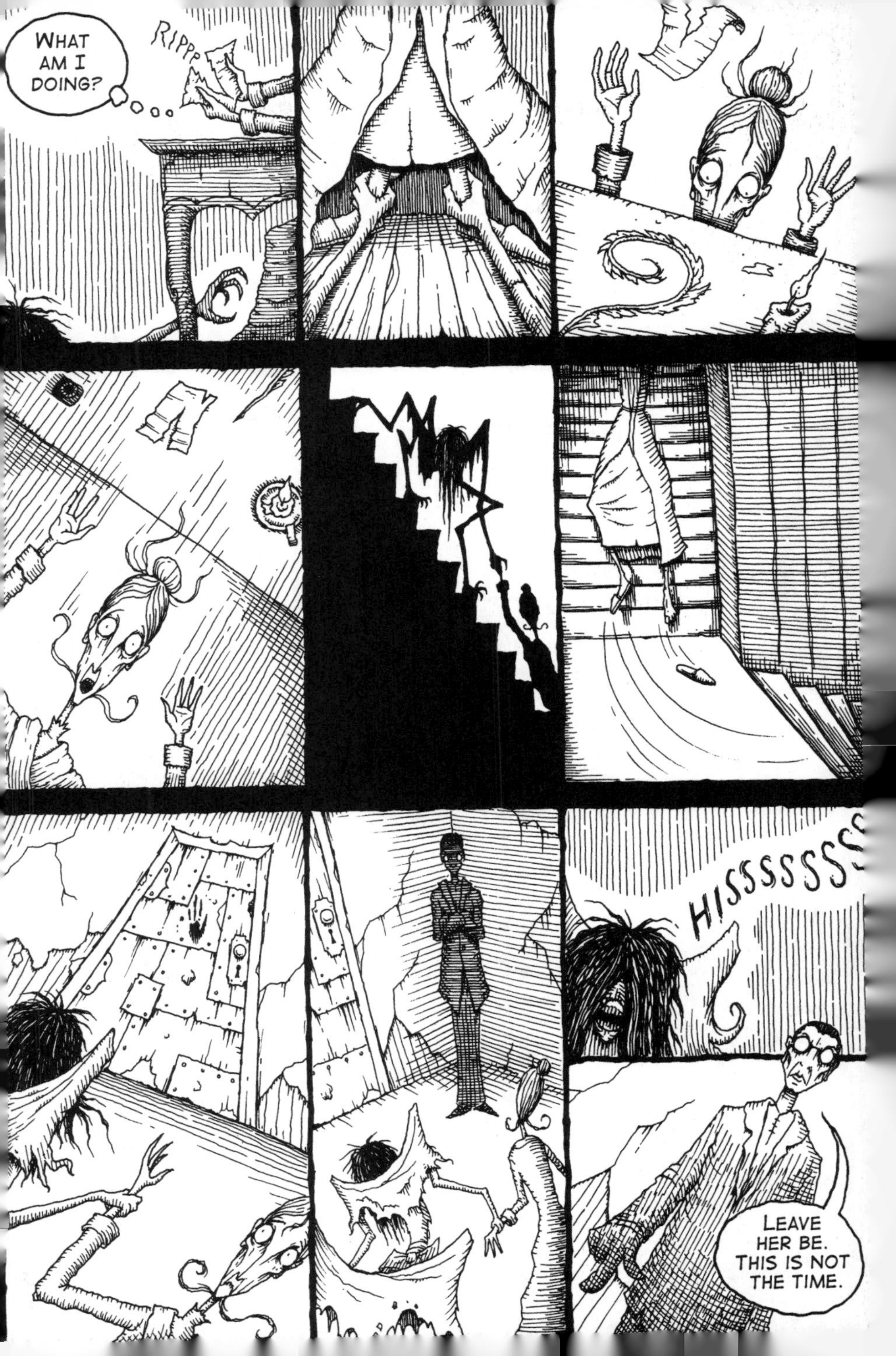
WHAT AM I DOING?
RIPPP
HISSSSSSSS
LEAVE HER BE. THIS IS NOT THE TIME.

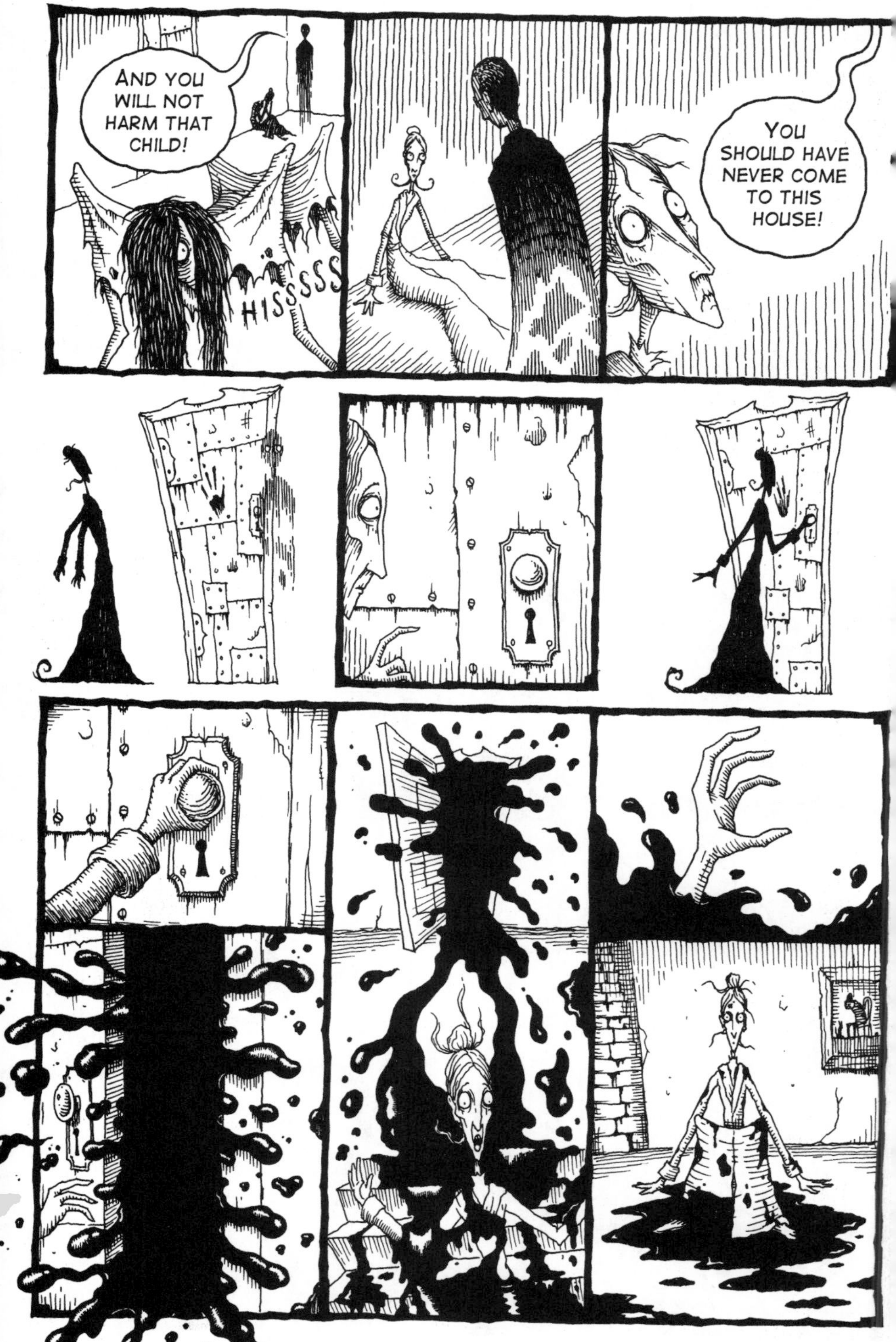
AND YOU WILL NOT HARM THAT CHILD!
HISSSSS
YOU SHOULD HAVE NEVER COME TO THIS HOUSE!

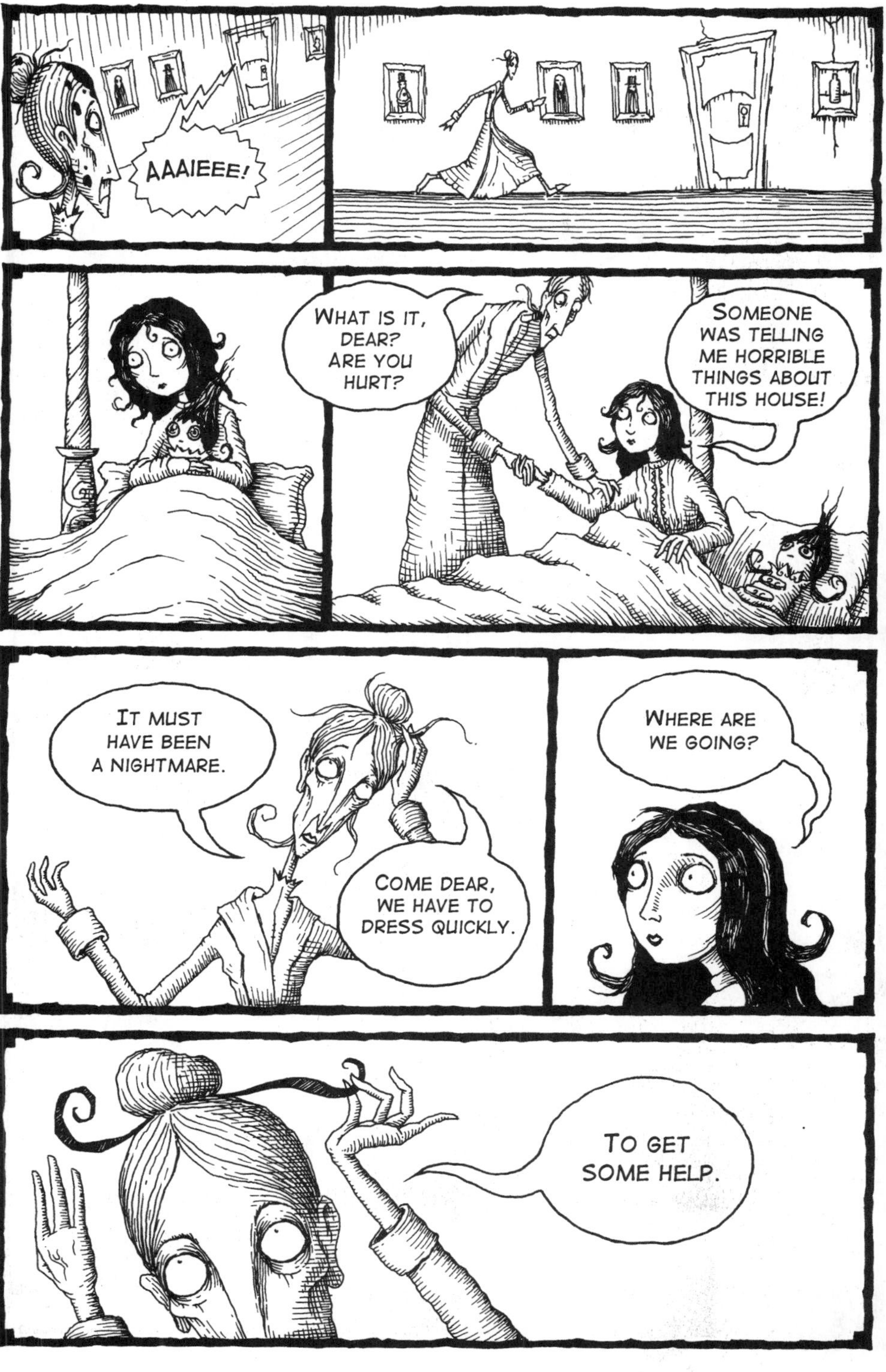
AAAIEEE!
WHAT IS IT, DEAR? ARE YOU HURT?
SOMEONE WAS TELLING ME HORRIBLE THINGS ABOUT THIS HOUSE!
IT MUST HAVE BEEN A NIGHTMARE.
COME DEAR, WE HAVE TO DRESS QUICKLY.
WHERE ARE WE GOING?
TO GET SOME HELP.

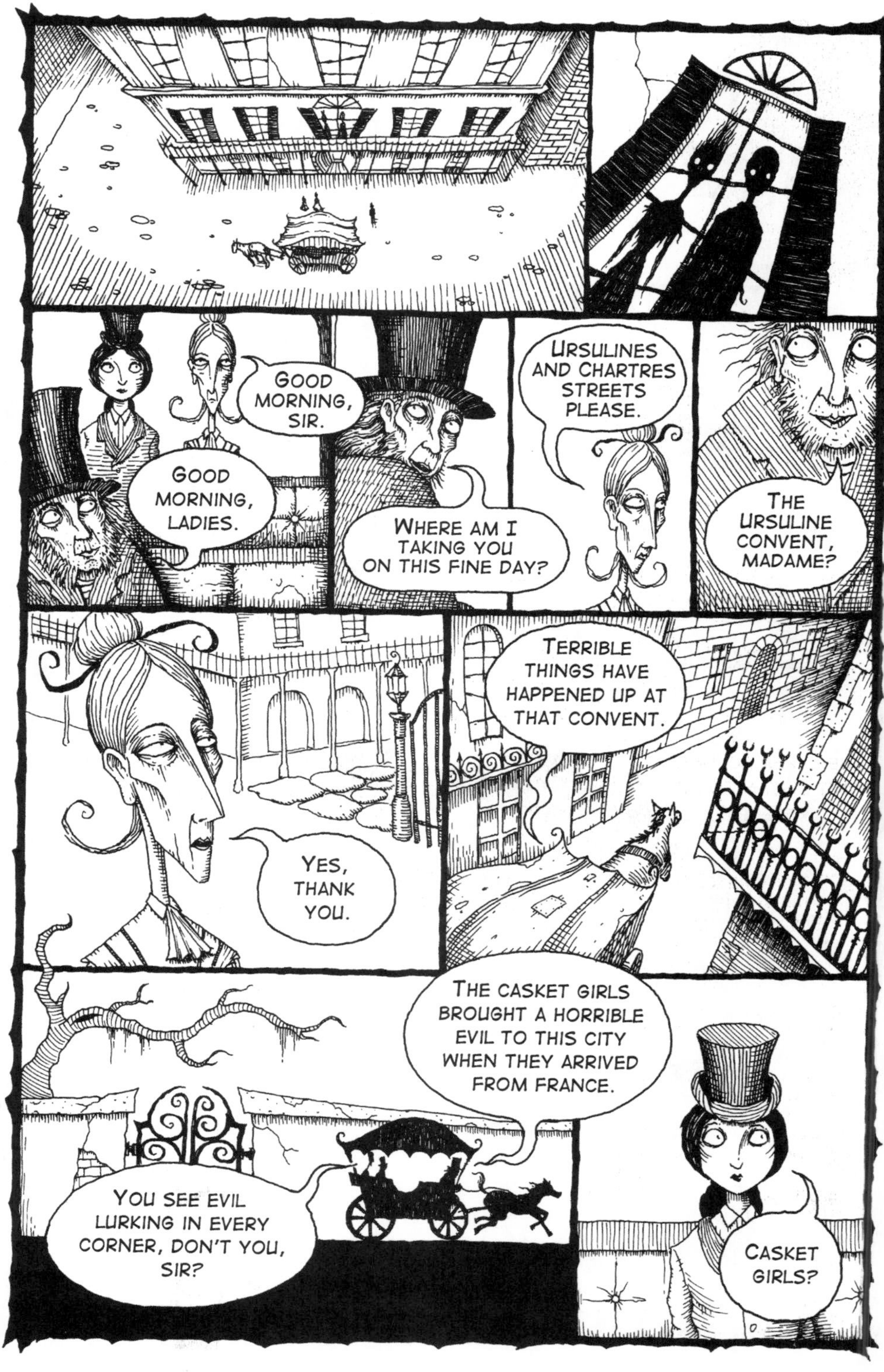
GOOD MORNING, SIR.
GOOD MORNING, LADIES.
WHERE AM I TAKING YOU ON THIS FINE DAY?
URSULINES AND CHARTRES STREETS PLEASE.
THE URSULINE CONVENT, MADAME?
YES, THANK YOU.
TERRIBLE THINGS HAVE HAPPENED UP AT THAT CONVENT.
THE CASKET GIRLS BROUGHT A HORRIBLE EVIL TO THIS CITY WHEN THEY ARRIVED FROM FRANCE.
YOU SEE EVIL LURKING IN EVERY CORNER, DON'T YOU, SIR?
CASKET GIRLS?

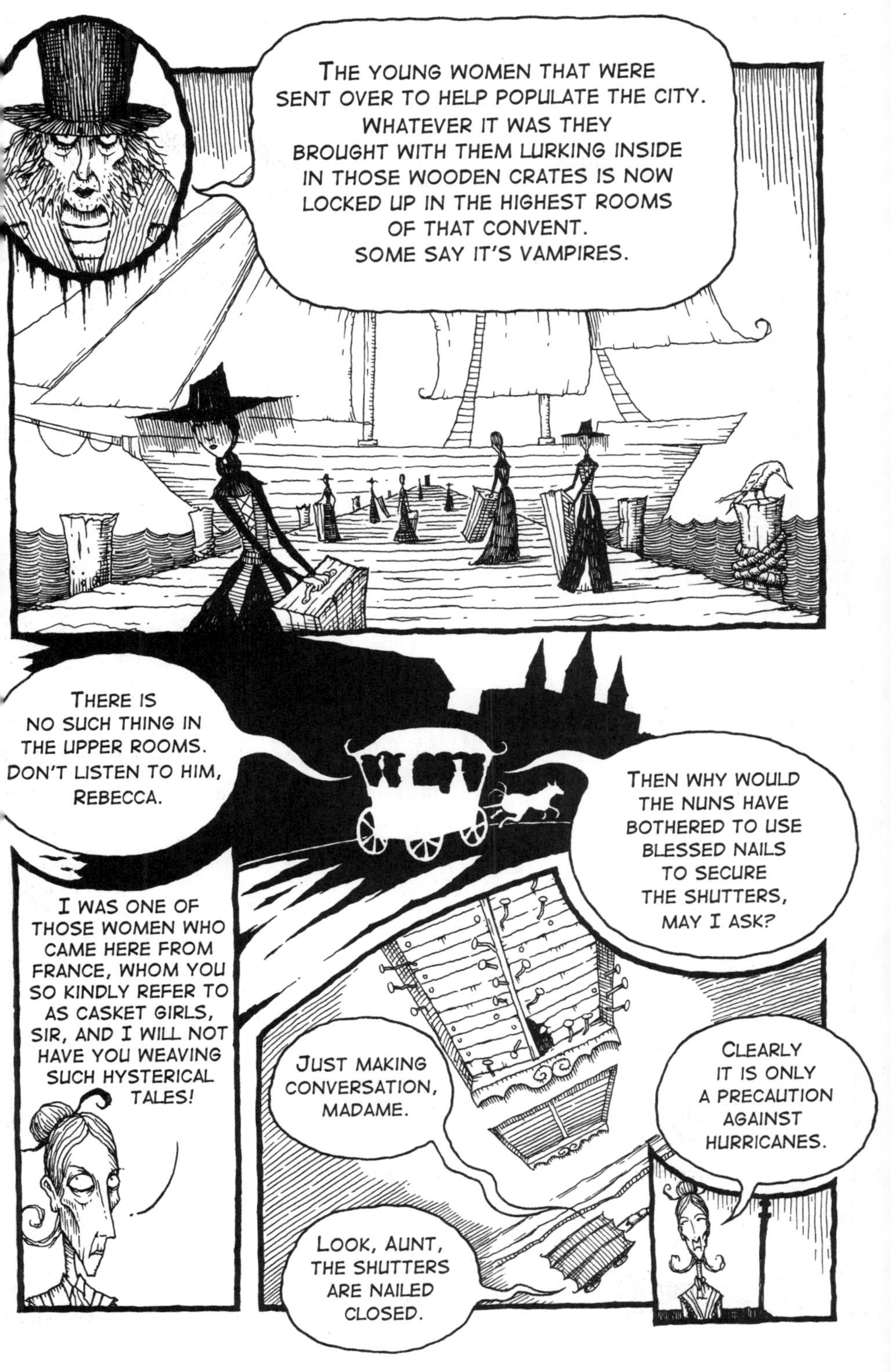
THE YOUNG WOMEN THAT WERE SENT OVER TO HELP POPULATE THE CITY. WHATEVER IT WAS THEY BROUGHT WITH THEM LURKING INSIDE IN THOSE WOODEN CRATES IS NOW LOCKED UP IN THE HIGHEST ROOMS OF THAT CONVENT. SOME SAY IT'S VAMPIRES.
THERE IS NO SUCH THING IN THE UPPER ROOMS. DON'T LISTEN TO HIM, REBECCA.
THEN WHY WOULD THE NUNS HAVE BOTHERED TO USE BLESSED NAILS TO SECURE THE SHUTTERS, MAY I ASK?
I WAS ONE OF THOSE WOMEN WHO CAME HERE FROM FRANCE, WHOM YOU SO KINDLY REFER TO AS CASKET GIRLS, SIR, AND I WILL NOT HAVE YOU WEAVING SUCH HYSTERICAL TALES!
JUST MAKING CONVERSATION, MADAME.
CLEARLY IT IS ONLY A PRECAUTION AGAINST HURRICANES.
LOOK, AUNT, THE SHUTTERS ARE NAILED CLOSED.

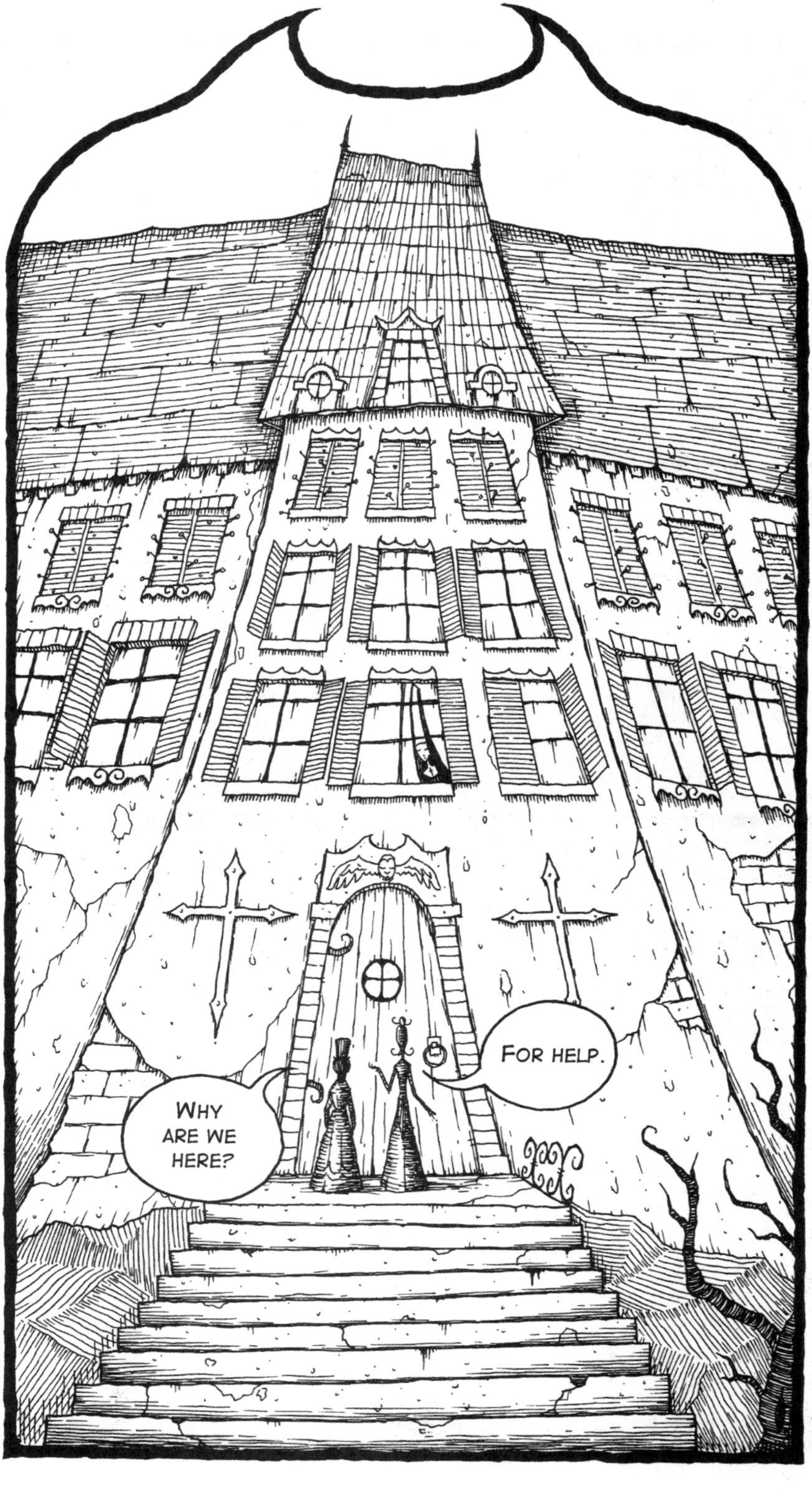
WHY ARE WE HERE?
FOR HELP.

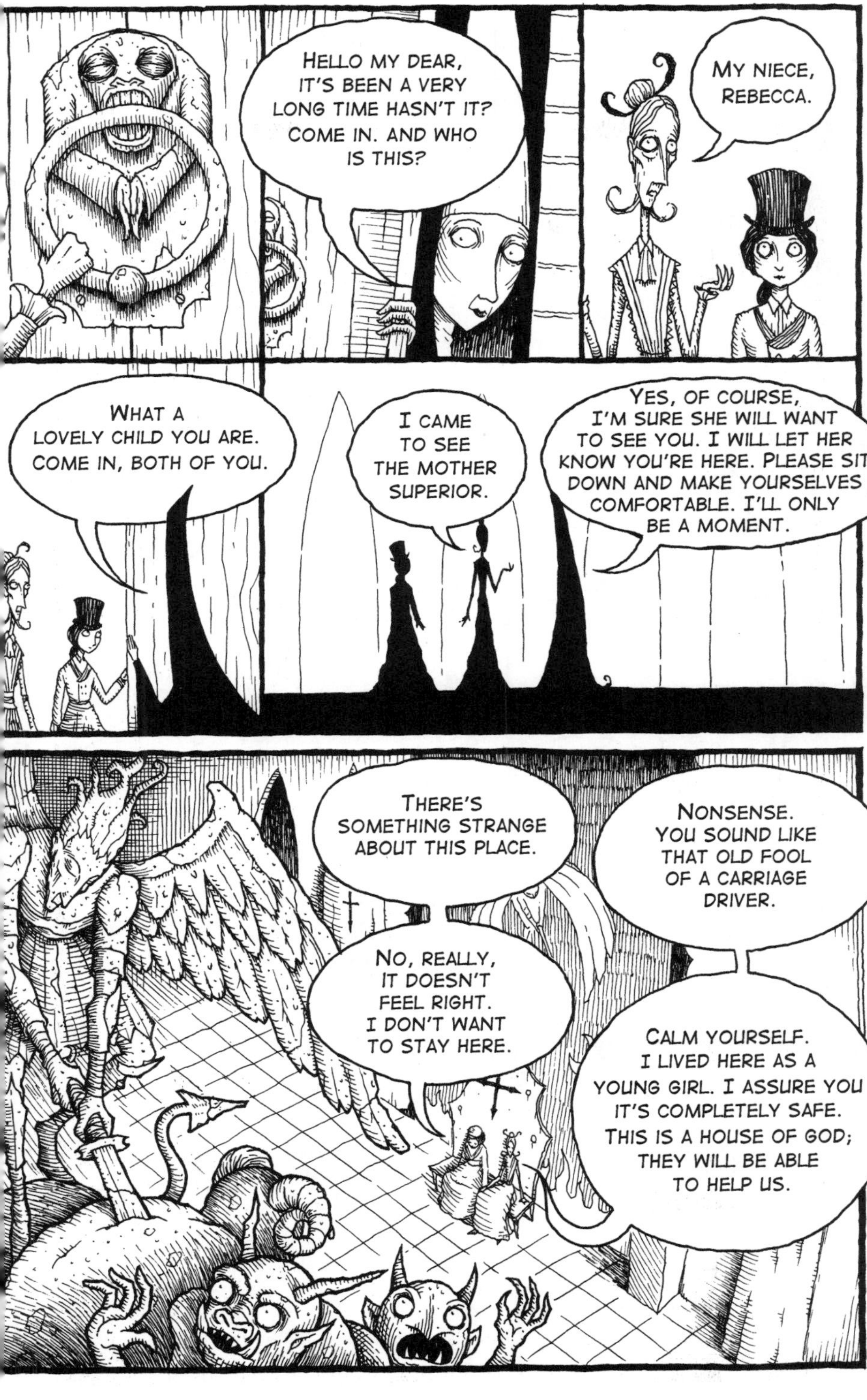
Hello my dear,
it's been a very long time hasn't it? come in. And who is this?
My niece, Rebecca.
What a lovely child you are. Come in, both of you.
I came to see the Mother Superior.
Yes, of course, I'm sure she will want to see you. I will let her know you're here. Please sit down and make yourselves comfortable. I'll only be a moment.
There's something strange about this place.
No, really, it doesn't feel right. I don't want to stay here.
Nonsense. You sound like that old fool of a carriage driver.
Calm yourself. I lived here as a young girl. I assure you it's completely safe. This is a house of God; they will be able to help us.

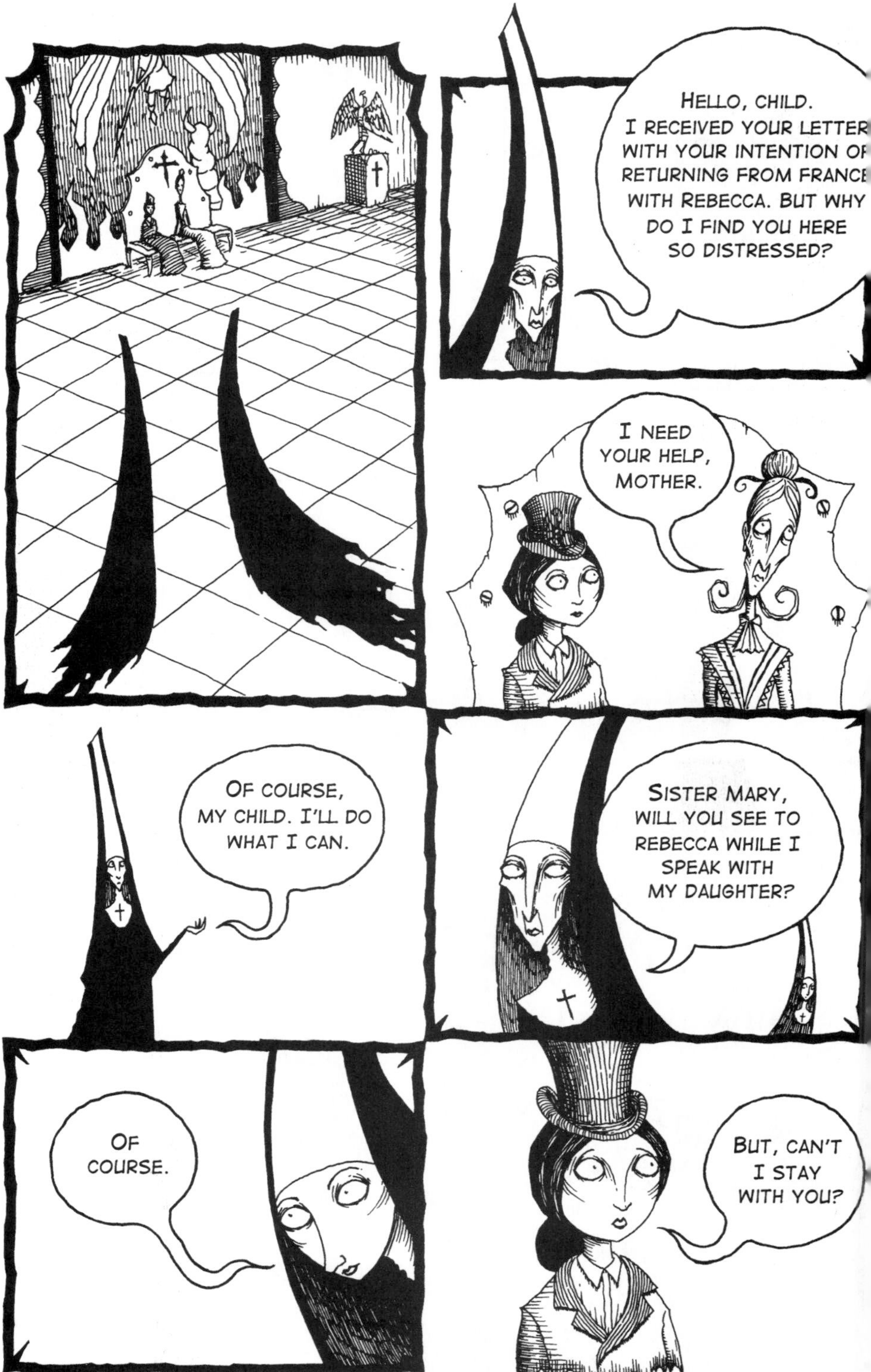
HELLO, CHILD. I RECEIVED YOUR LETTER WITH YOUR INTENTION OF RETURNING FROM FRANCE WITH REBECCA. BUT WHY DO I FIND YOU HERE SO DISTRESSED?
I NEED YOUR HELP, MOTHER.
OF COURSE, MY CHILD. I'LL DO WHAT I CAN.
SISTER MARY, WILL YOU SEE TO REBECCA WHILE I SPEAK WITH MY DAUGHTER?
OF COURSE.
BUT, CAN'T I STAY WITH YOU?

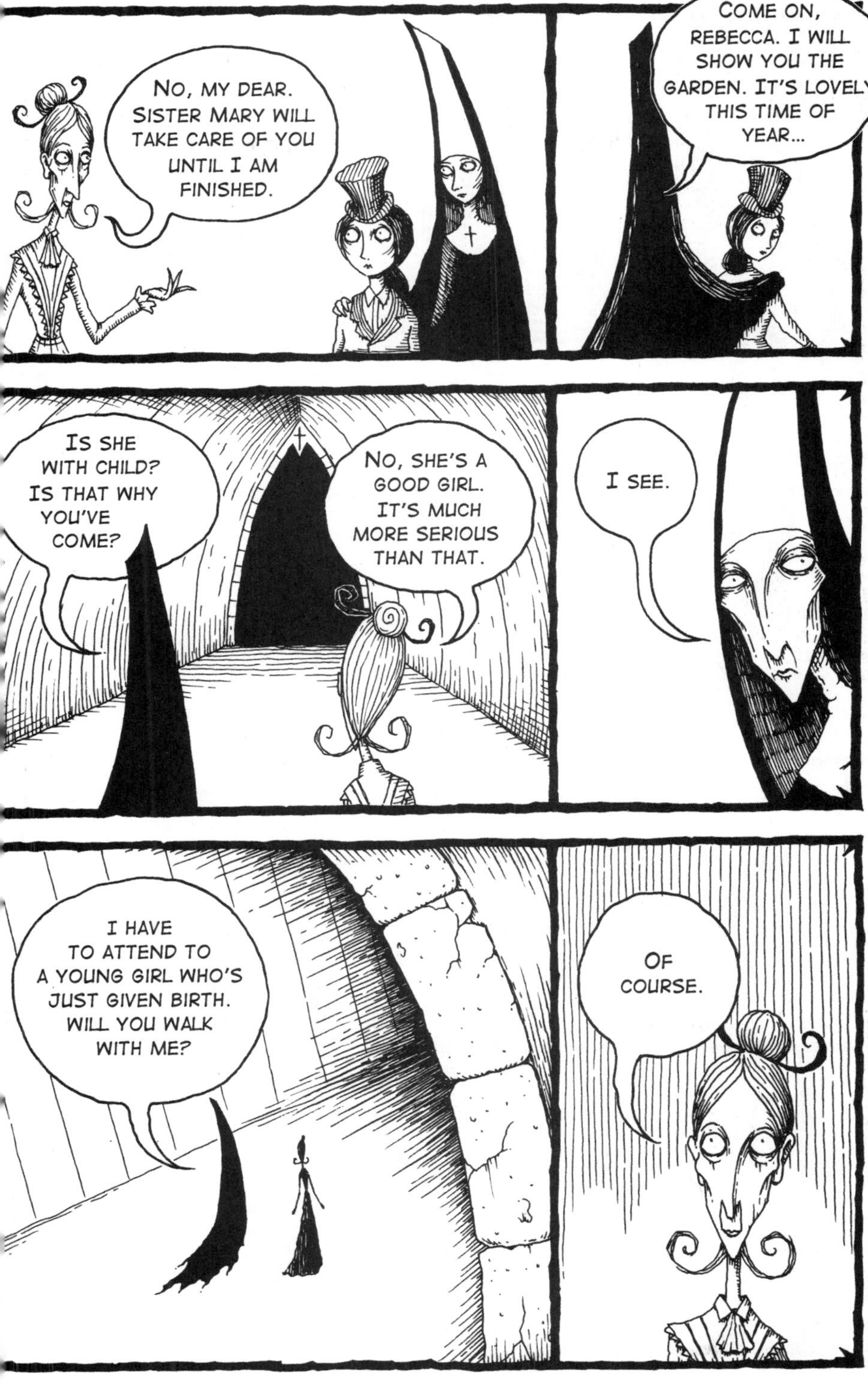
NO, MY DEAR. SISTER MARY WILL TAKE CARE OF YOU UNTIL I AM FINISHED.
COME ON, REBECCA. I WILL SHOW YOU THE GARDEN. IT'S LOVELY THIS TIME OF YEAR...
IS SHE WITH CHILD? IS THAT WHY YOU'VE COME?
NO, SHE'S A GOOD GIRL. IT'S MUCH MORE SERIOUS THAN THAT.
I SEE.
I HAVE TO ATTEND TO A YOUNG GIRL WHO'S JUST GIVEN BIRTH. WILL YOU WALK WITH ME?
OF COURSE.

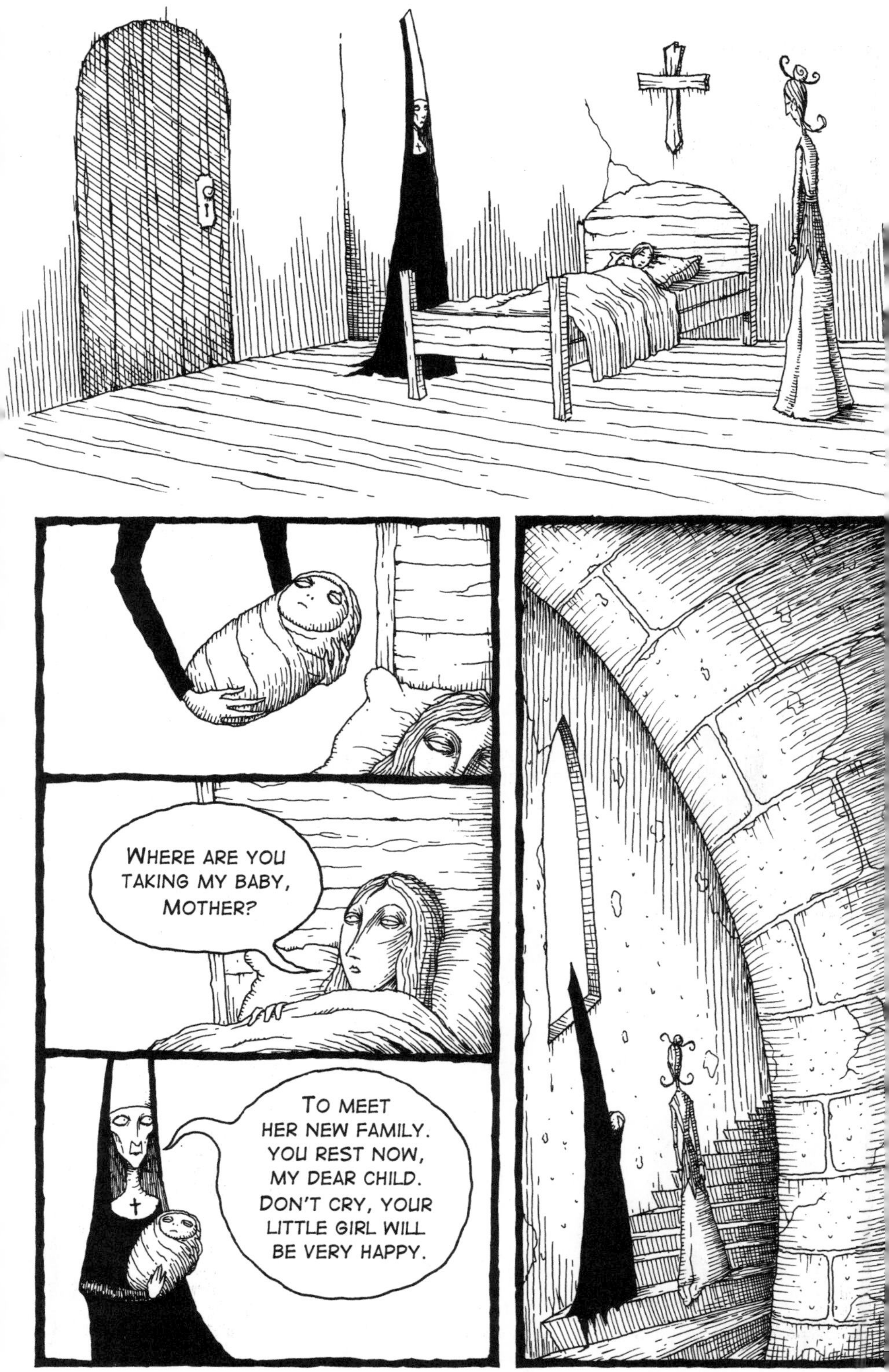
WHERE ARE YOU TAKING MY BABY, MOTHER?
TO MEET HER NEW FAMILY. YOU REST NOW, MY DEAR CHILD. DON'T CRY, YOUR LITTLE GIRL WILL BE VERY HAPPY.

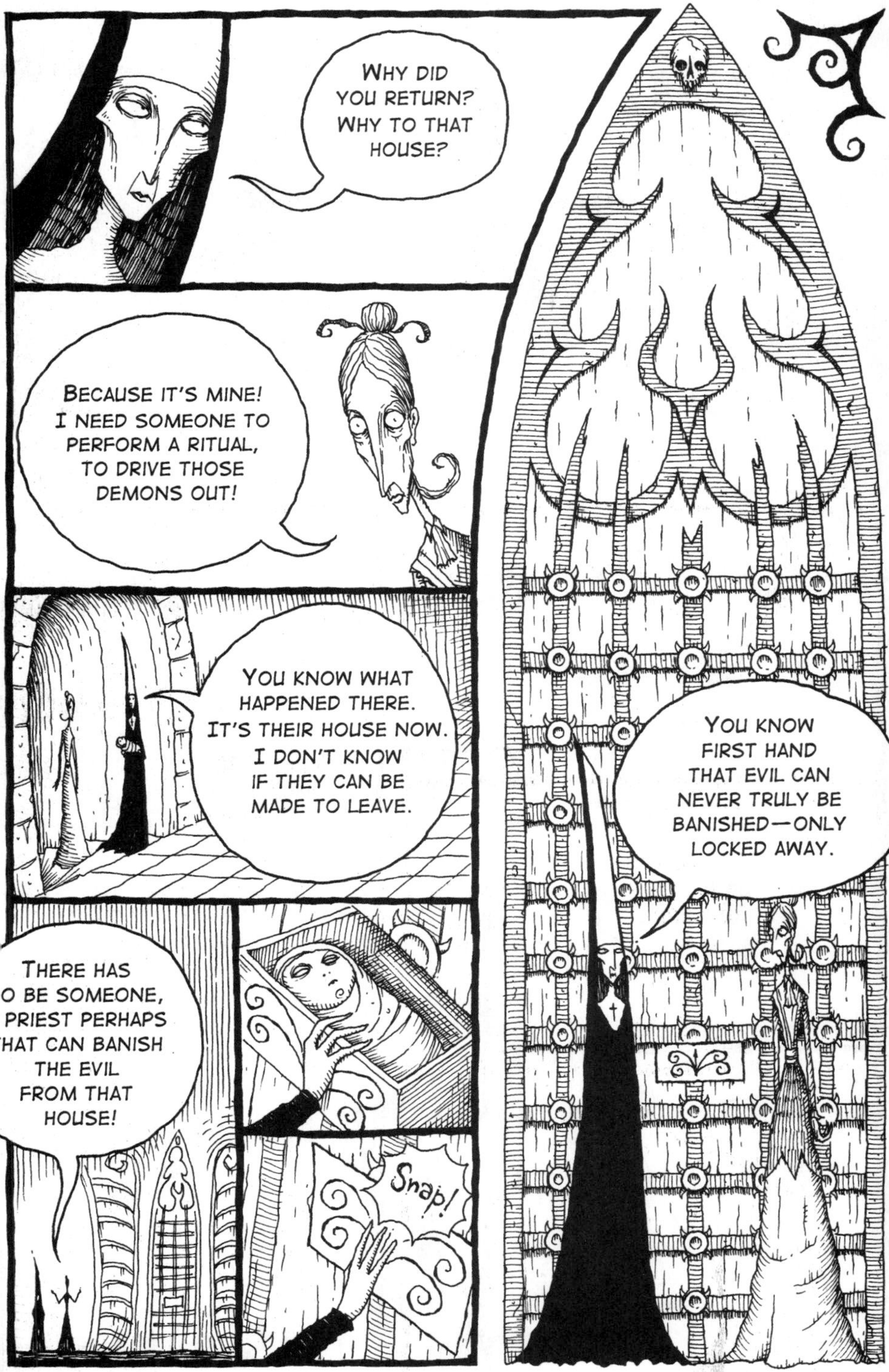
WHY DID YOU RETURN? WHY TO THAT HOUSE?
BECAUSE IT'S MINE! I NEED SOMEONE TO PERFORM A RITUAL, TO DRIVE THOSE DEMONS OUT!
YOU KNOW WHAT HAPPENED THERE. IT'S THEIR HOUSE NOW. I DON'T KNOW IF THEY CAN BE MADE TO LEAVE.
THERE HAS O BE SOMEONE, PRIEST PERHAPS HAT CAN BANISH THE EVIL FROM THAT HOUSE!
Snap!
YOU KNOW FIRST HAND THAT EVIL CAN NEVER TRULY BE BANISHED—ONLY LOCKED AWAY.

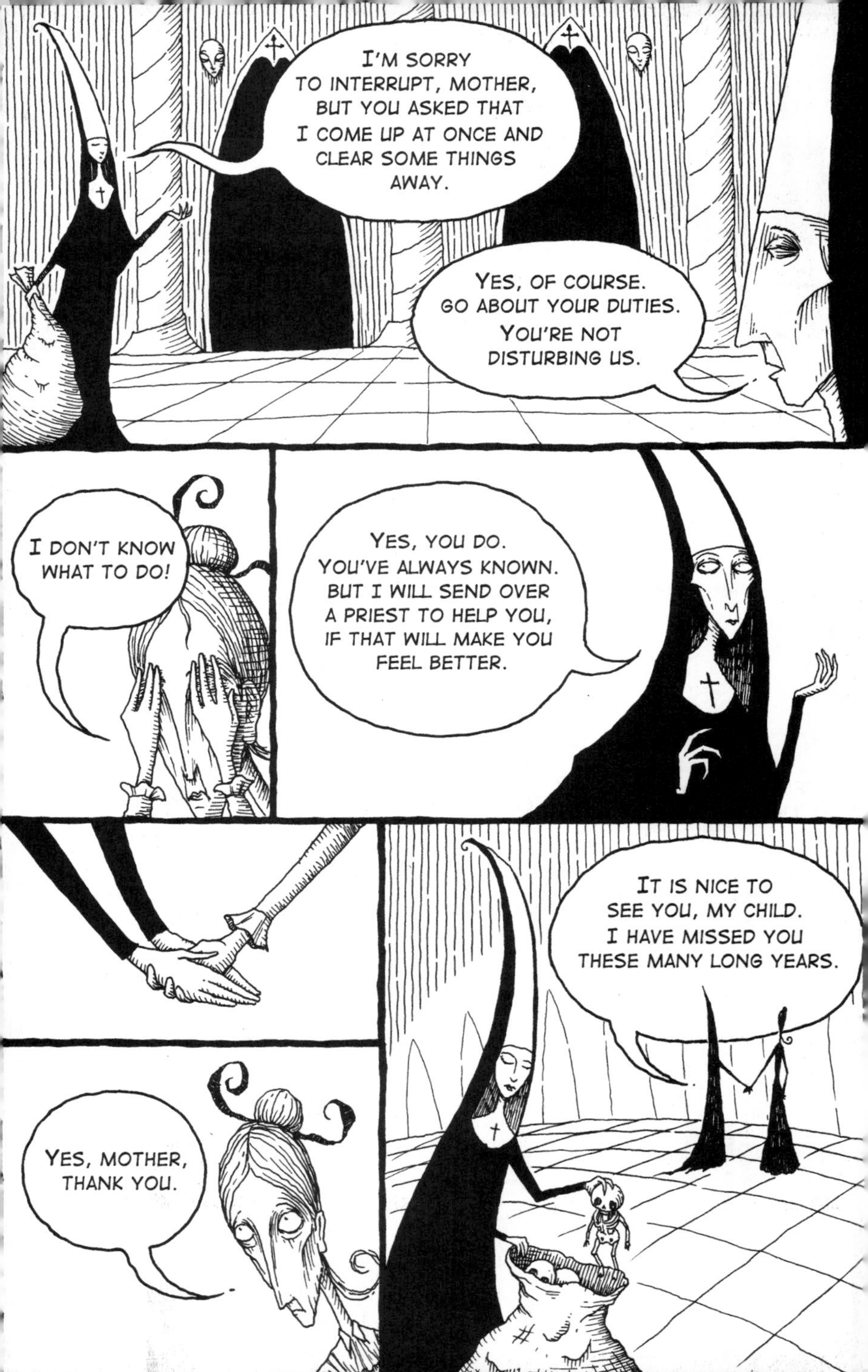
I'M SORRY TO INTERRUPT, MOTHER, BUT YOU ASKED THAT I COME UP AT ONCE AND CLEAR SOME THINGS AWAY.
YES, OF COURSE. GO ABOUT YOUR DUTIES. YOU'RE NOT DISTURBING US.
I DON'T KNOW WHAT TO DO!
YES, YOU DO. YOU'VE ALWAYS KNOWN. BUT I WILL SEND OVER A PRIEST TO HELP YOU, IF THAT WILL MAKE YOU FEEL BETTER.
YES, MOTHER, THANK YOU.
IT IS NICE TO SEE YOU, MY CHILD. I HAVE MISSED YOU THESE MANY LONG YEARS.

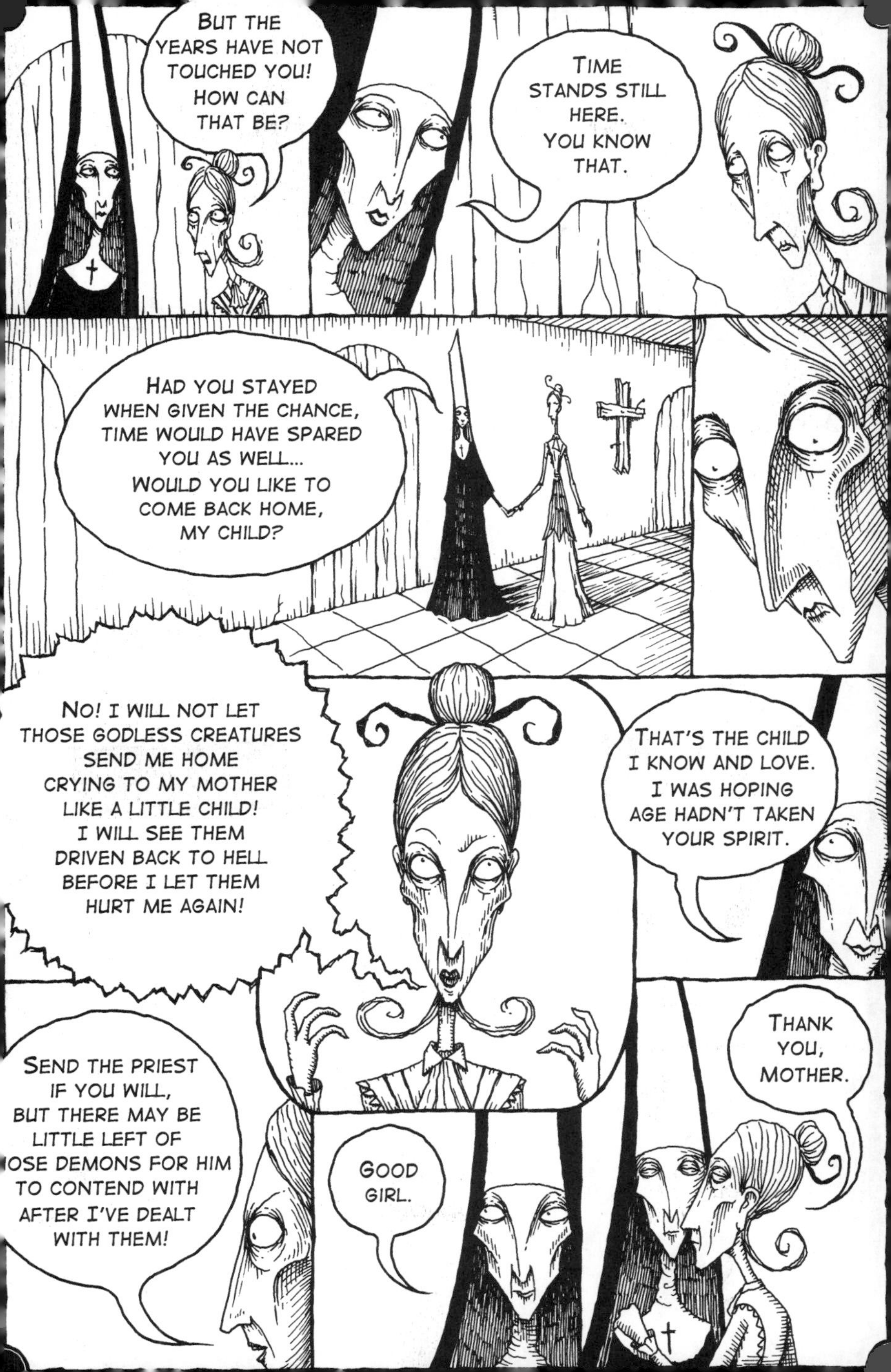
But the years have not touched you! How can that be?
Time stands still here. You know that.
Had you stayed when given the chance, time would have spared you as well... Would you like to come back home, my child?
No! I will not let those godless creatures send me home crying to my mother like a little child! I will see them driven back to hell before I let them hurt me again!
That's the child I know and love. I was hoping age hadn't taken your spirit.
Send the priest if you will, but there may be little left of ose demons for him to contend with after I've dealt with them!
Good girl.
Thank you, Mother.

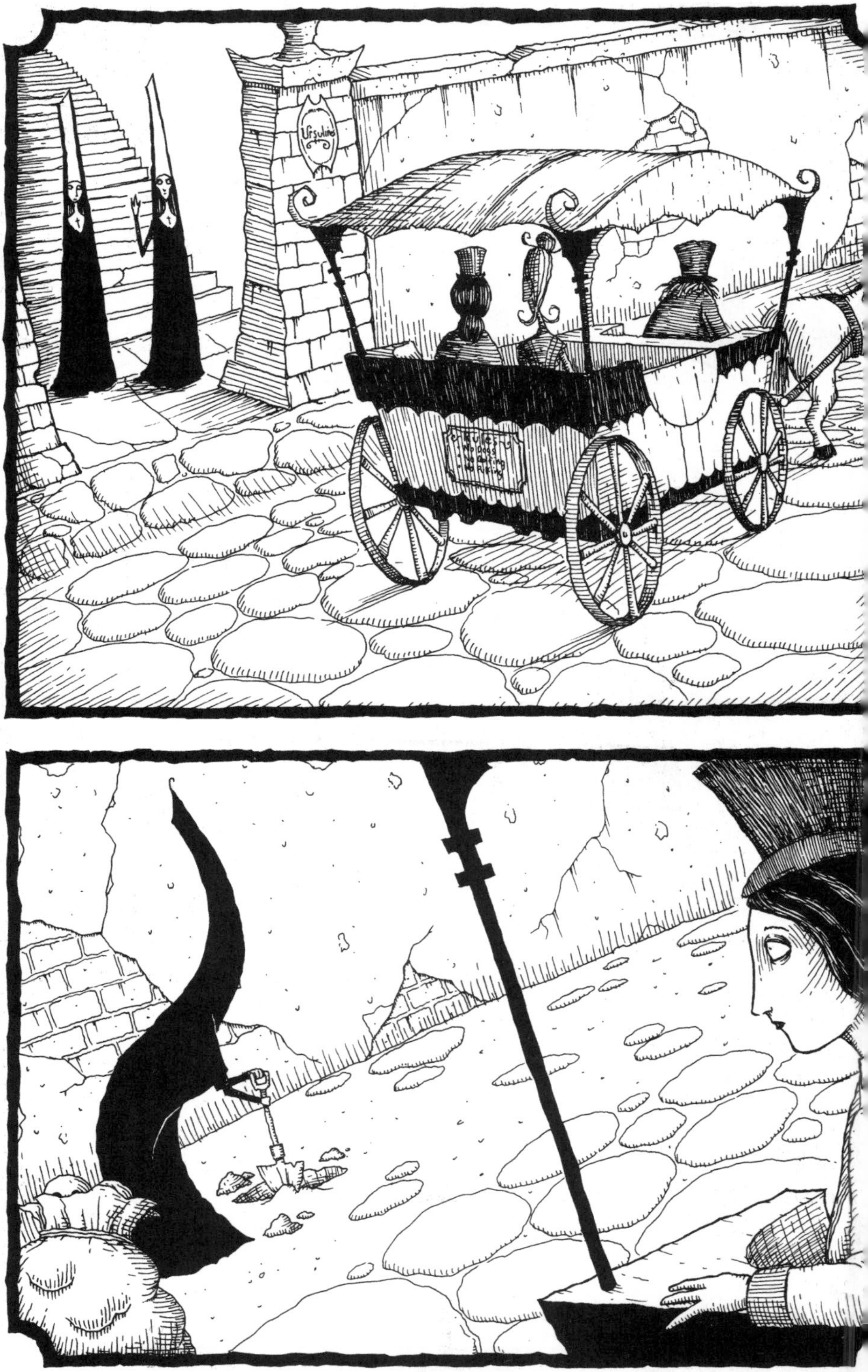
Ursuline
Rules
No Dogs

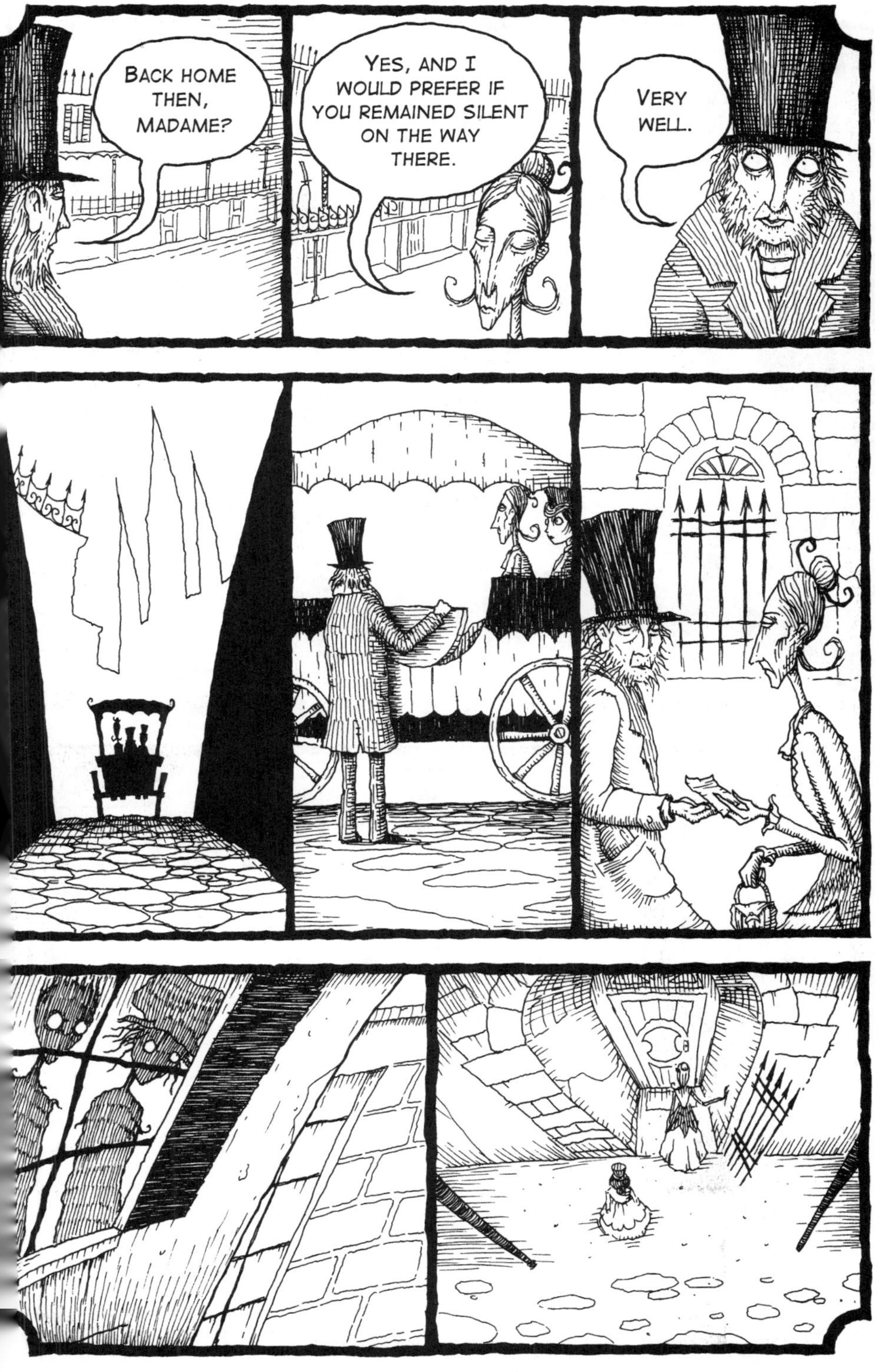
Back home then, Madame?
Yes, and I would prefer if you remained silent on the way there.
Very well.

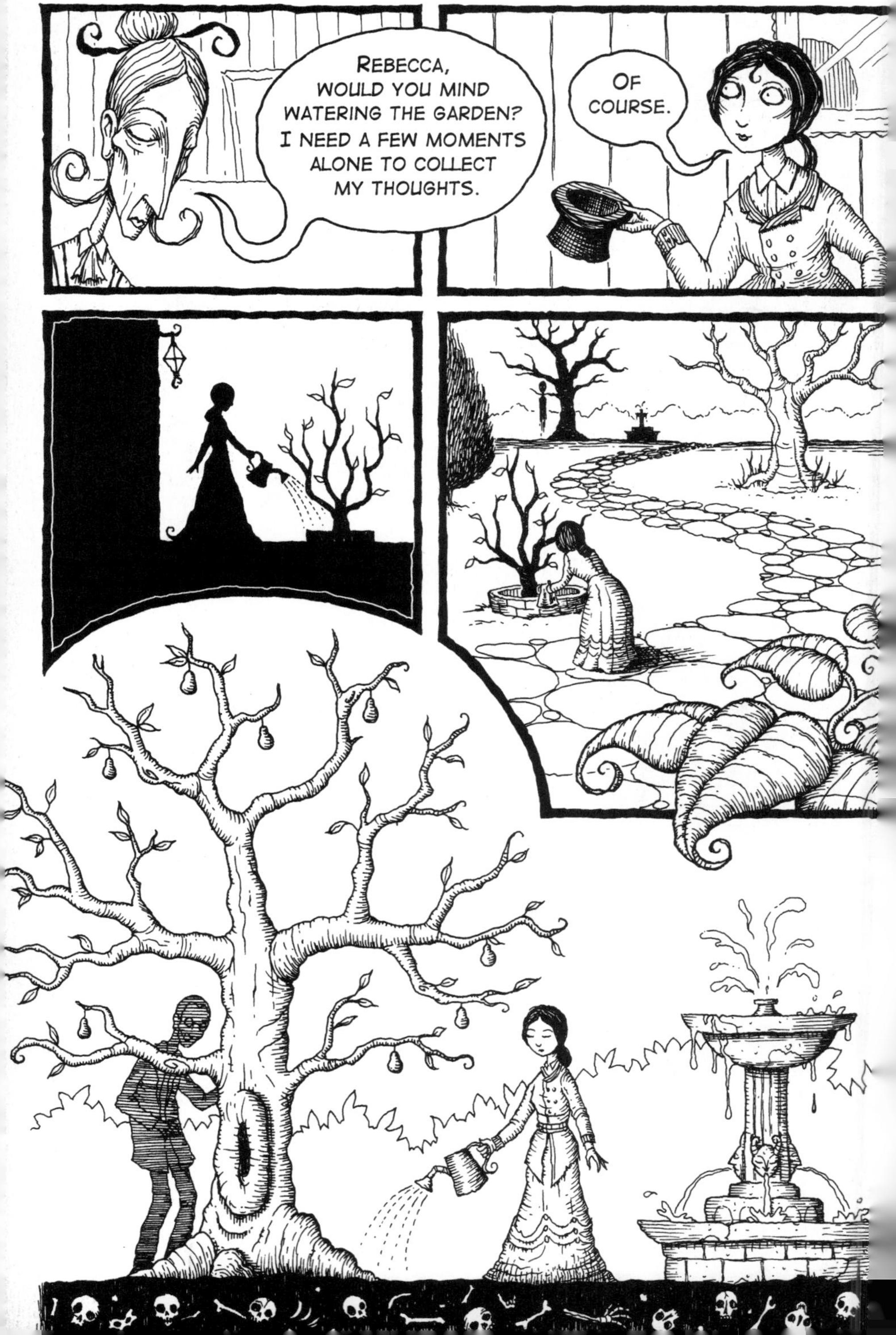
REBECCA, WOULD YOU MIND WATERING THE GARDEN? I NEED A FEW MOMENTS ALONE TO COLLECT MY THOUGHTS.
OF COURSE.

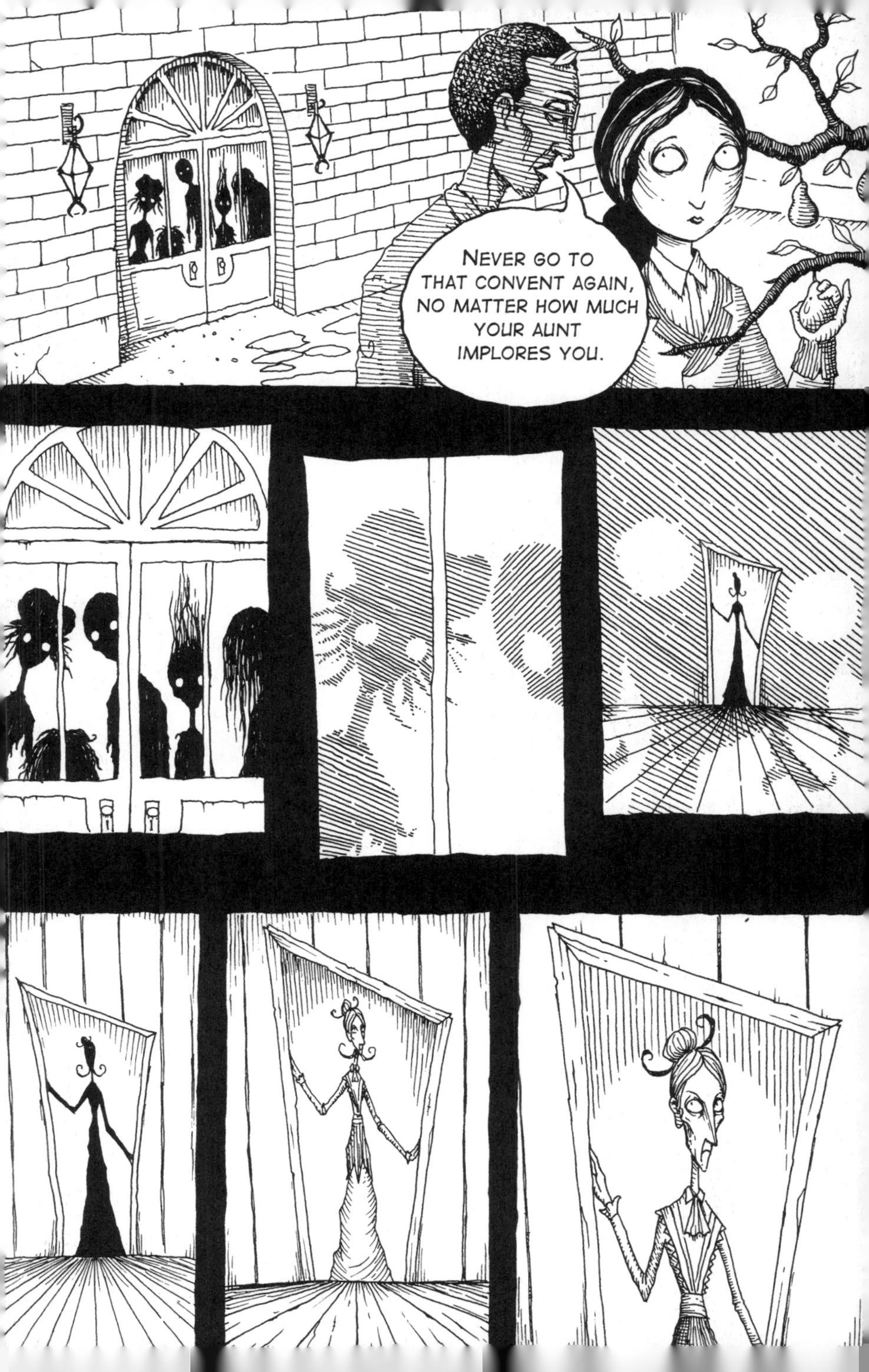
NEVER GO TO THAT CONVENT AGAIN, NO MATTER HOW MUCH YOUR AUNT IMPLORES YOU.

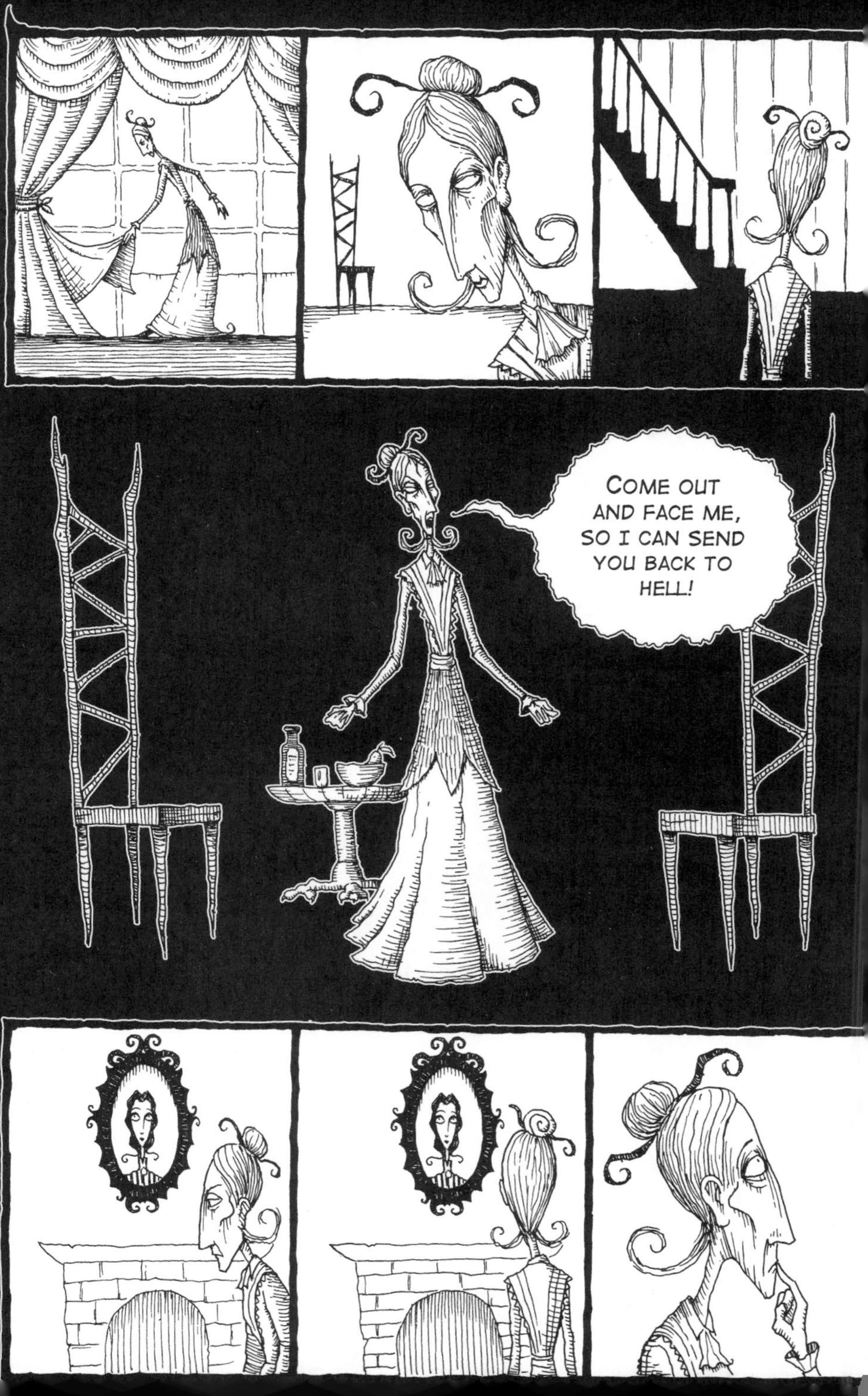
COME OUT AND FACE ME, SO I CAN SEND YOU BACK TO HELL!

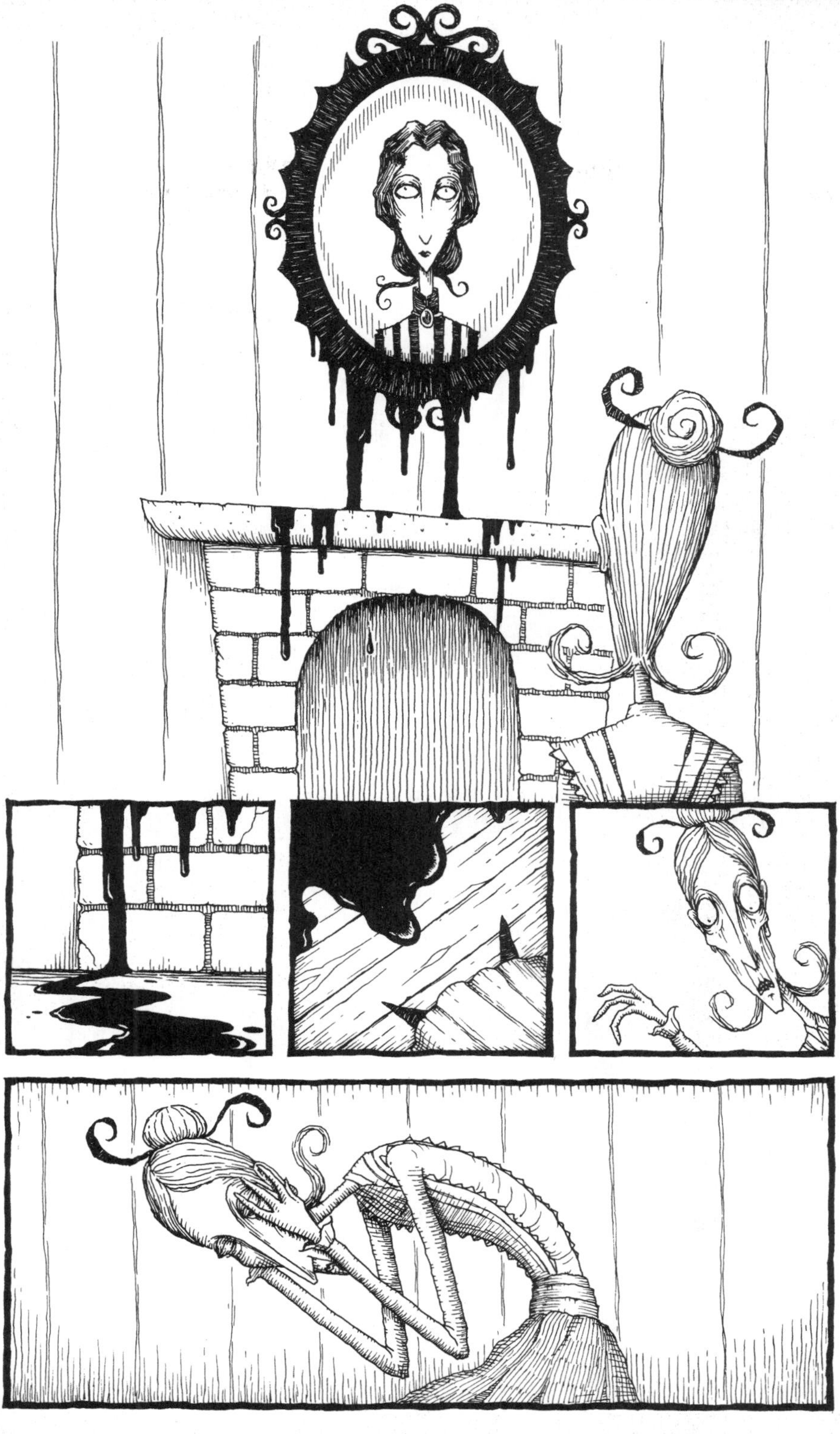

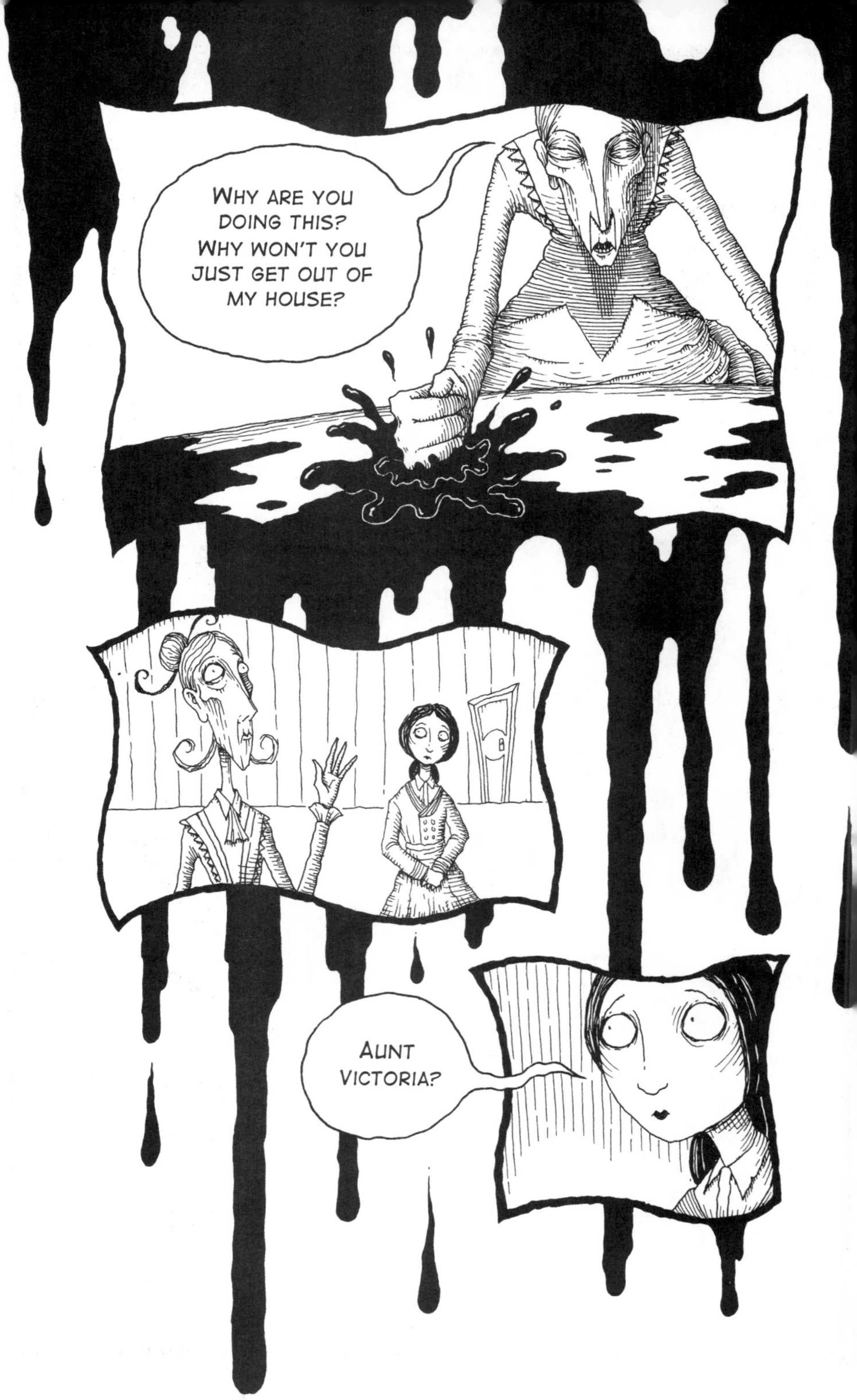
WHY ARE YOU DOING THIS? WHY WON'T YOU JUST GET OUT OF MY HOUSE?
AUNT VICTORIA?

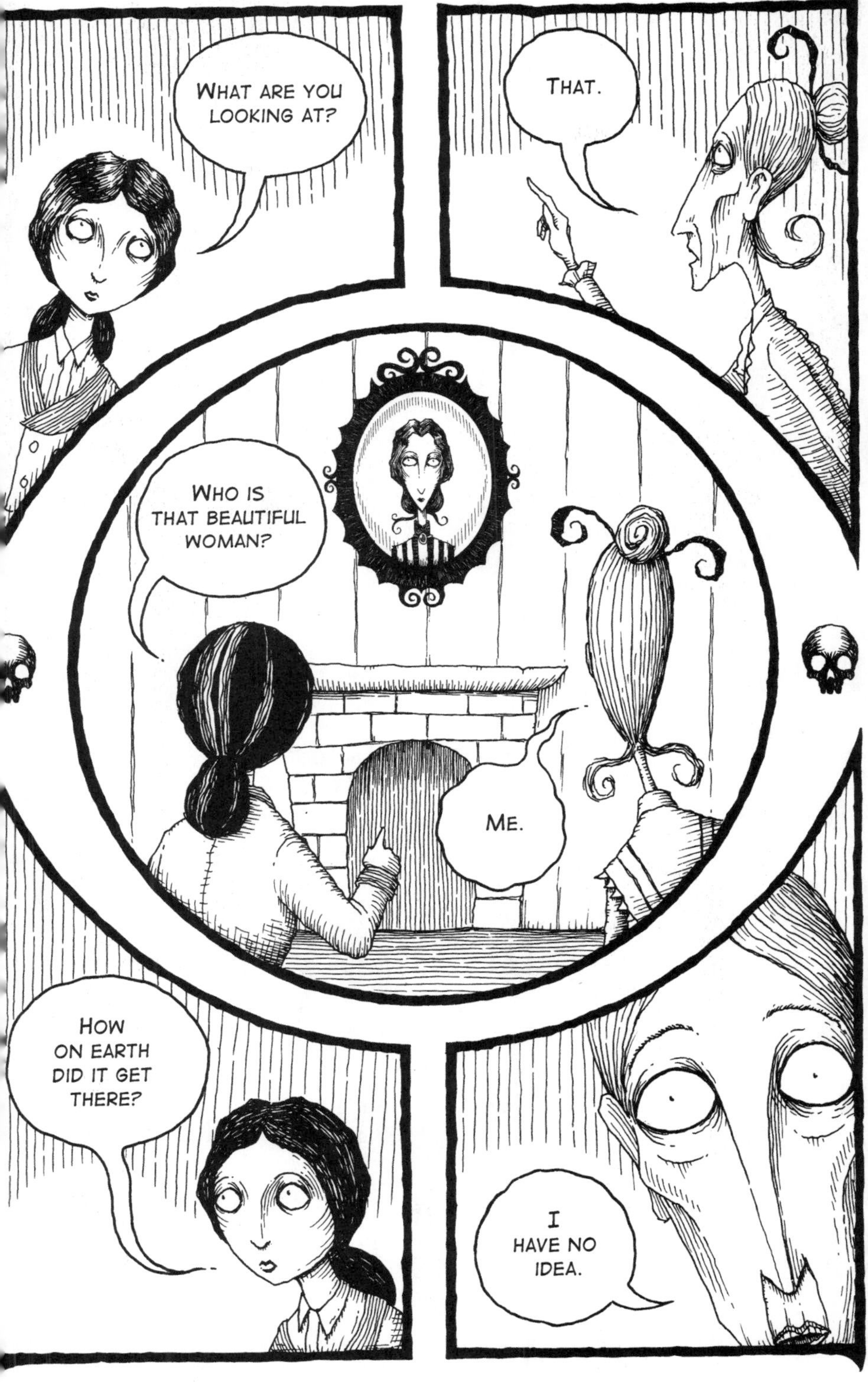
WHAT ARE YOU LOOKING AT?
THAT.
WHO IS THAT BEAUTIFUL WOMAN?
ME.
HOW ON EARTH DID IT GET THERE?
I HAVE NO IDEA.

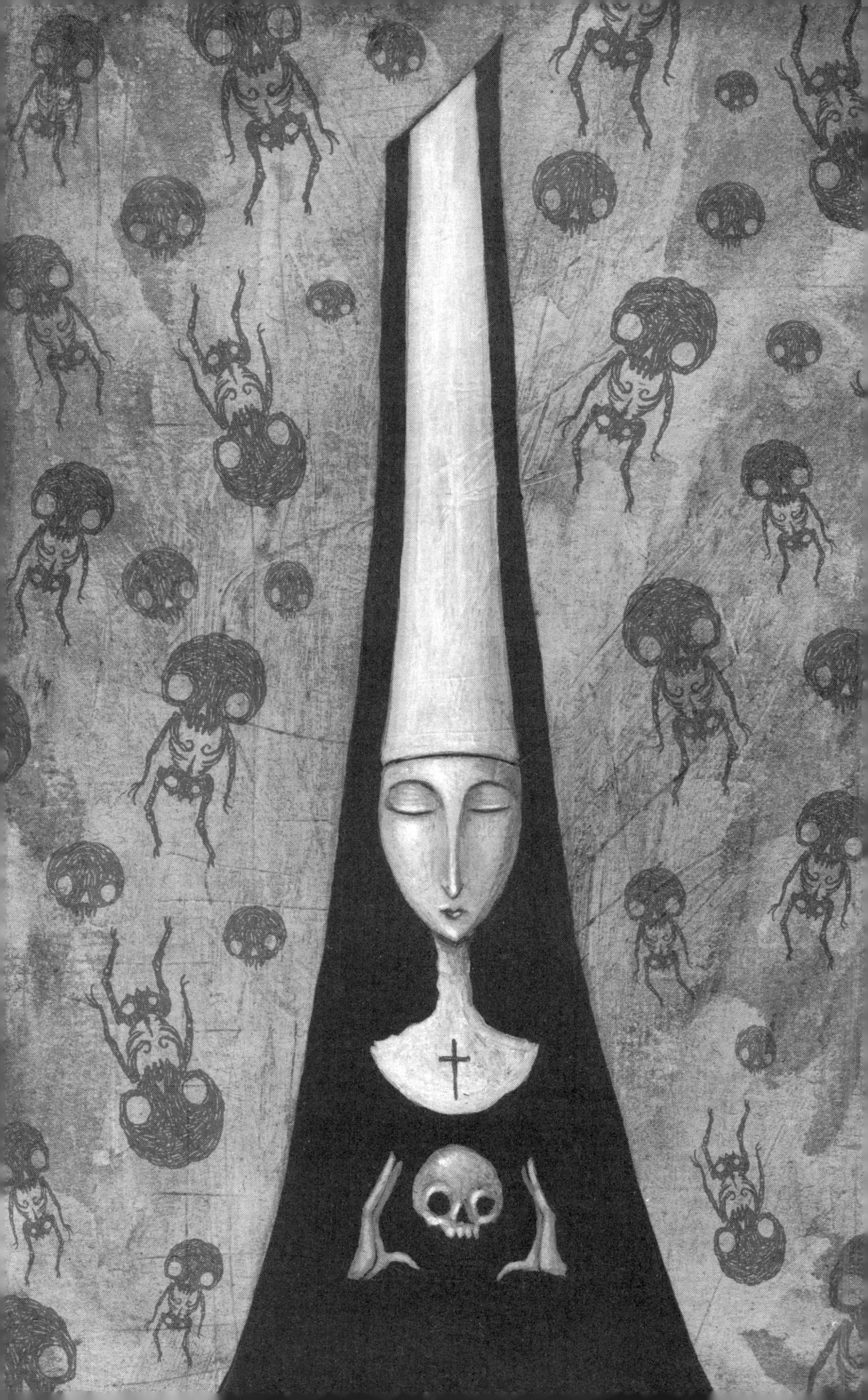

Chapter 3

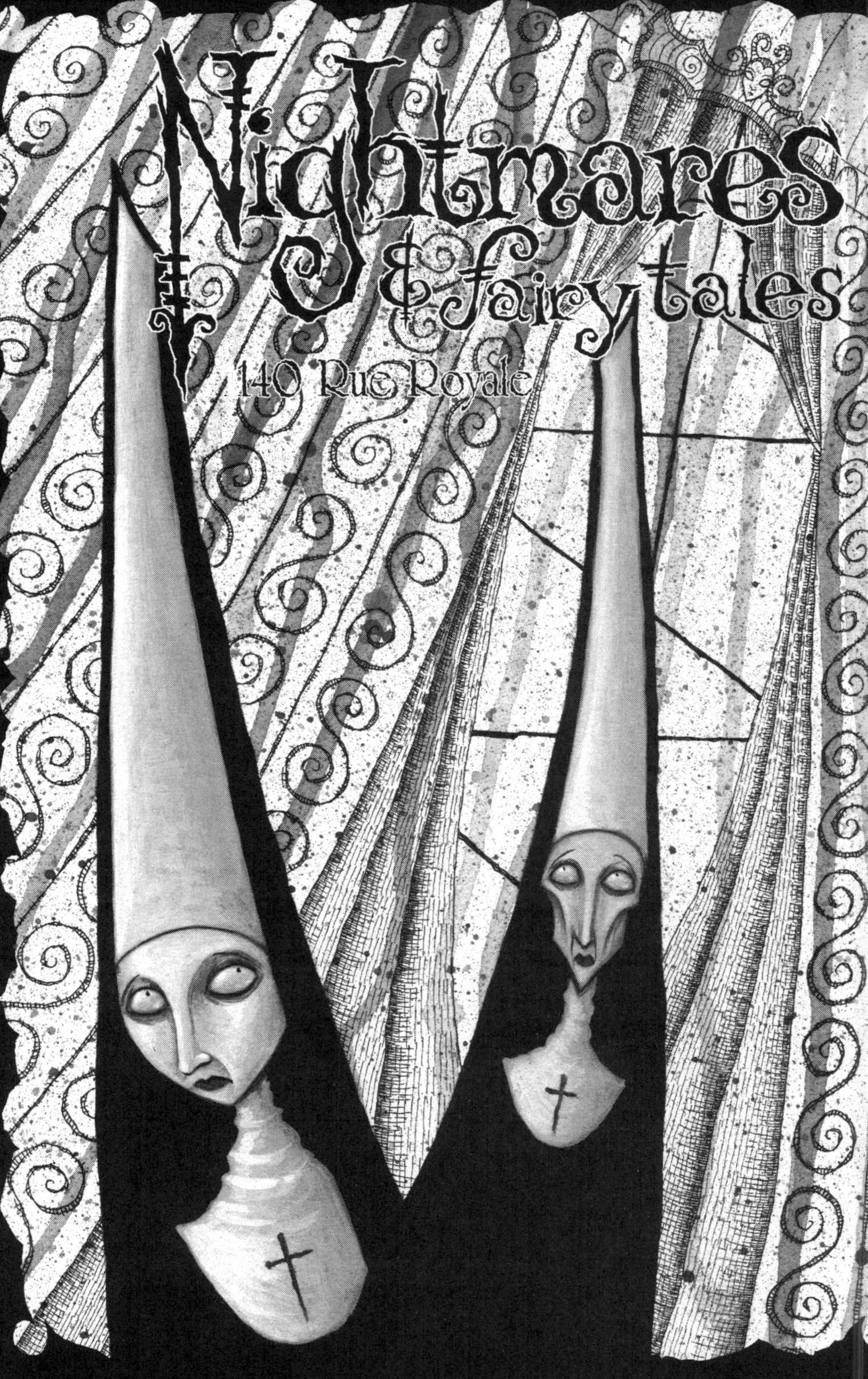
Nightmares
& fairy tales
140 Rue Royale

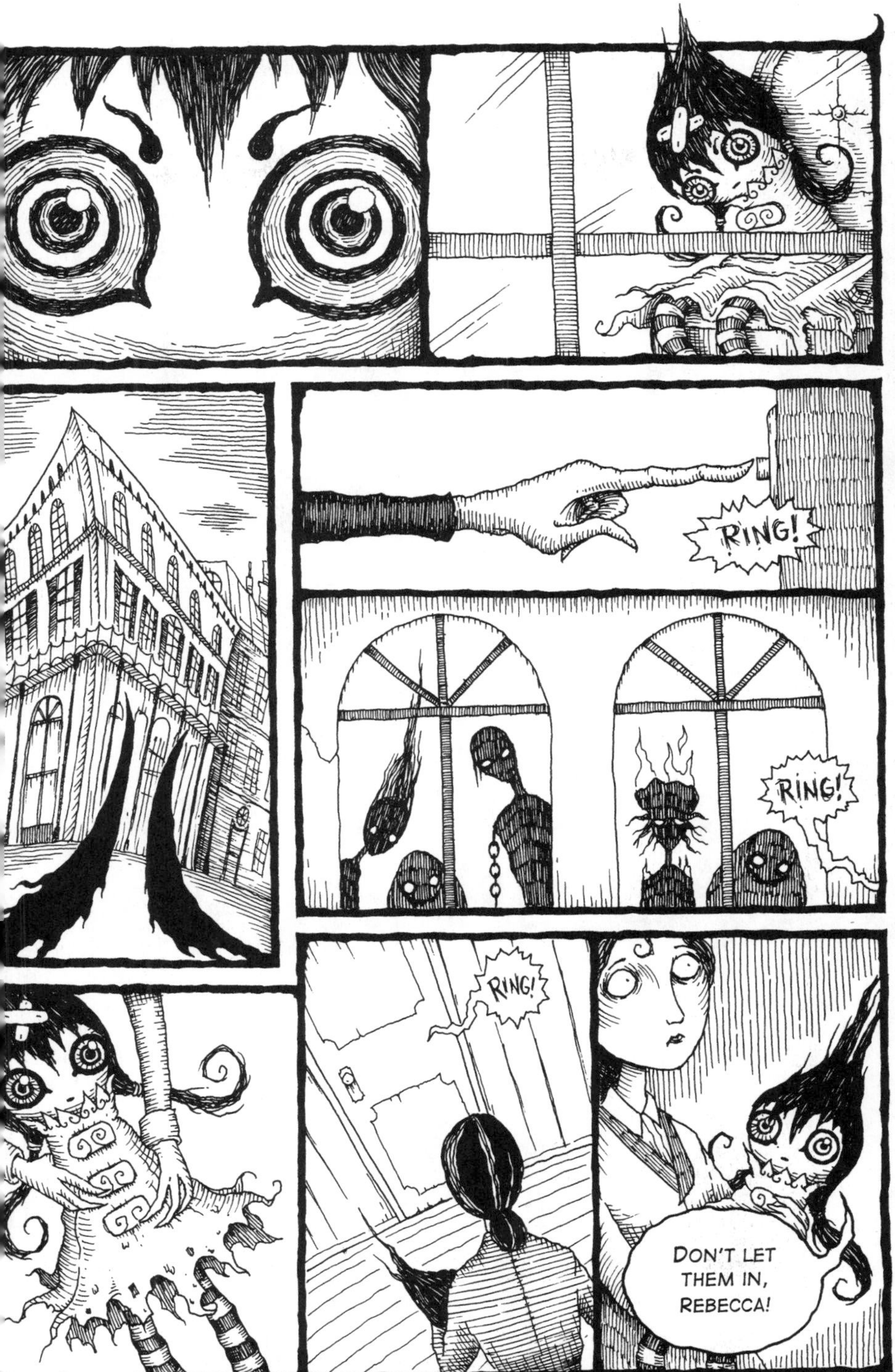
RING!
RING!
RING!
DON'T LET THEM IN, REBECCA!

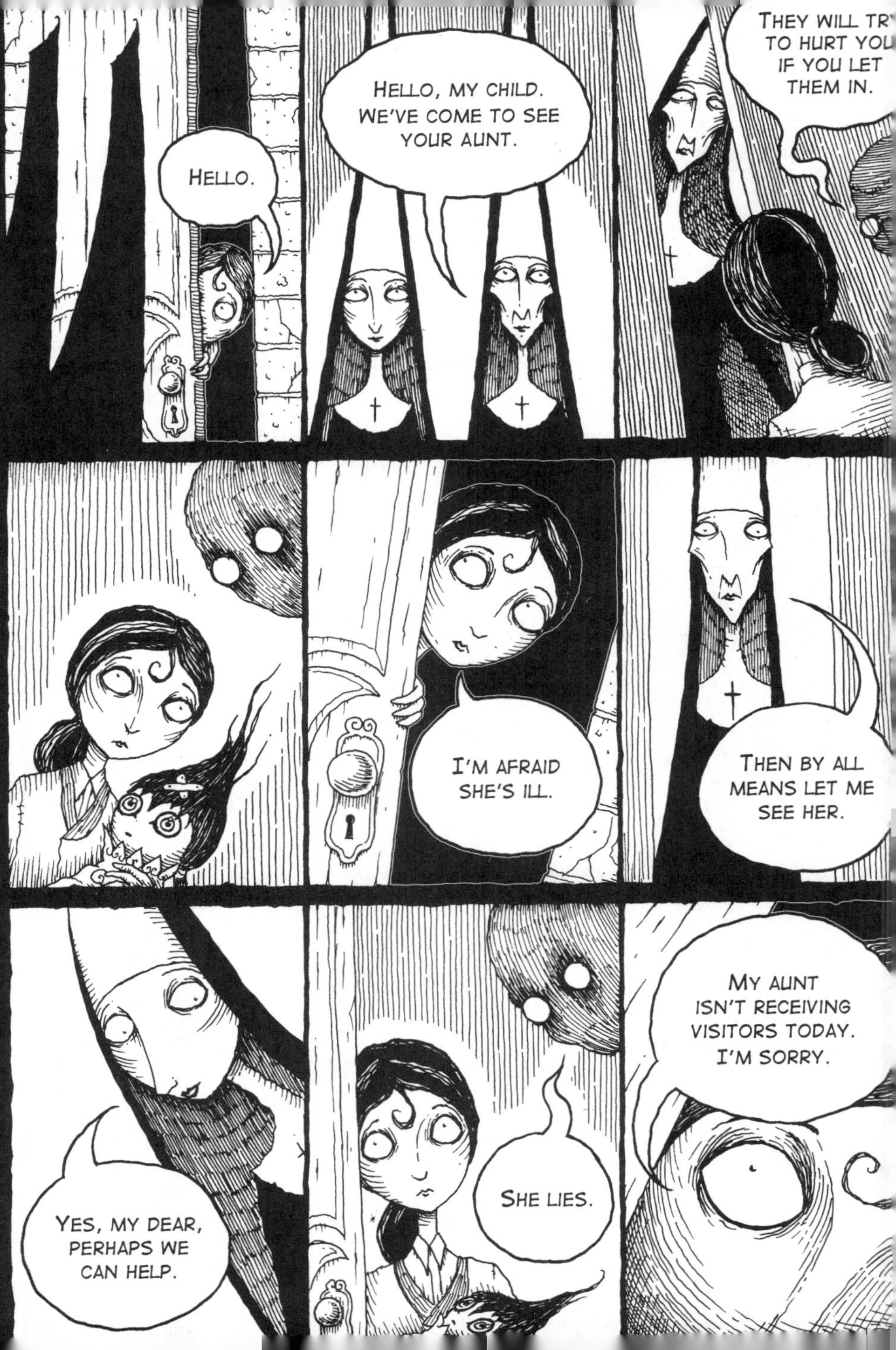
HELLO.
HELLO, MY CHILD. WE'VE COME TO SEE YOUR AUNT.
THEY WILL TRY TO HURT YOU IF YOU LET THEM IN.
I'M AFRAID SHE'S ILL.
THEN BY ALL MEANS LET ME SEE HER.
YES, MY DEAR, PERHAPS WE CAN HELP.
SHE LIES.
MY AUNT ISN'T RECEIVING VISITORS TODAY. I'M SORRY.

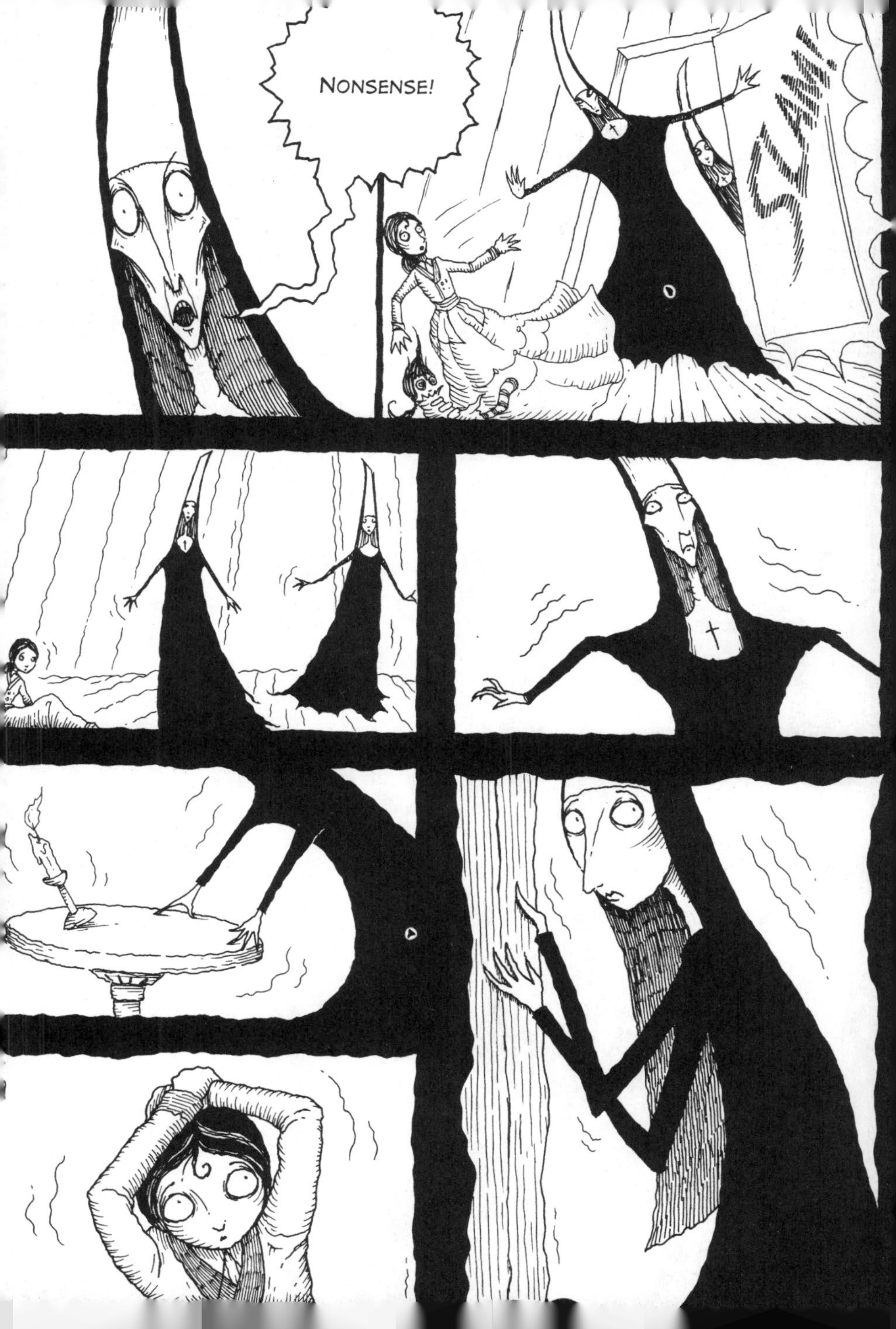
NONSENSE!
SLAM!

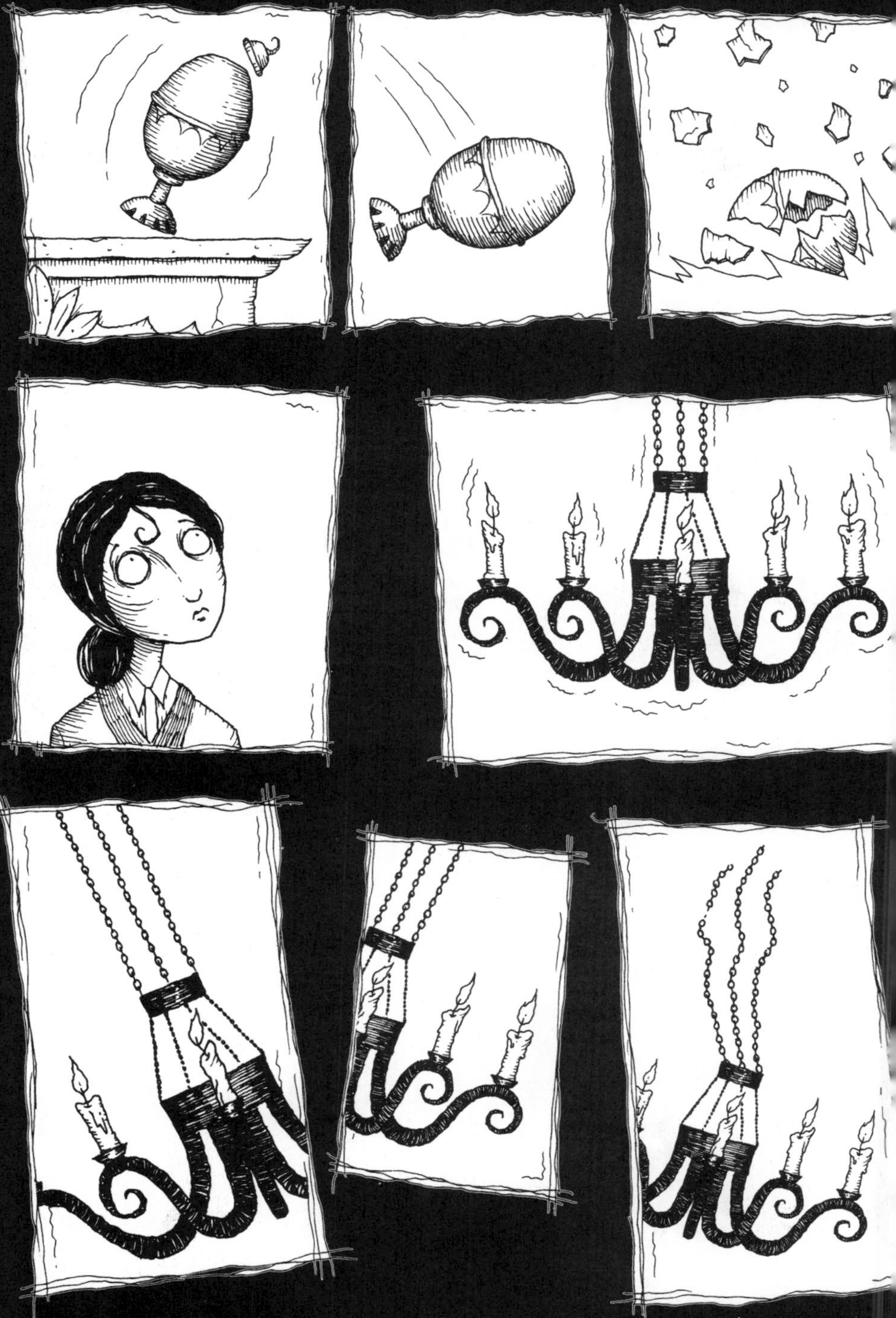

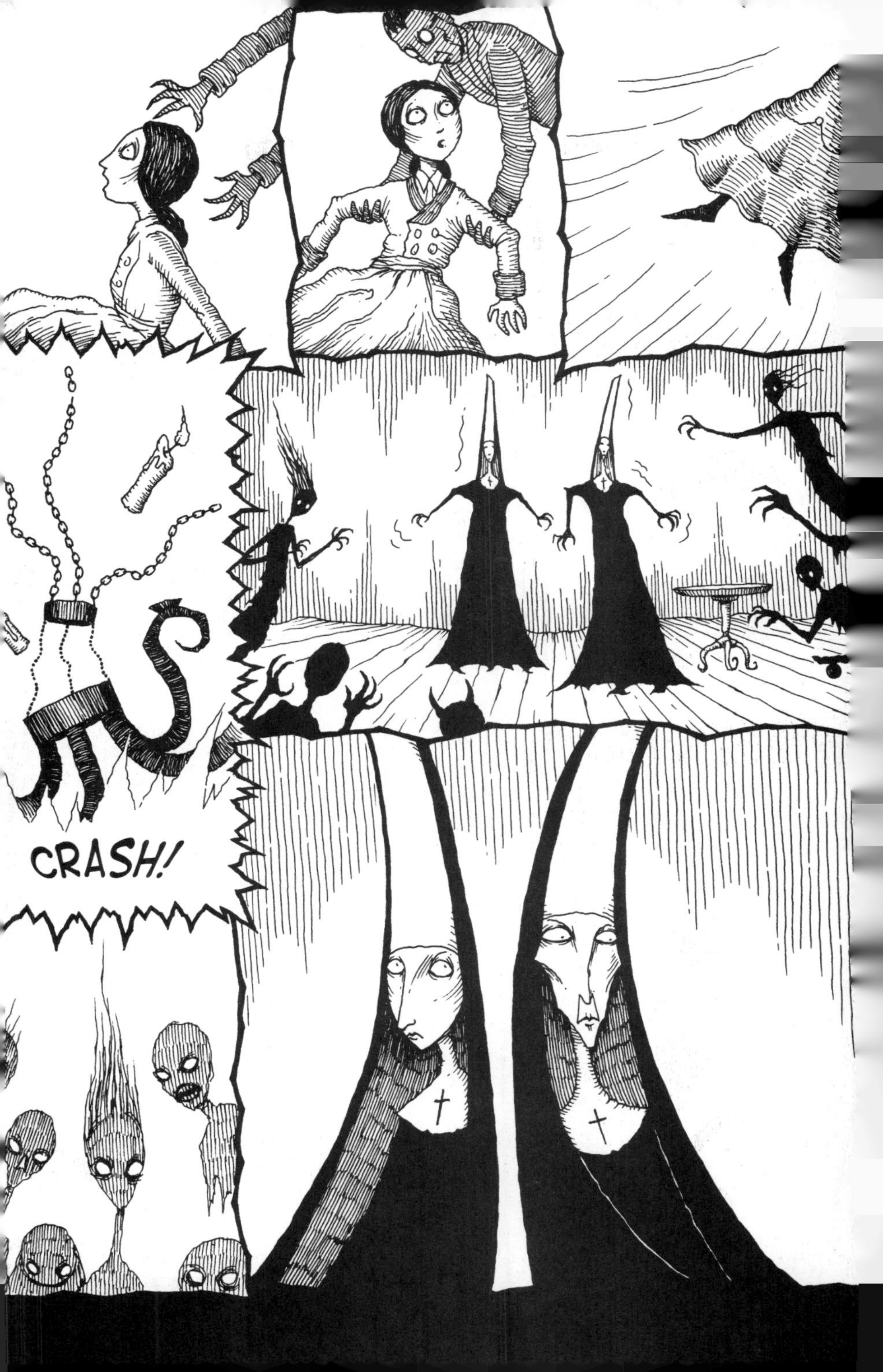
CRASH!

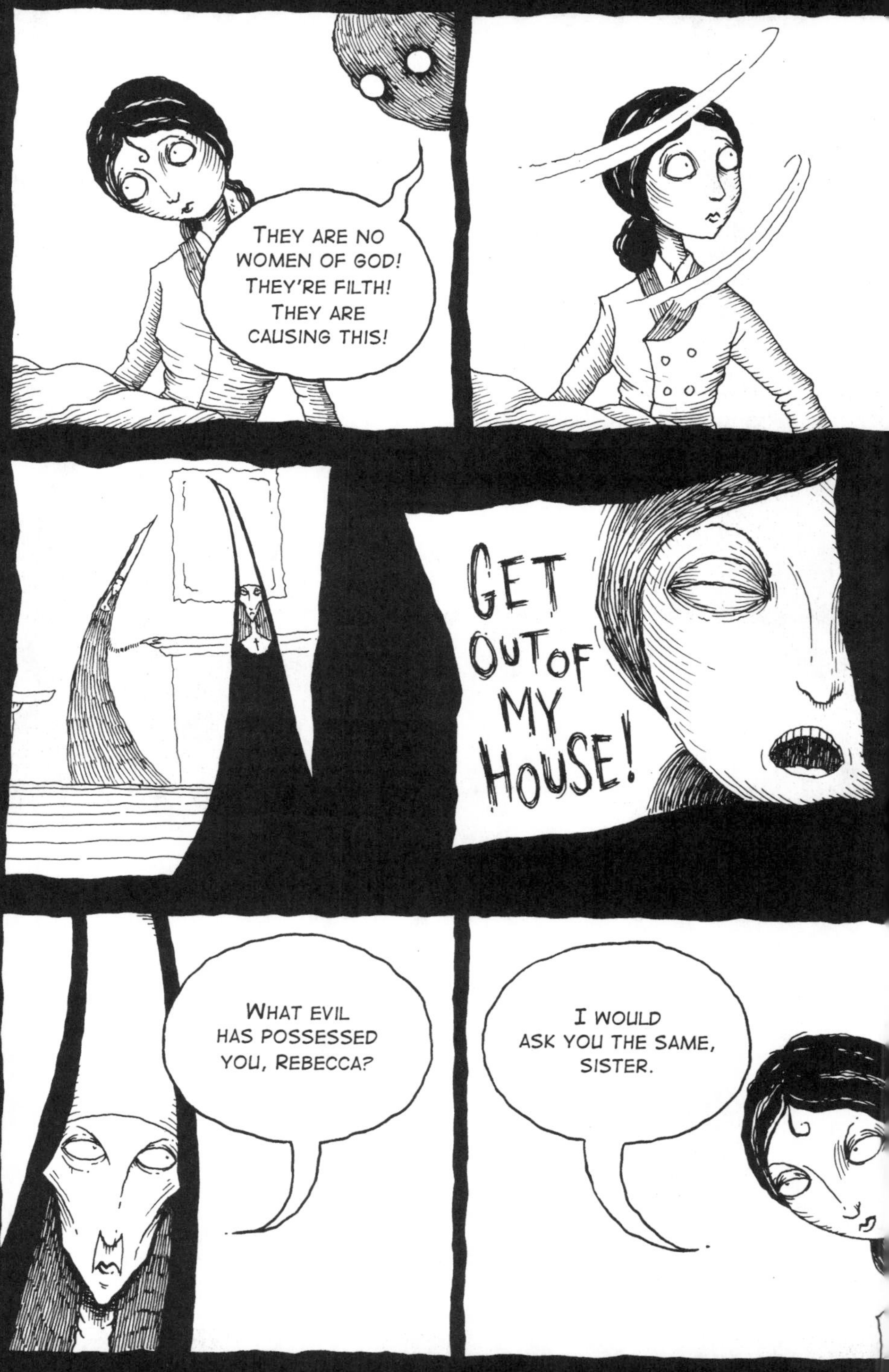
THEY ARE NO WOMEN OF GOD! THEY'RE FILTH! THEY ARE CAUSING THIS!
GET OUT OF MY HOUSE!
WHAT EVIL HAS POSSESSED YOU, REBECCA?
I WOULD ASK YOU THE SAME, SISTER.

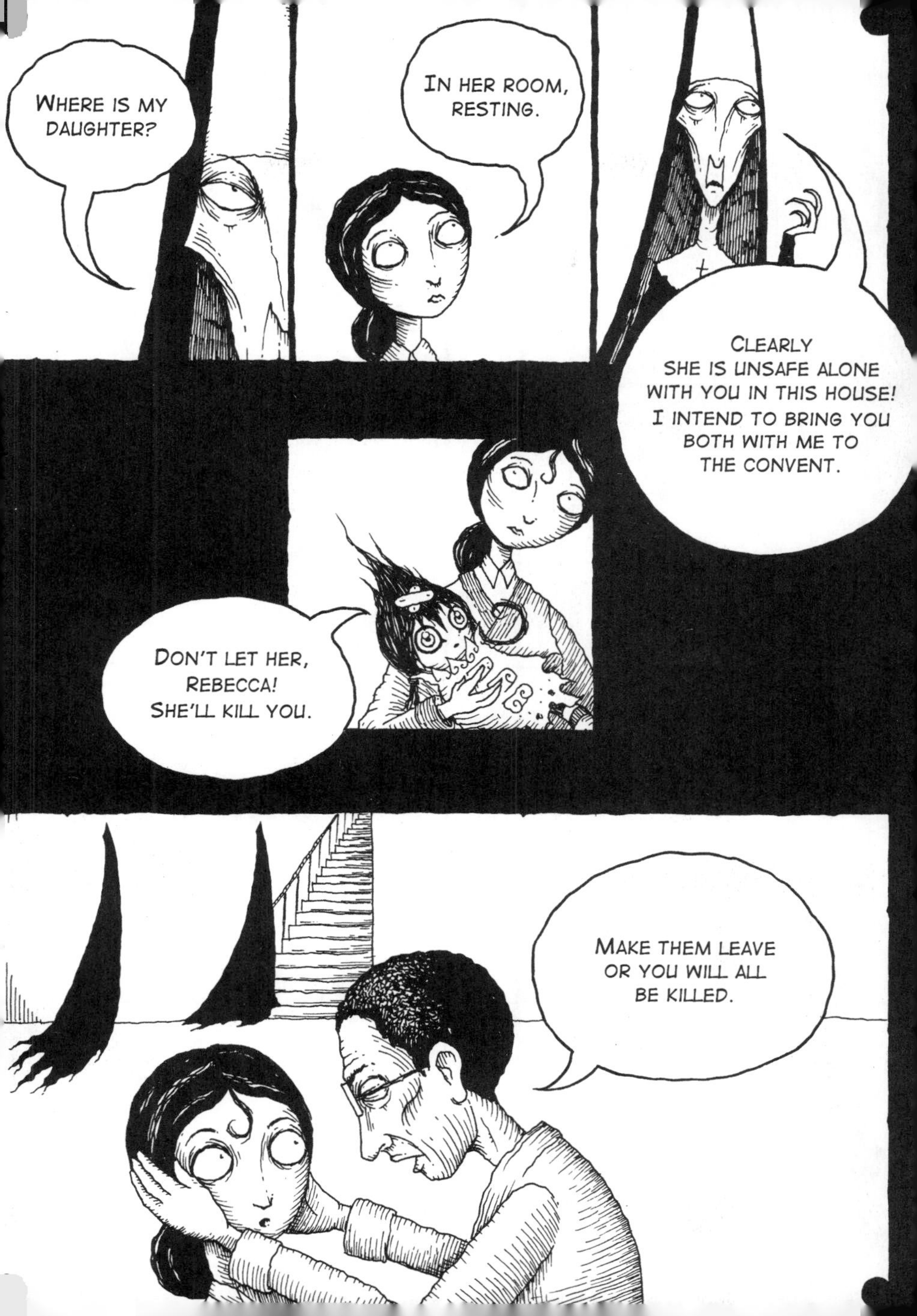

WHERE IS MY DAUGHTER?
IN HER ROOM, RESTING.
CLEARLY SHE IS UNSAFE ALONE WITH YOU IN THIS HOUSE! I INTEND TO BRING YOU BOTH WITH ME TO THE CONVENT.
DON'T LET HER, REBECCA! SHE'LL KILL YOU.
MAKE THEM LEAVE OR YOU WILL ALL BE KILLED.

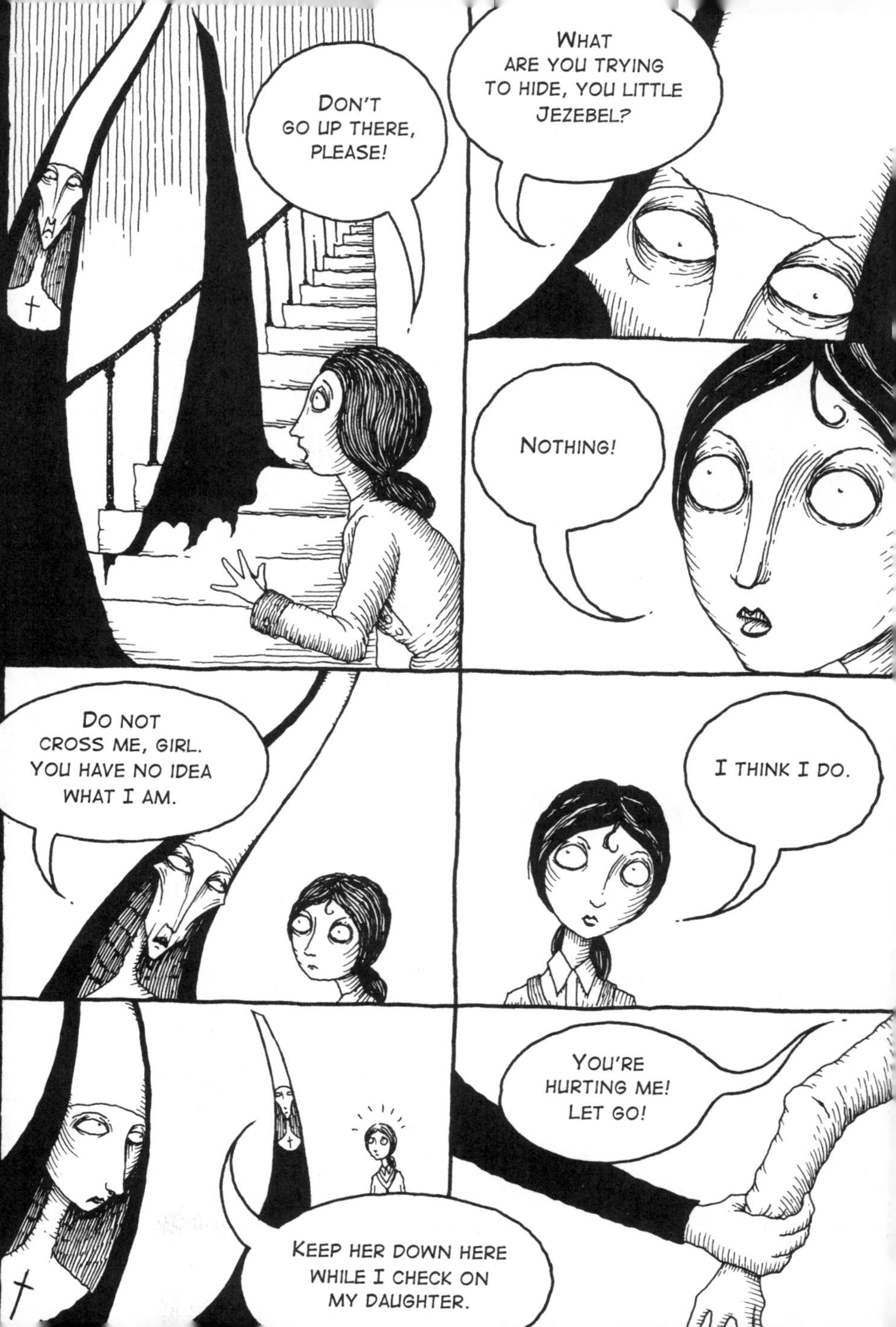
DON'T GO UP THERE, PLEASE!
WHAT ARE YOU TRYING TO HIDE, YOU LITTLE JEZEBEL?
NOTHING!
DO NOT CROSS ME, GIRL. YOU HAVE NO IDEA WHAT I AM.
I THINK I DO.
KEEP HER DOWN HERE WHILE I CHECK ON MY DAUGHTER.
YOU'RE HURTING ME! LET GO!

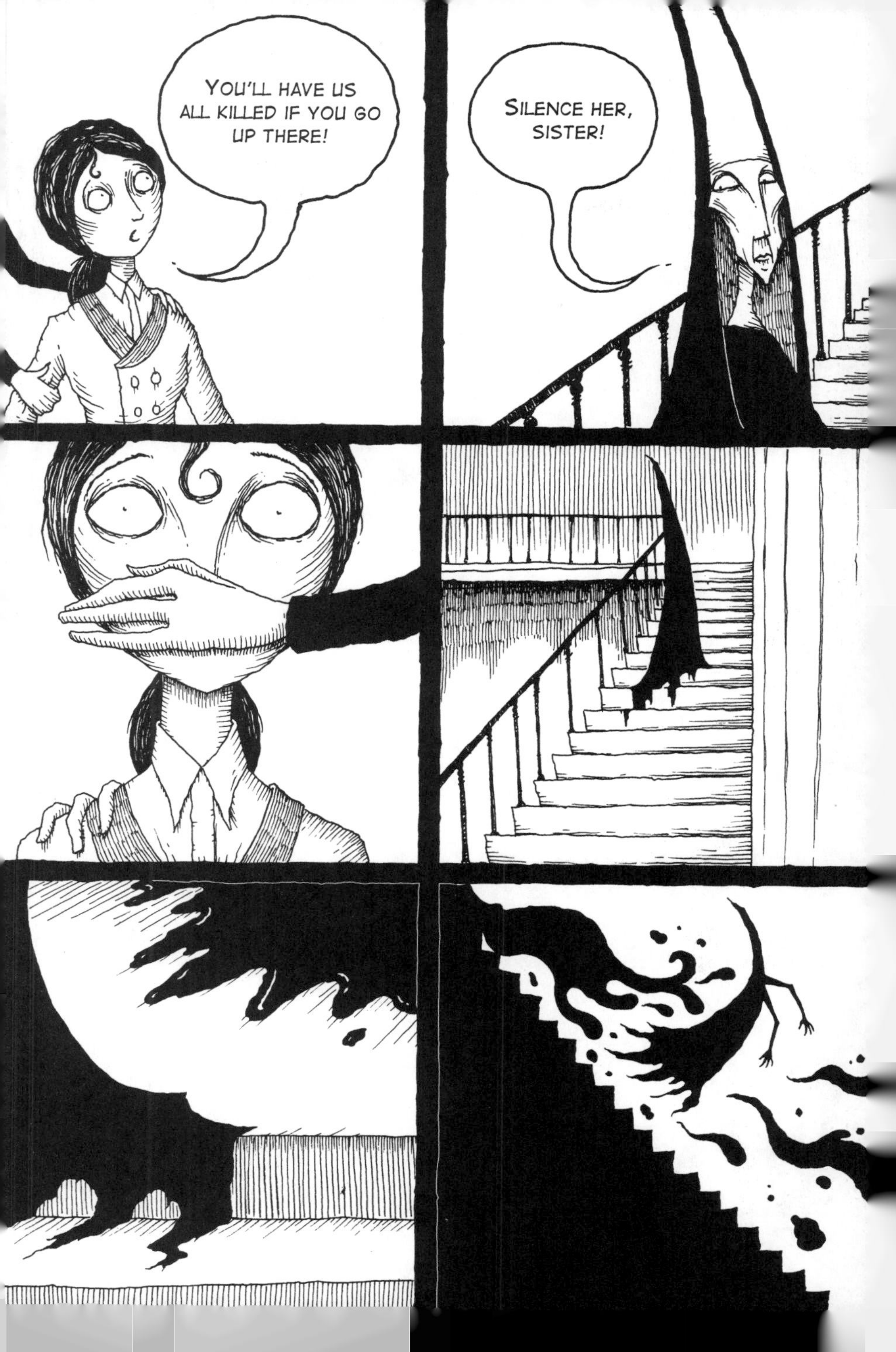
YOU'LL HAVE US ALL KILLED IF YOU GO UP THERE!
SILENCE HER, SISTER!

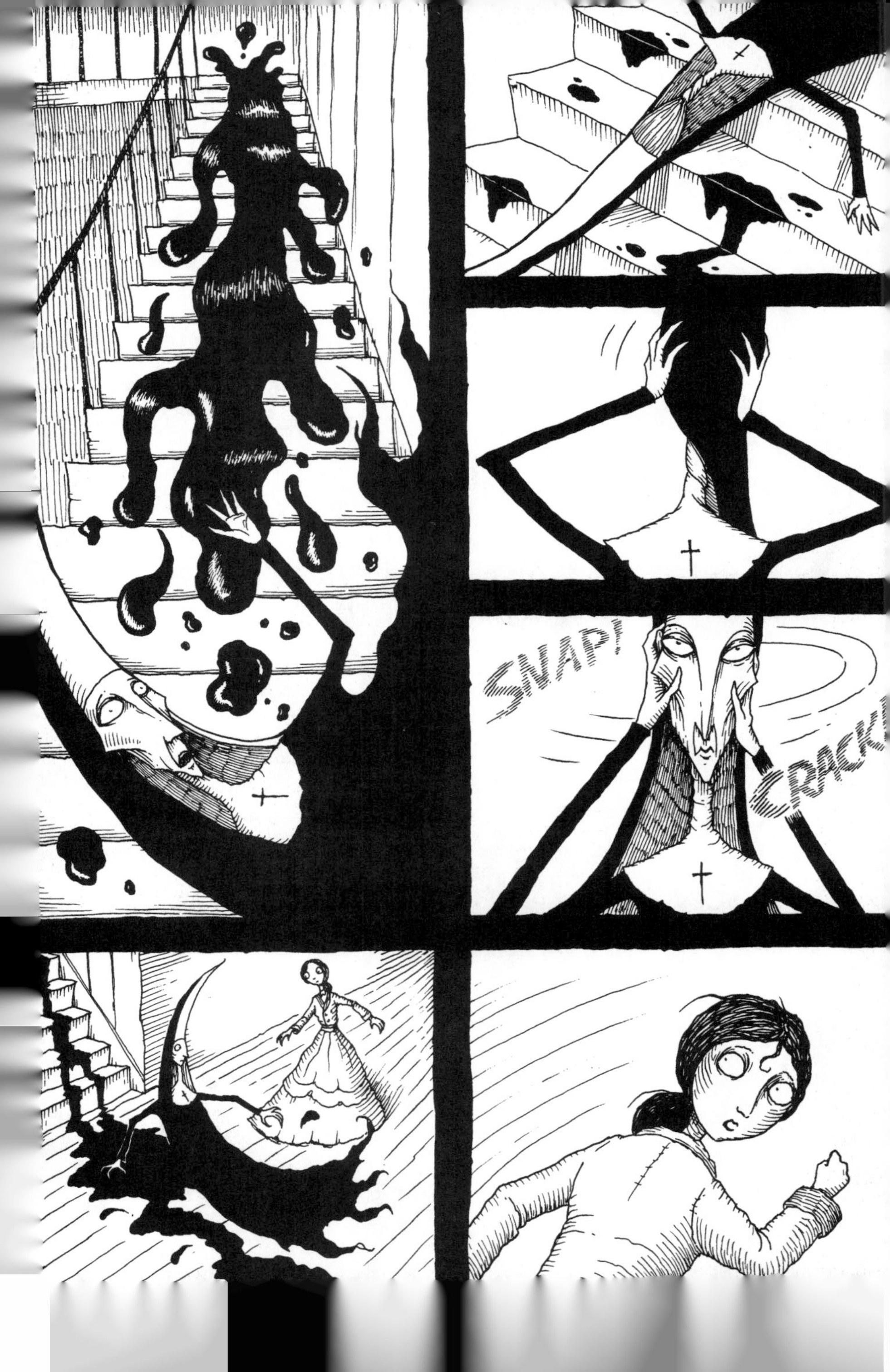
SNAP!
CRACK

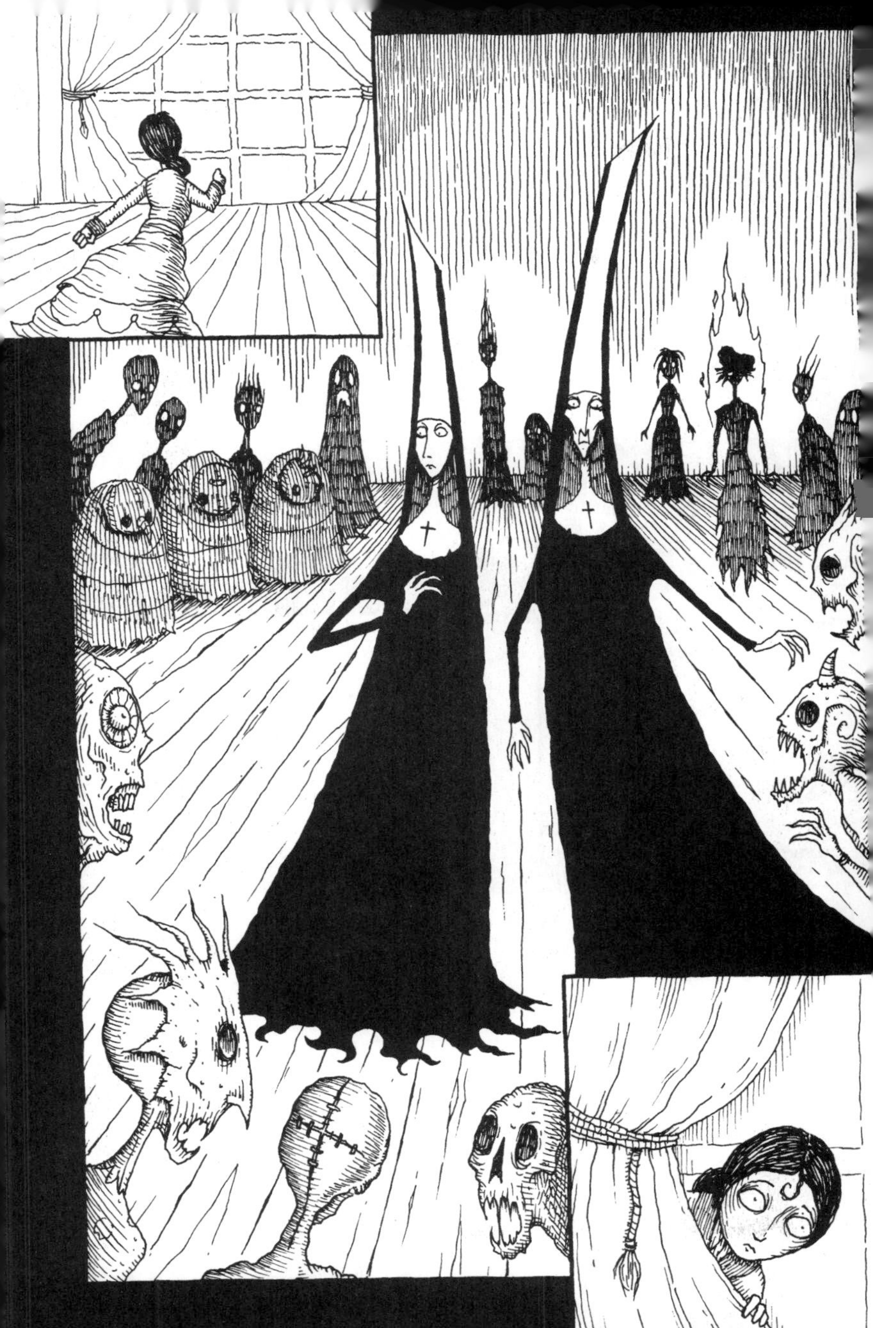

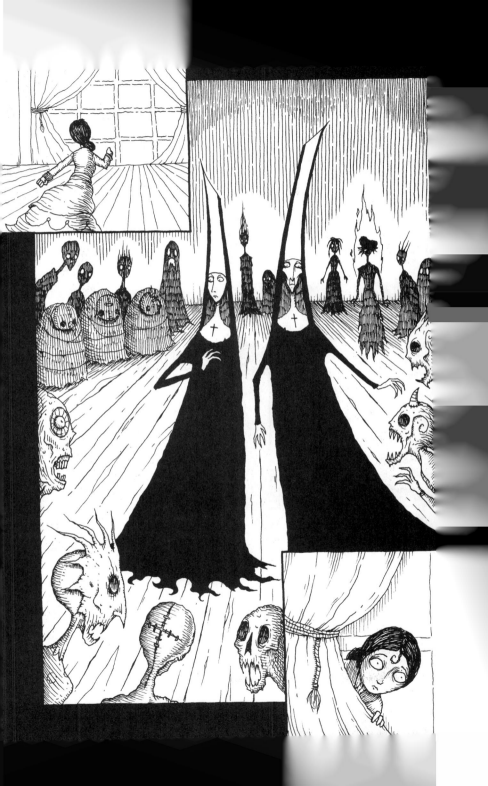

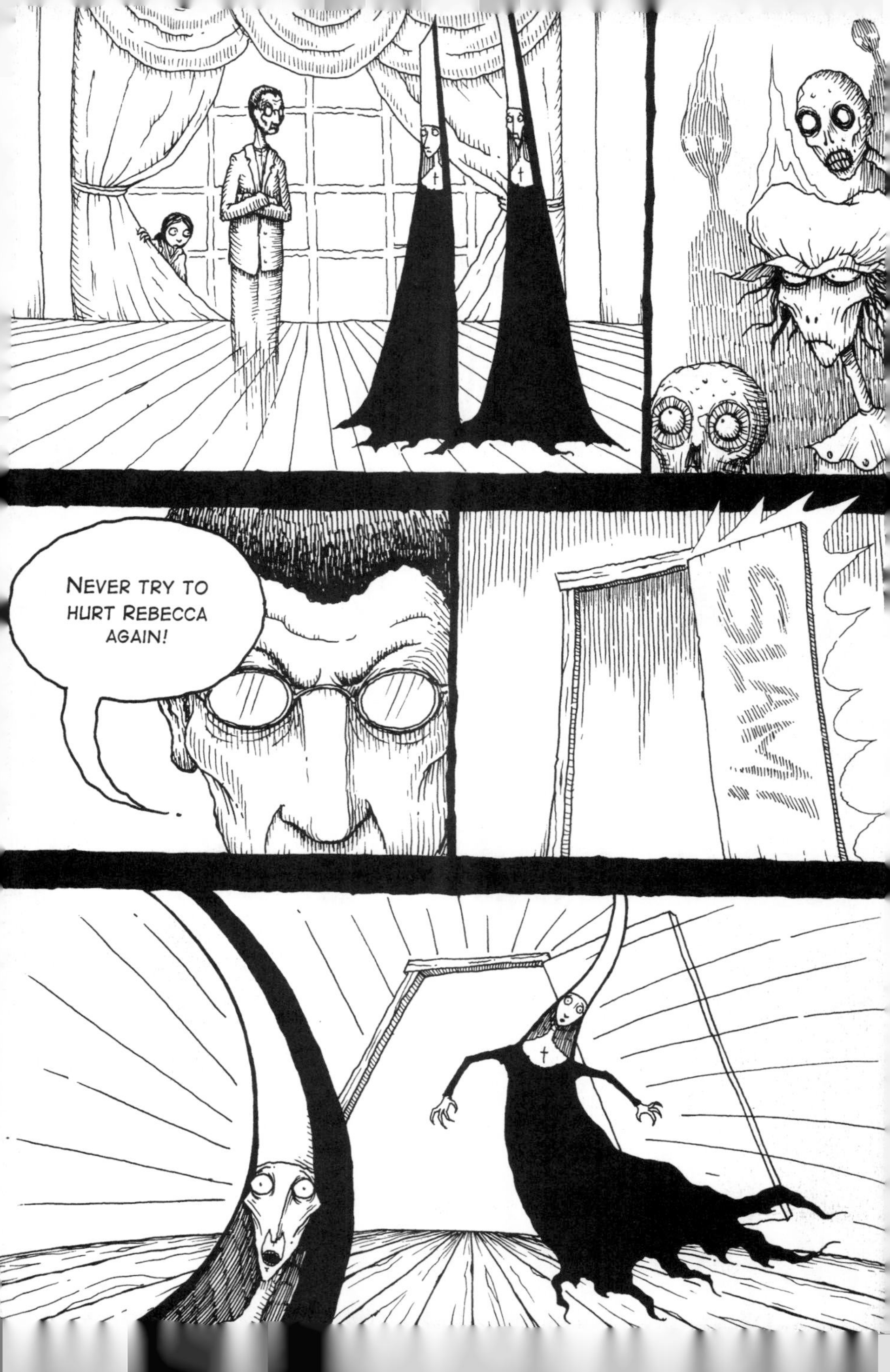
NEVER TRY TO HURT REBECCA AGAIN!
SLAM

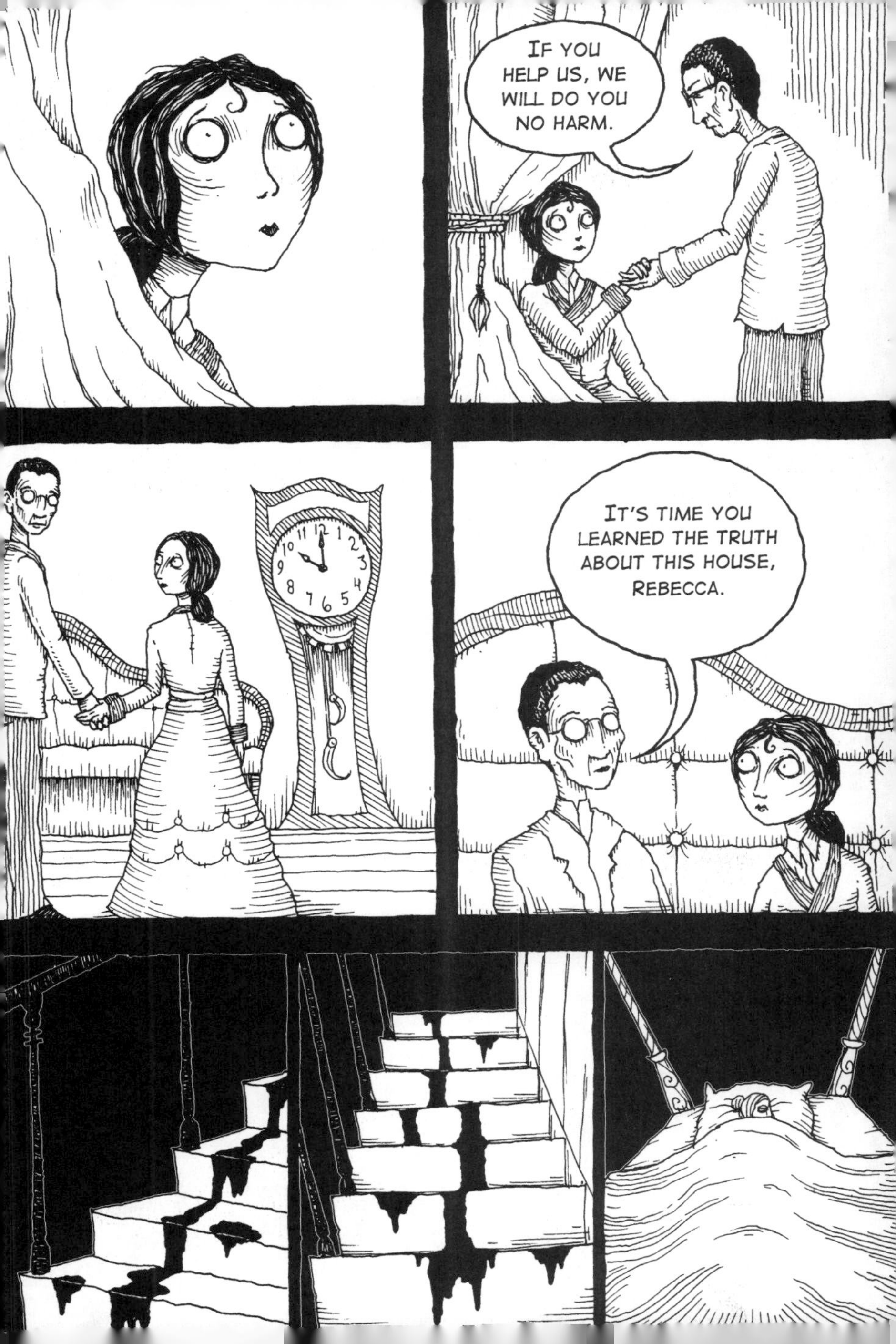
IF YOU HELP US, WE WILL DO YOU NO HARM.
IT'S TIME YOU LEARNED THE TRUTH ABOUT THIS HOUSE, REBECCA.

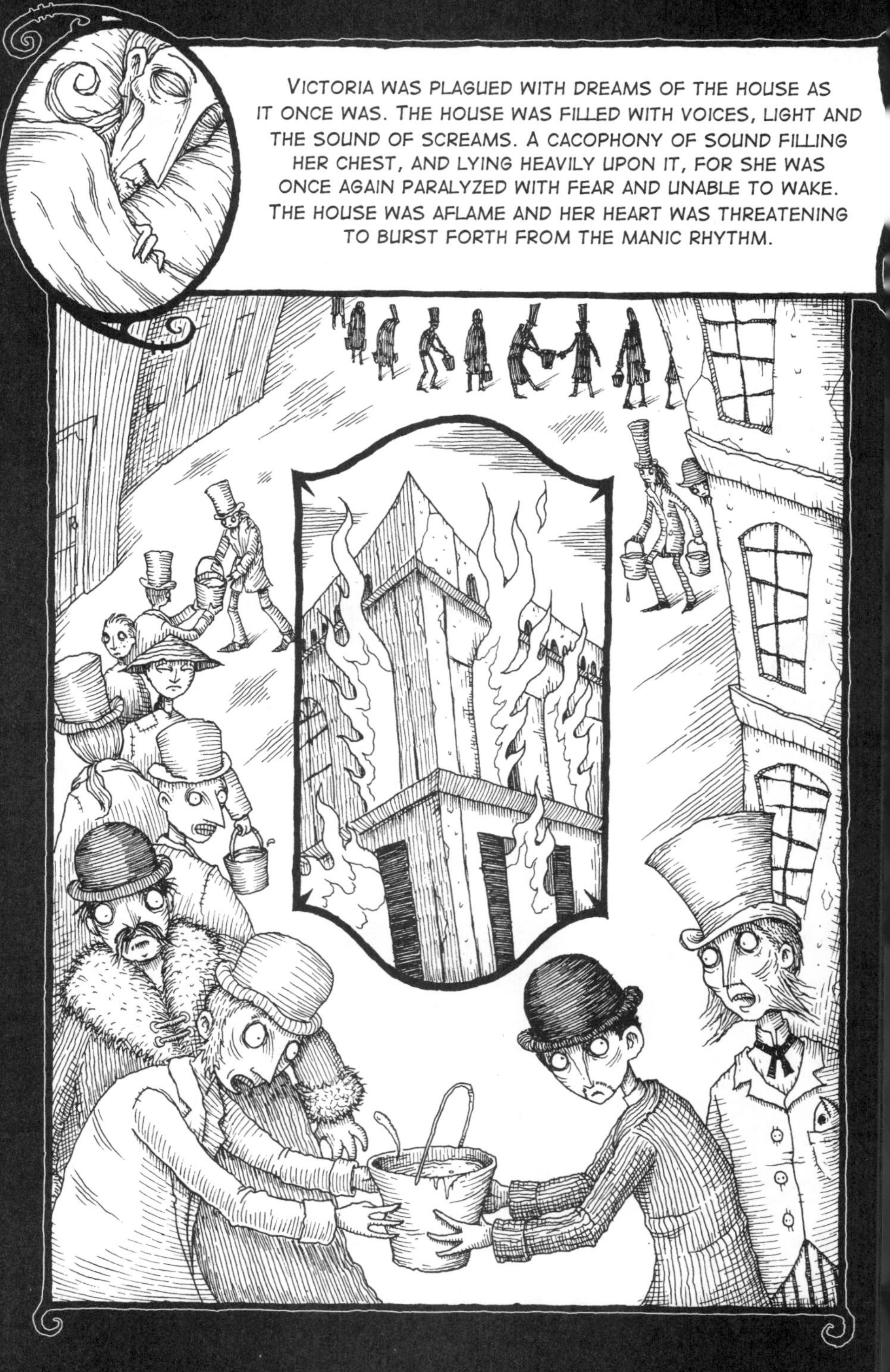
VICTORIA WAS PLAGUED WITH DREAMS OF THE HOUSE AS IT ONCE WAS. THE HOUSE WAS FILLED WITH VOICES, LIGHT AND THE SOUND OF SCREAMS. A CACOPHONY OF SOUND FILLING HER CHEST, AND LYING HEAVILY UPON IT, FOR SHE WAS ONCE AGAIN PARALYZED WITH FEAR AND UNABLE TO WAKE. THE HOUSE WAS AFLAME AND HER HEART WAS THREATENING TO BURST FORTH FROM THE MANIC RHYTHM.

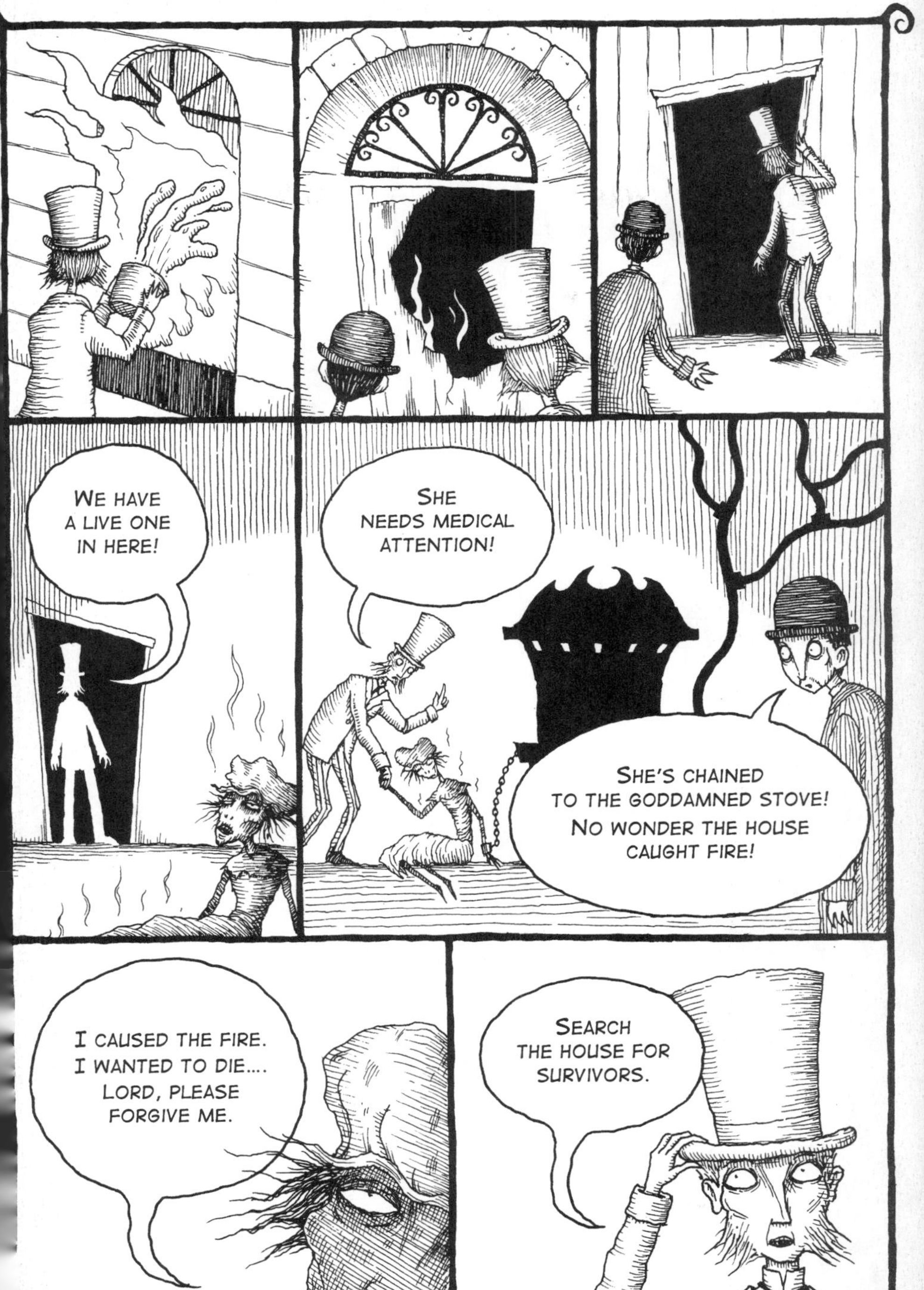
We have a live one in here!
She needs medical attention!
She's chained to the goddamned stove! No wonder the house caught fire!
I caused the fire. I wanted to die.... Lord, please forgive me.
Search the house for survivors.

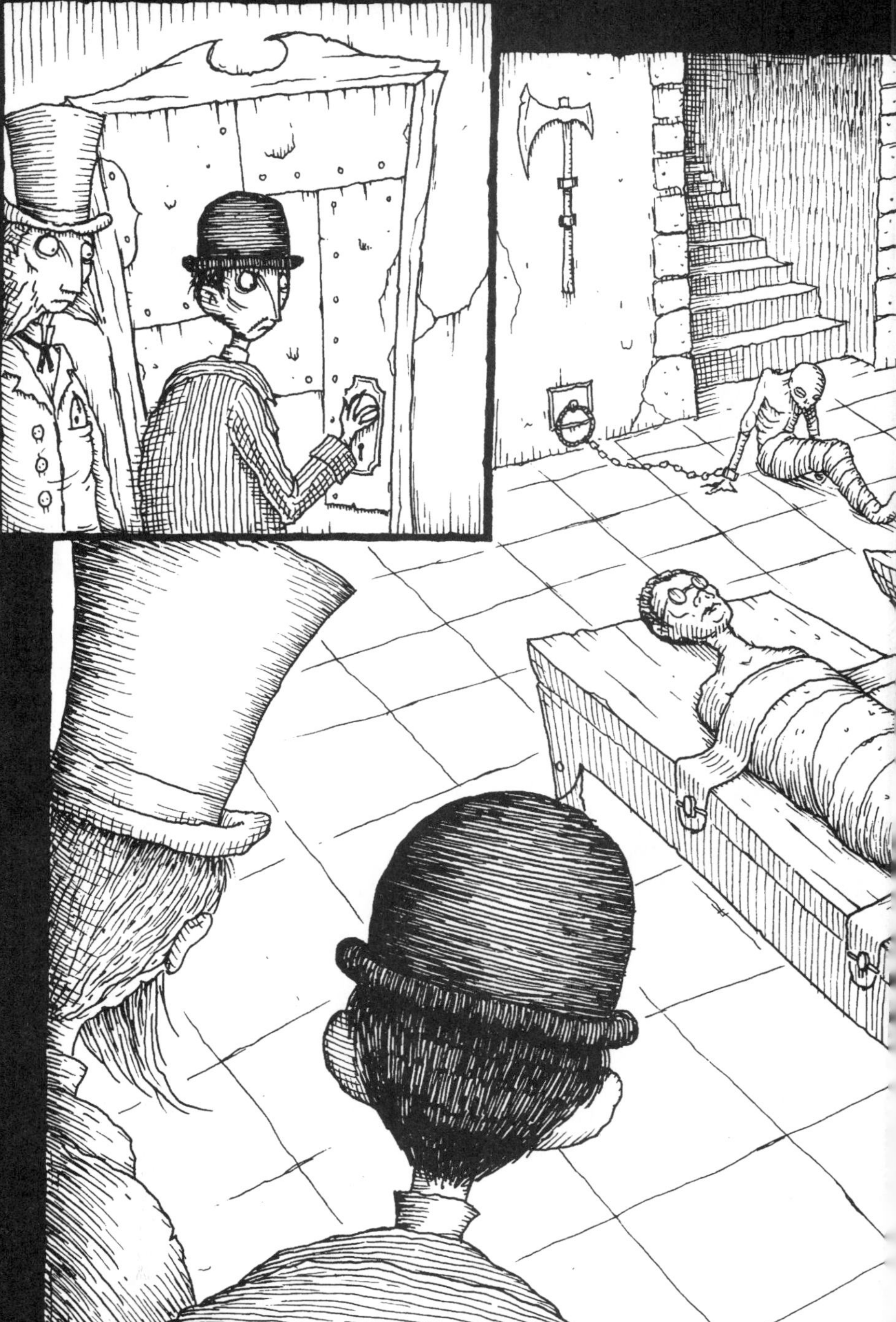

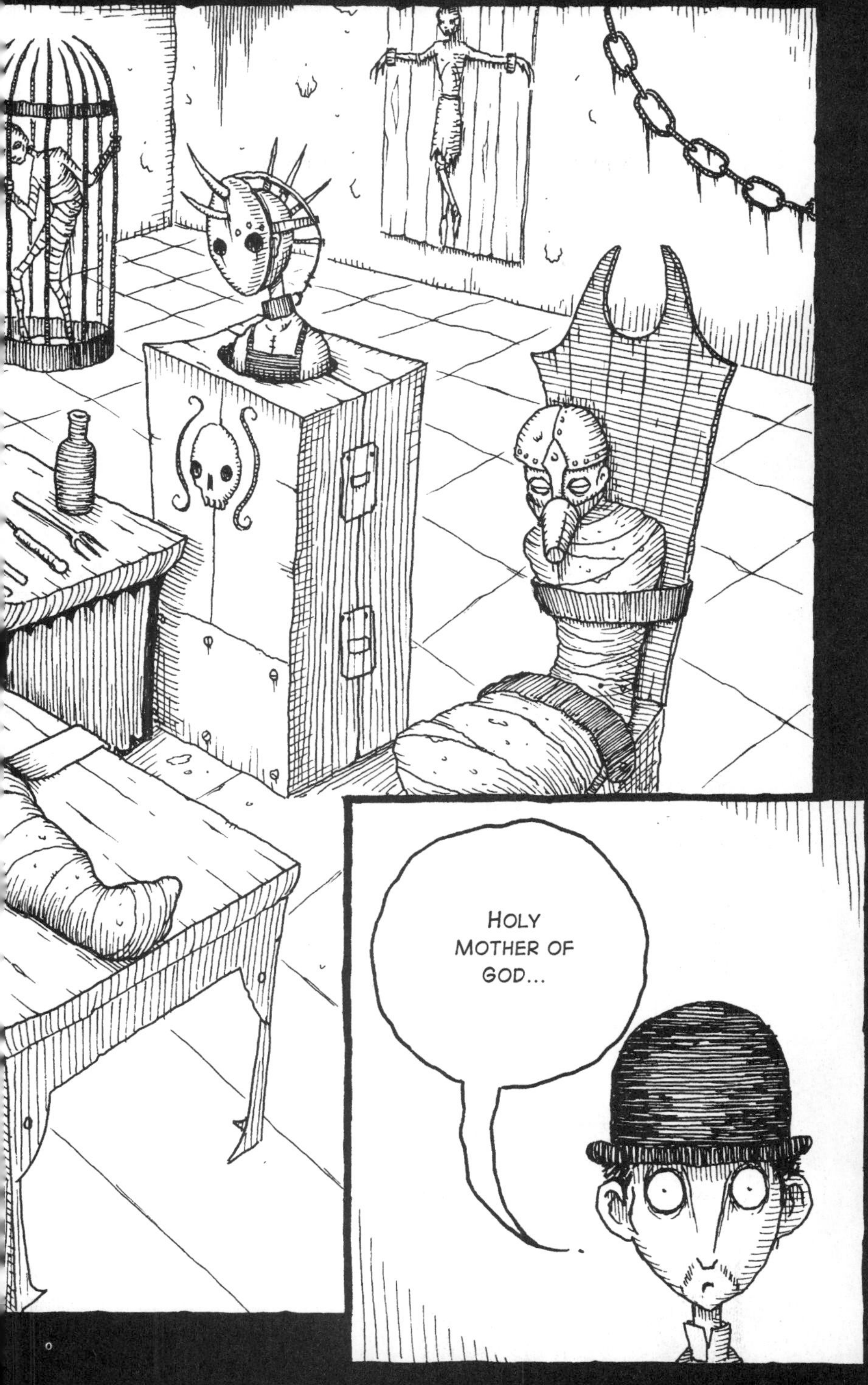
HOLY MOTHER OF GOD...

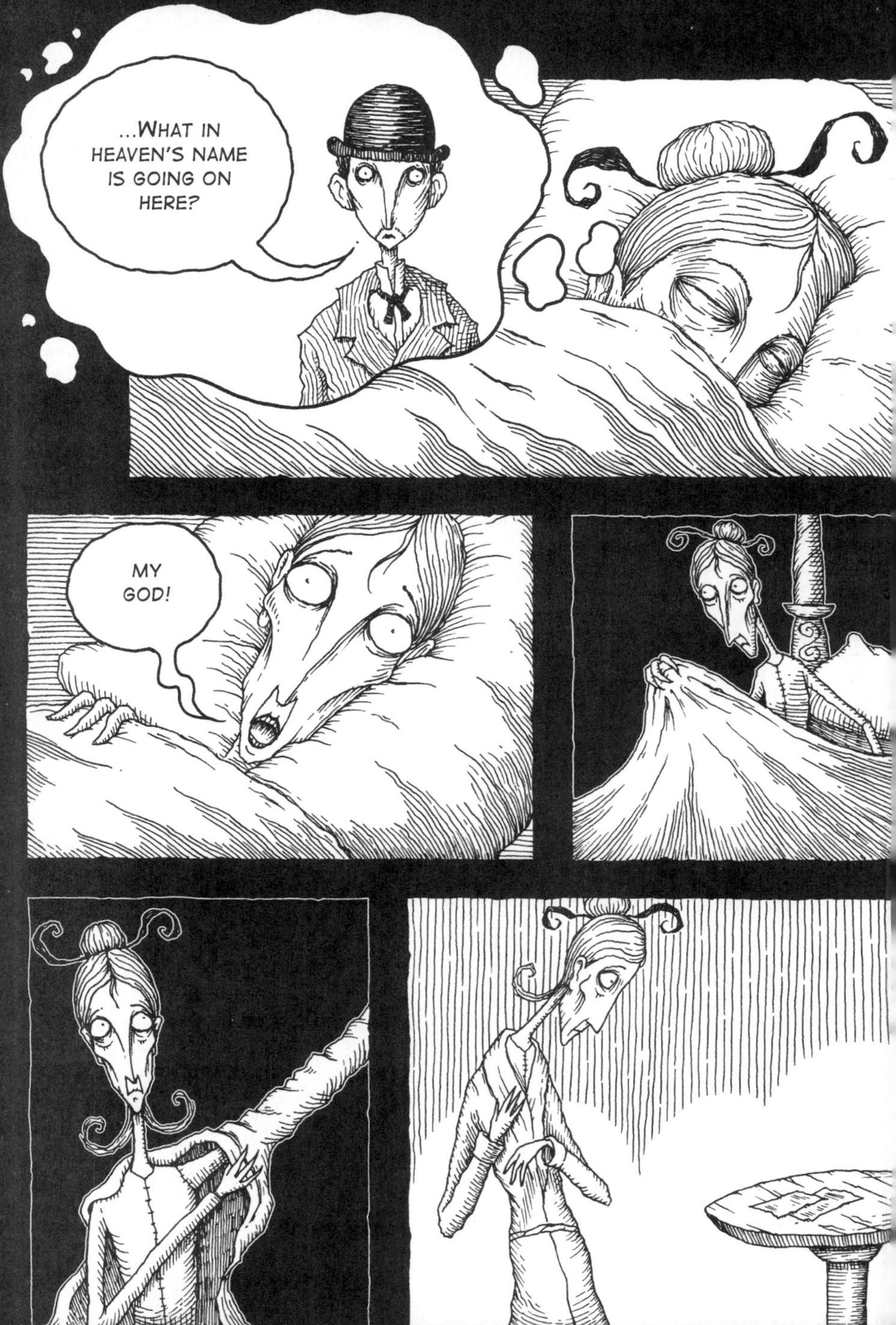
...WHAT IN HEAVEN'S NAME IS GOING ON HERE?
MY GOD!

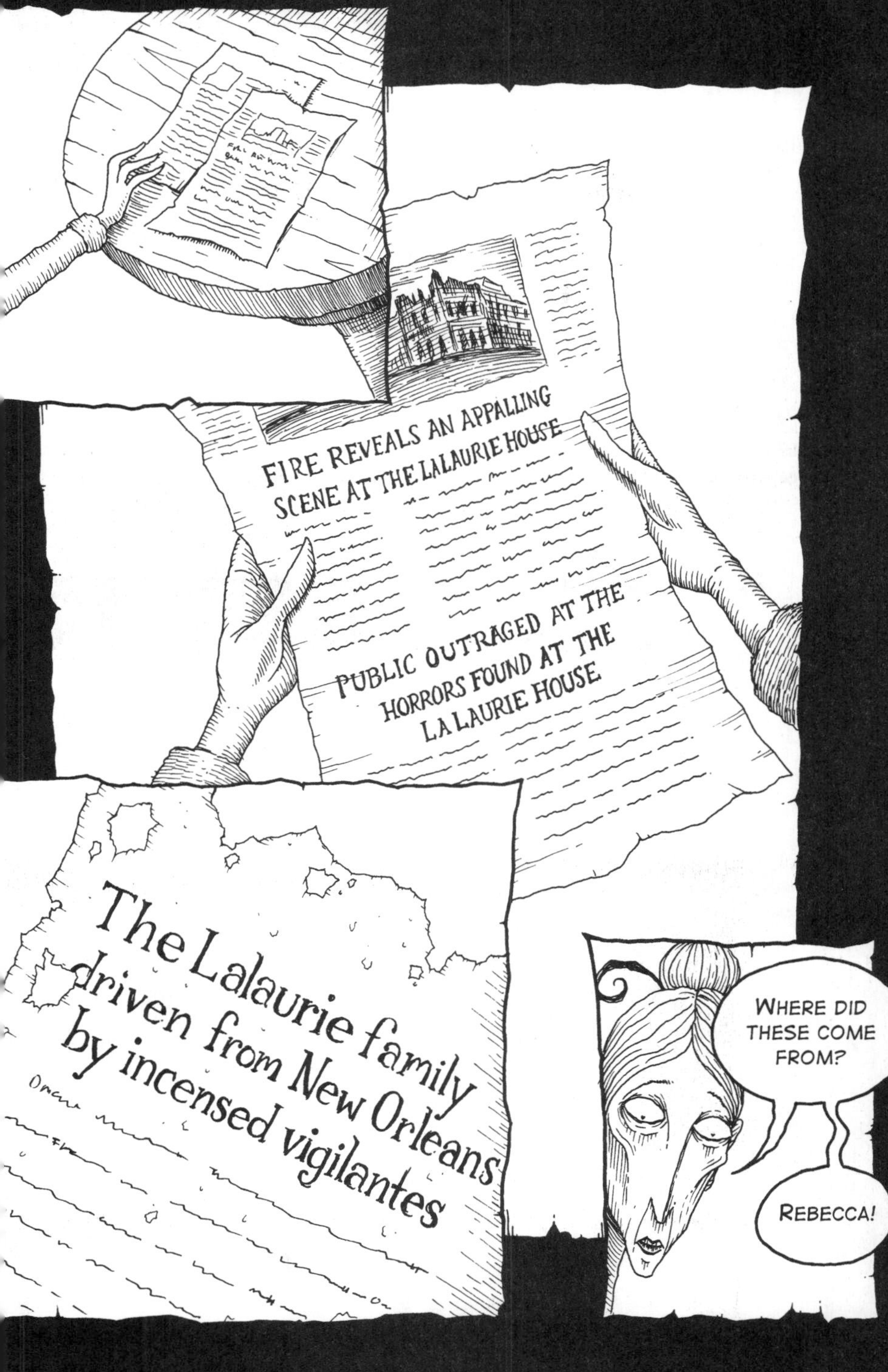
FIRE REVEALS AN APPALLING SCENE AT THE LALAURIE HOUSE
PUBLIC OUTRAGED AT THE HORRORS FOUND AT THE LA LAURIE HOUSE
The Lalaurie family driven from New Orleans by incensed vigilantes
WHERE DID THESE COME FROM?
REBECCA!

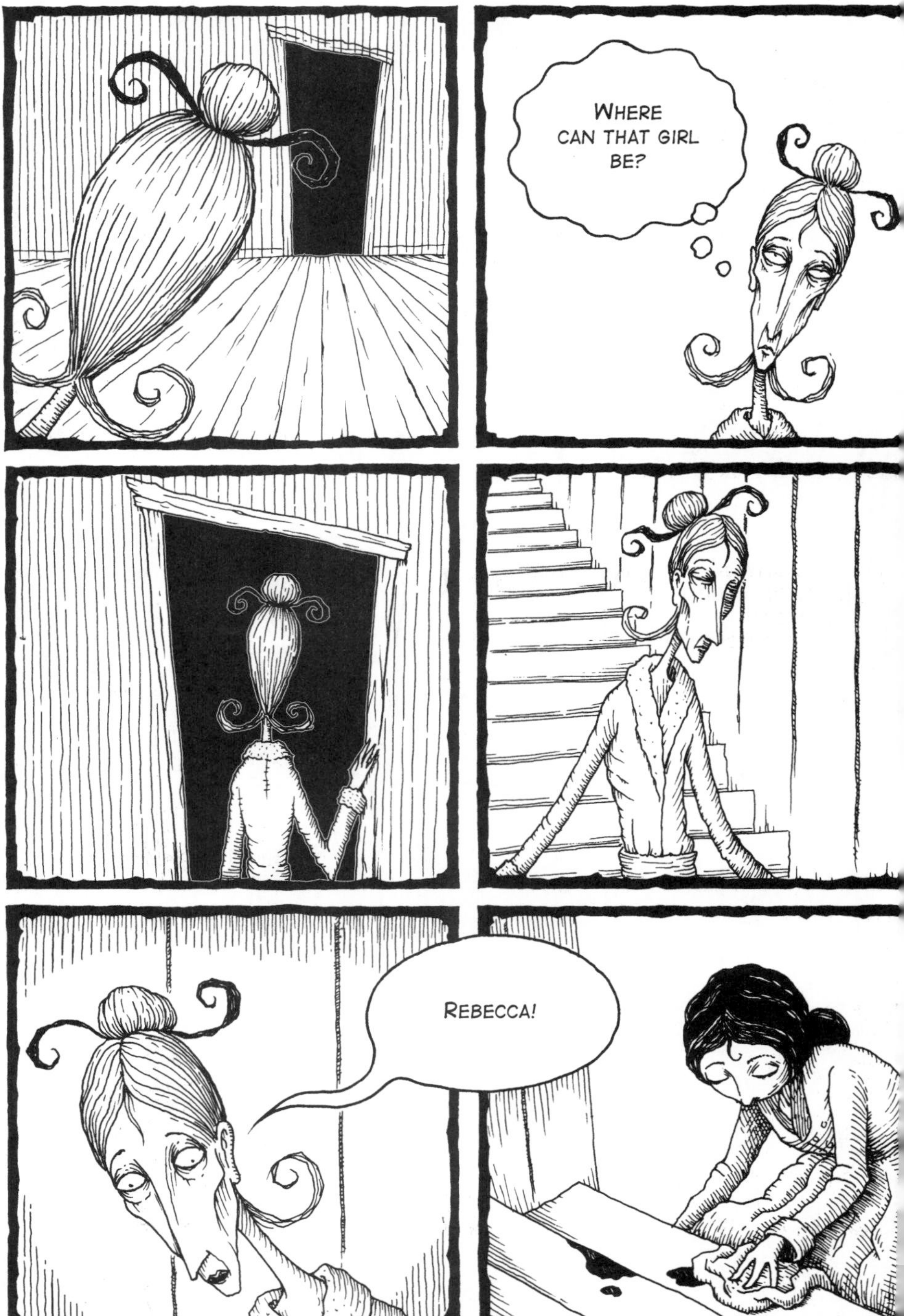
WHERE CAN THAT GIRL BE?
REBECCA!

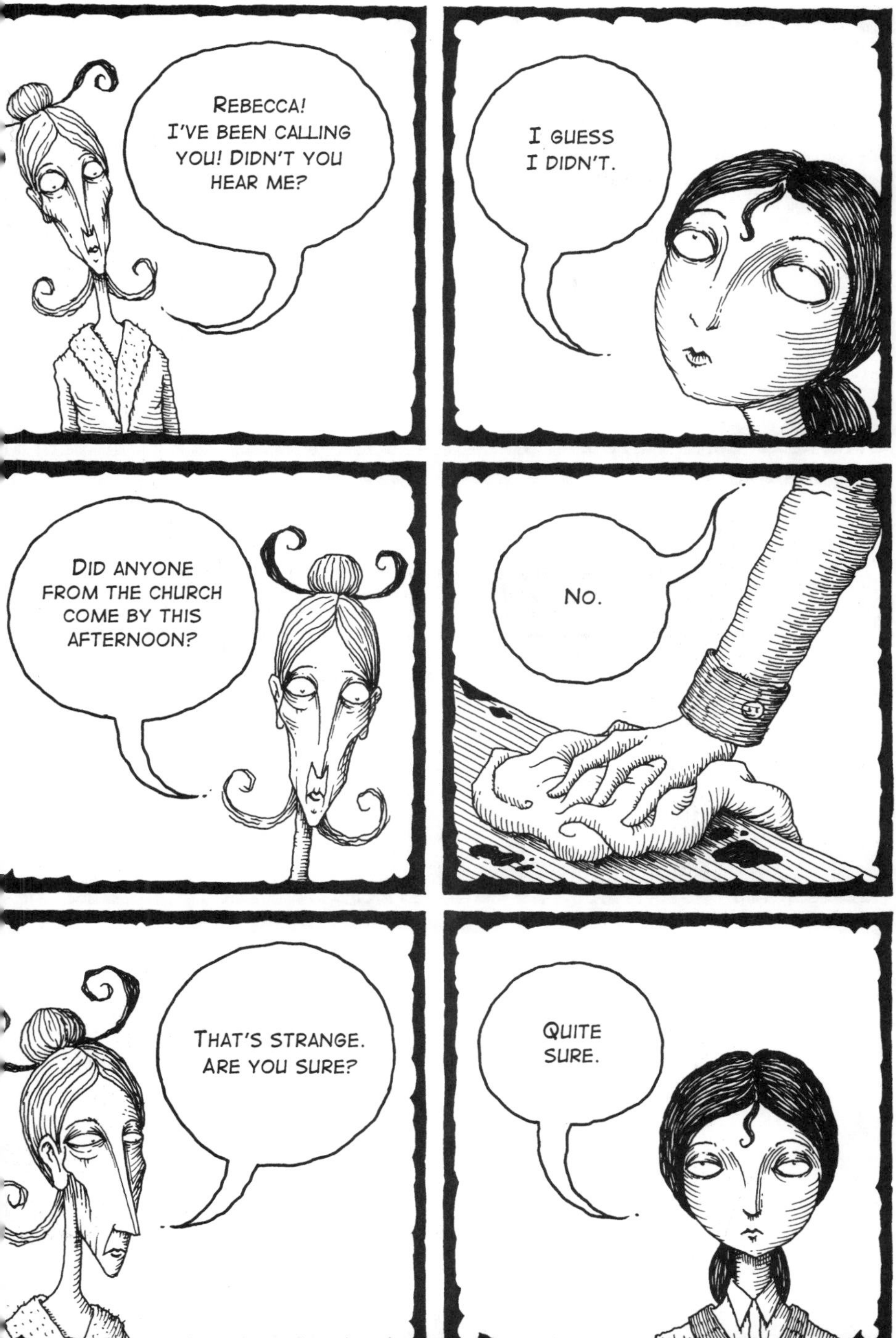
REBECCA! I'VE BEEN CALLING YOU! DIDN'T YOU HEAR ME?
I GUESS I DIDN'T.
DID ANYONE FROM THE CHURCH COME BY THIS AFTERNOON?
NO.
THAT'S STRANGE. ARE YOU SURE?
QUITE SURE.

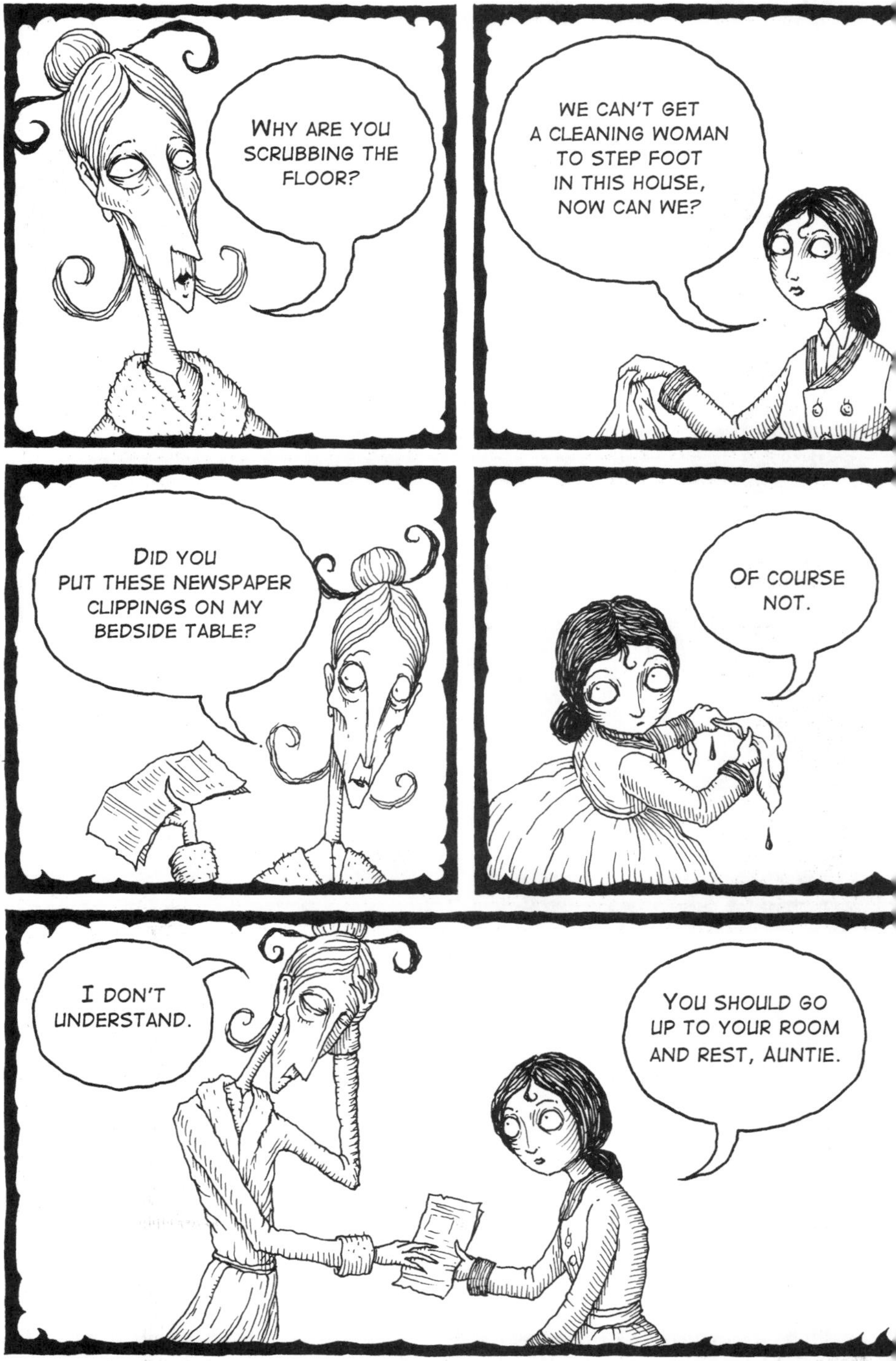
WHY ARE YOU SCRUBBING THE FLOOR?
WE CAN'T GET A CLEANING WOMAN TO STEP FOOT IN THIS HOUSE, NOW CAN WE?
DID YOU PUT THESE NEWSPAPER CLIPPINGS ON MY BEDSIDE TABLE?
OF COURSE NOT.
I DON'T UNDERSTAND.
YOU SHOULD GO UP TO YOUR ROOM AND REST, AUNTIE.

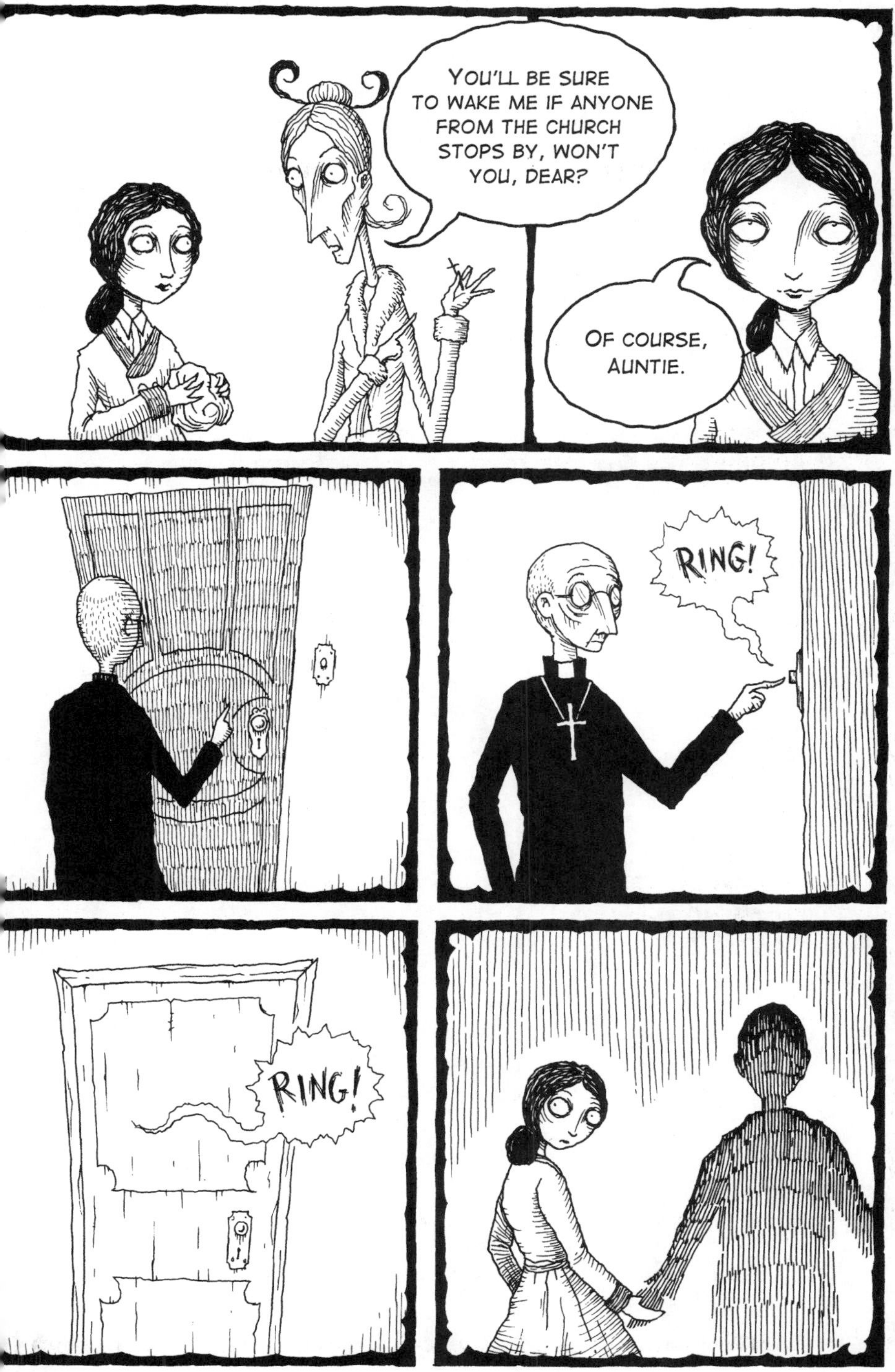
YOU'LL BE SURE TO WAKE ME IF ANYONE FROM THE CHURCH STOPS BY, WON'T YOU, DEAR?
OF COURSE, AUNTIE.
RING!
RING!

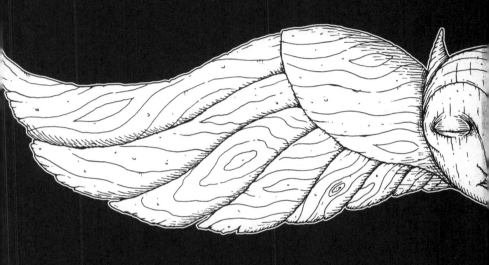

Chapter 4

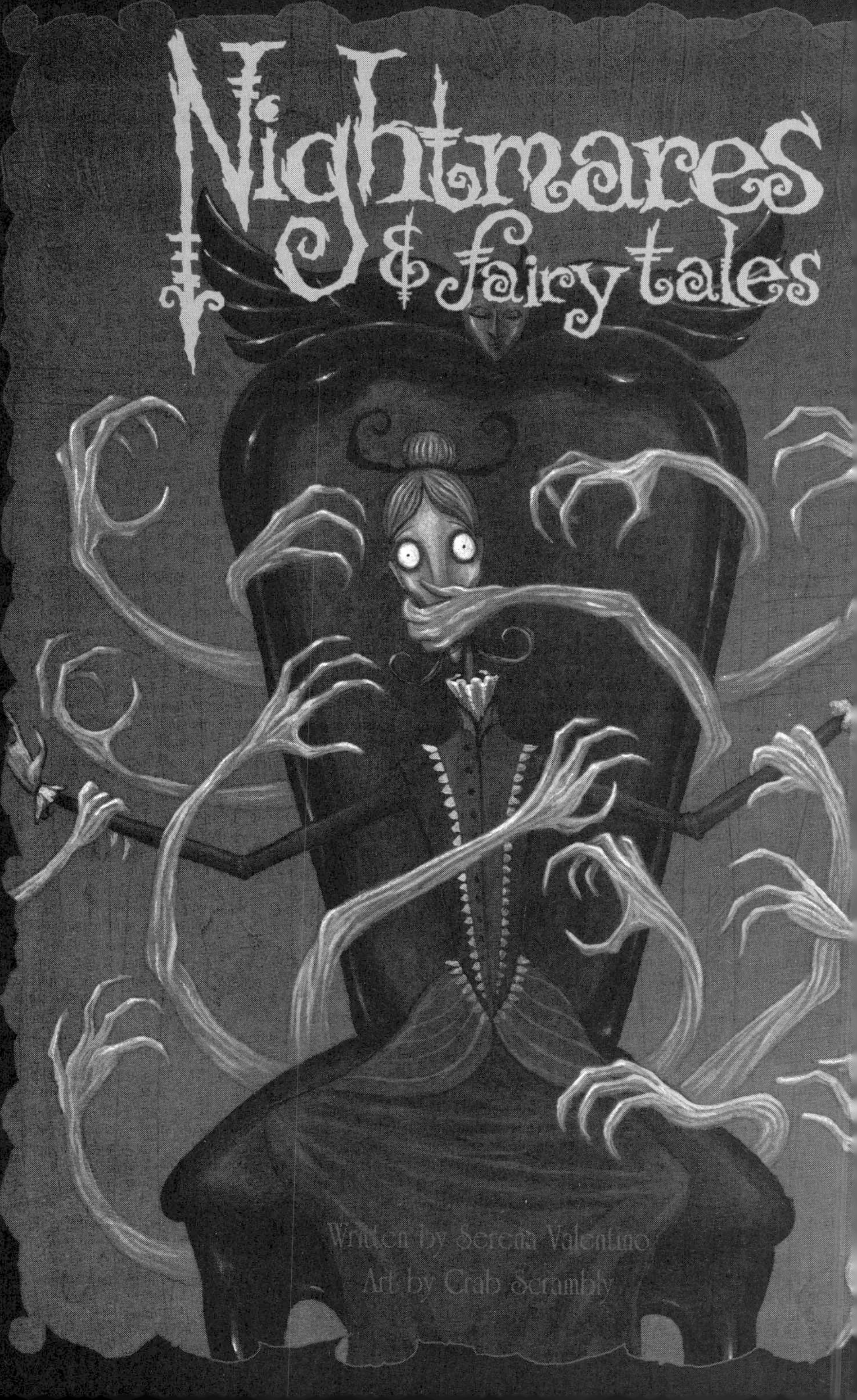
Nightmares & fairy tales
Written by Serena Valentino
Art by Crab Scrambly

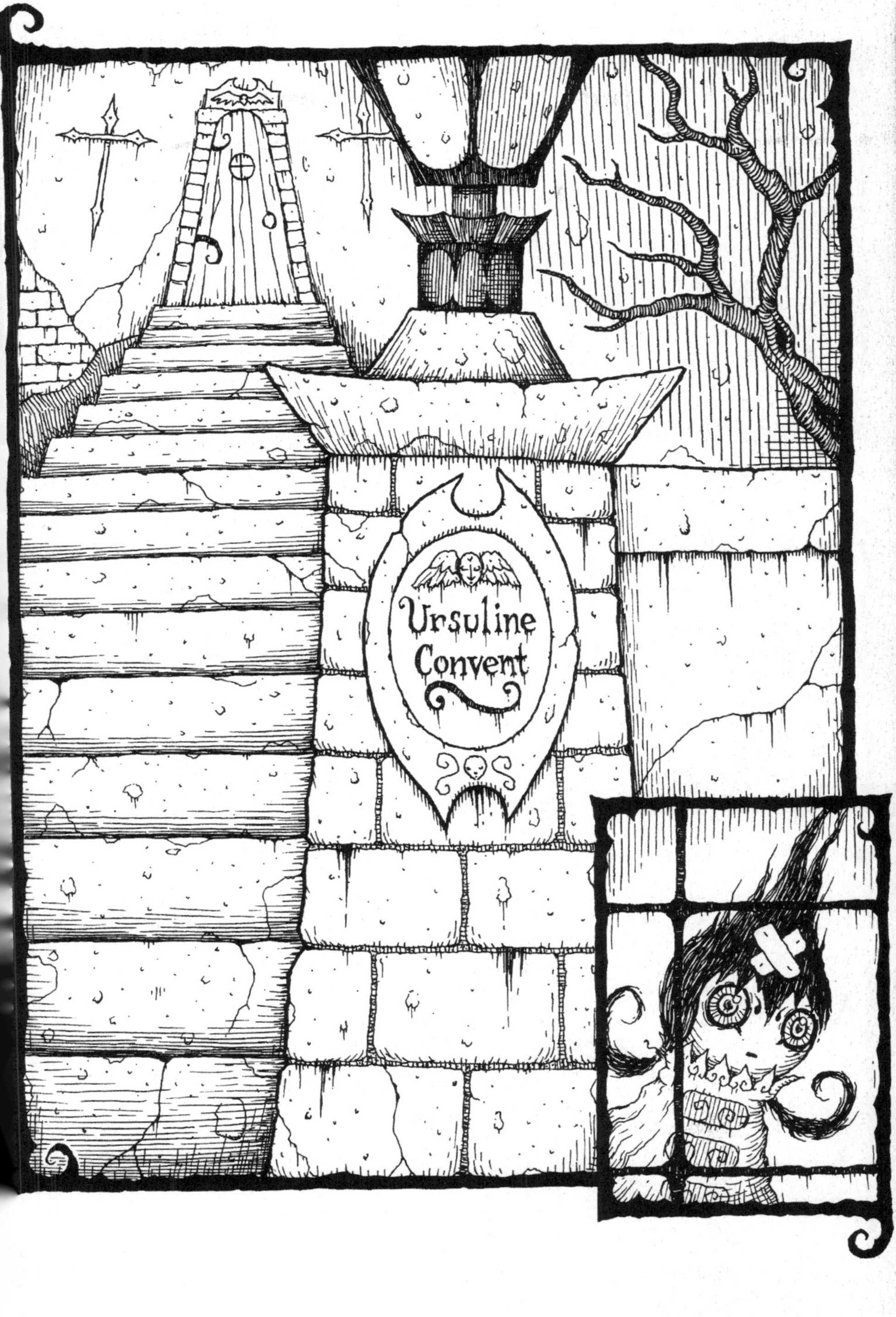
Ursuline Convent

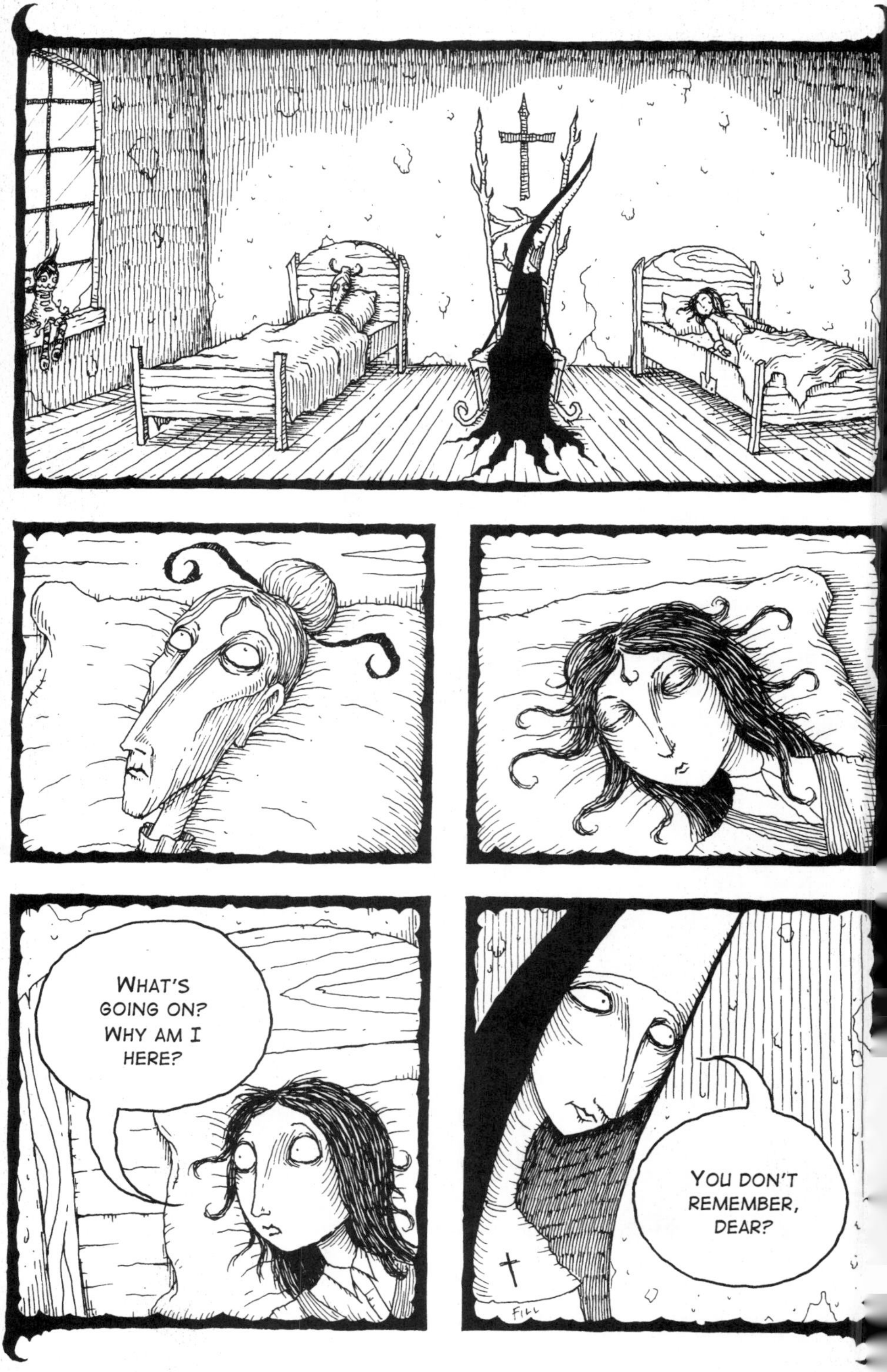
WHAT'S GOING ON? WHY AM I HERE?
YOU DON'T REMEMBER, DEAR?

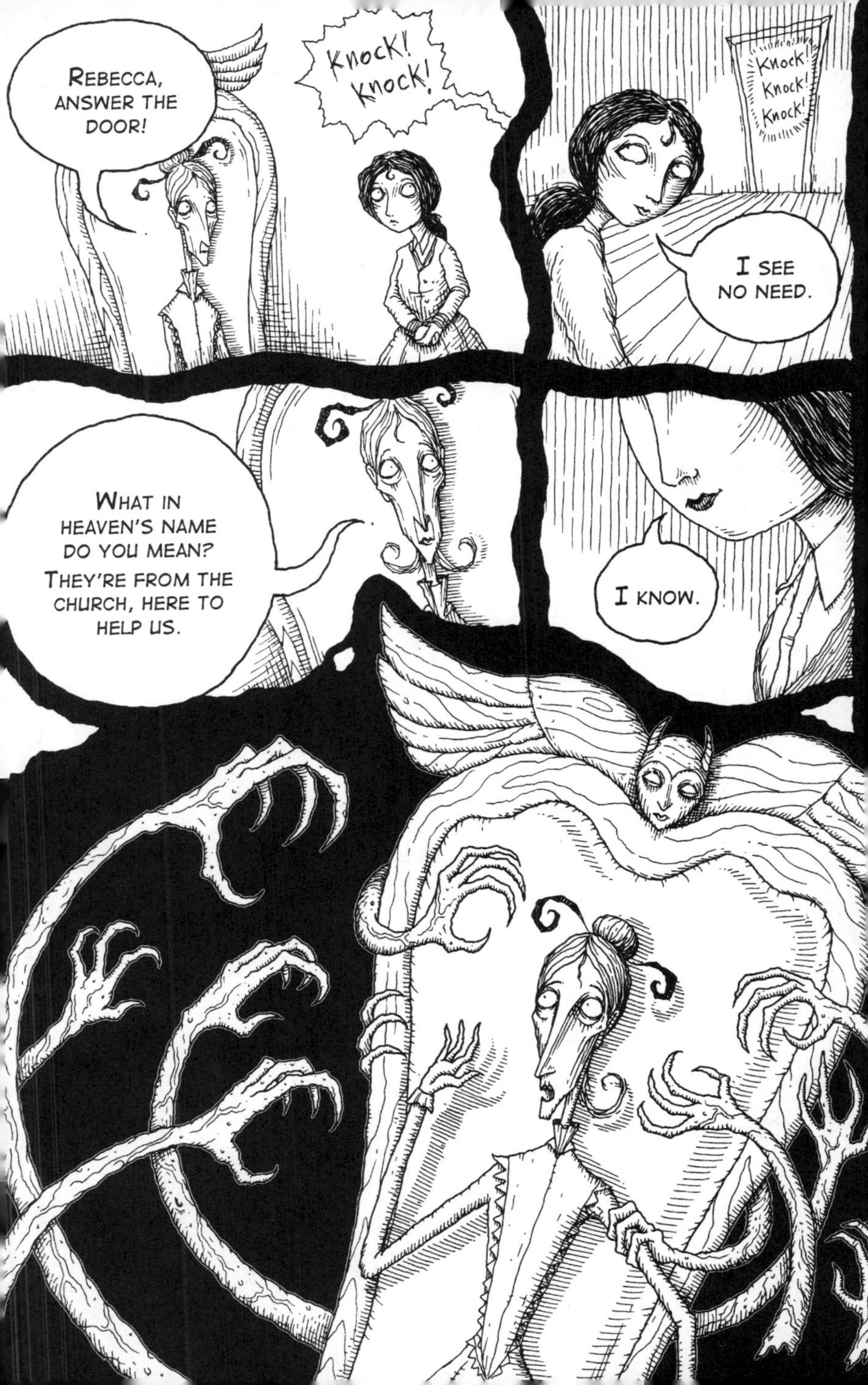
Rebecca, answer the door!
Knock! Knock!
Knock! Knock! Knock!
I see no need.
What in heaven's name do you mean? They're from the church, here to help us.
I know.

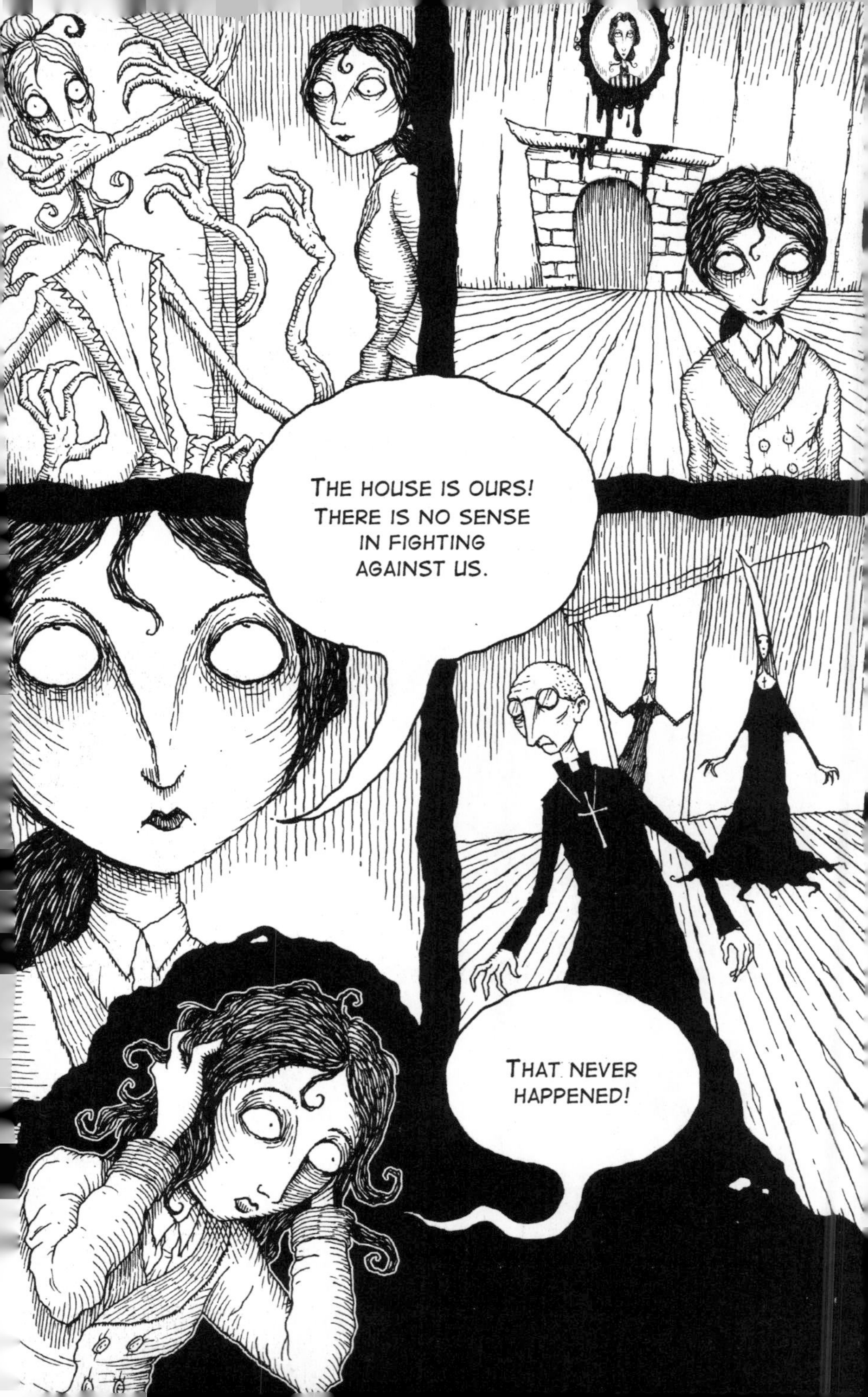
THE HOUSE IS OURS! THERE IS NO SENSE IN FIGHTING AGAINST US.
THAT NEVER HAPPENED!

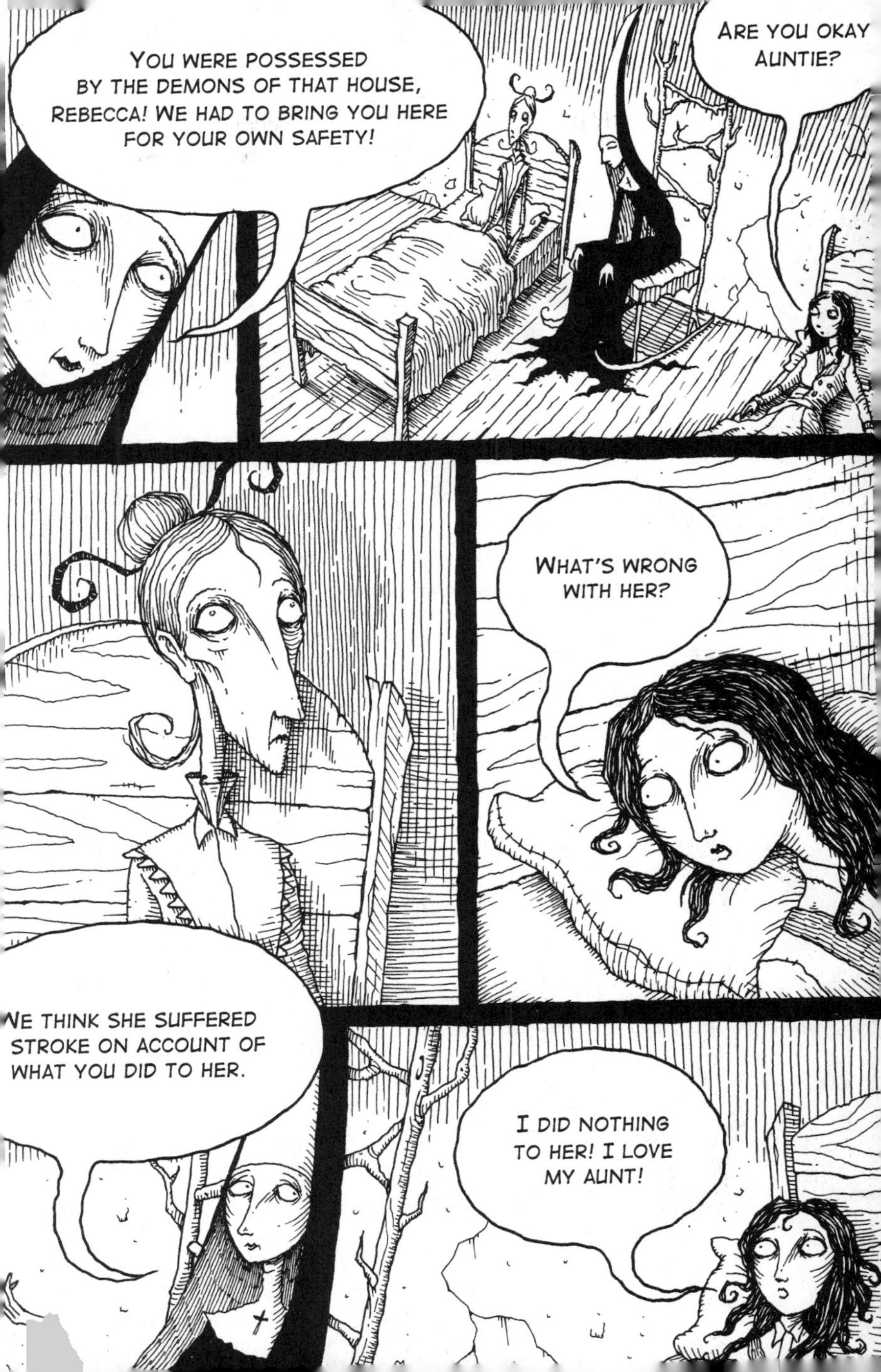
You were possessed by the demons of that house, Rebecca! We had to bring you here for your own safety!
Are you okay Auntie?
What's wrong with her?
We think she suffered stroke on account of what you did to her.
I did nothing to her! I love my aunt!

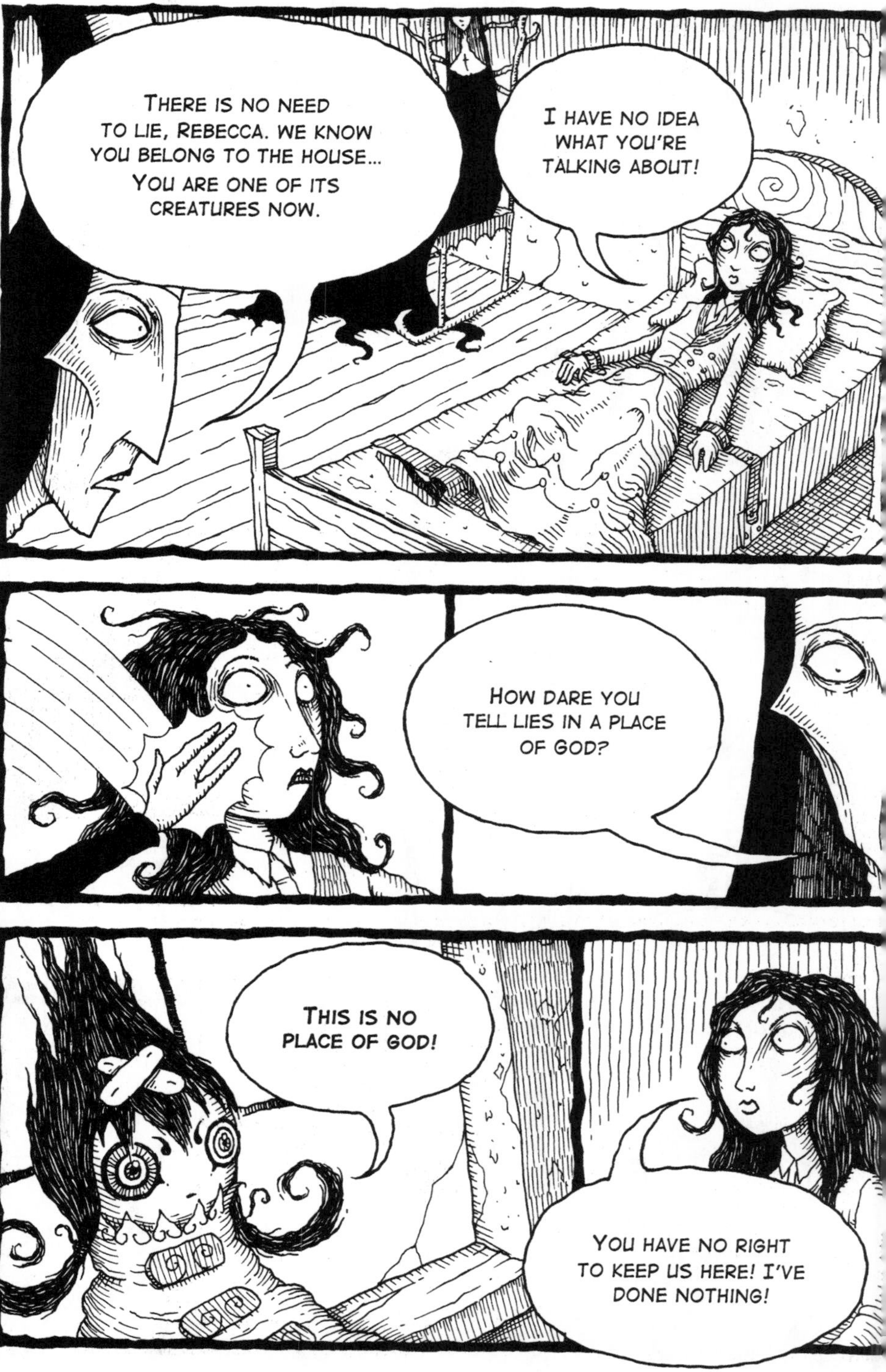
THERE IS NO NEED TO LIE, REBECCA. WE KNOW YOU BELONG TO THE HOUSE... YOU ARE ONE OF ITS CREATURES NOW.
I HAVE NO IDEA WHAT YOU'RE TALKING ABOUT!
HOW DARE YOU TELL LIES IN A PLACE OF GOD?
THIS IS NO PLACE OF GOD!
YOU HAVE NO RIGHT TO KEEP US HERE! I'VE DONE NOTHING!

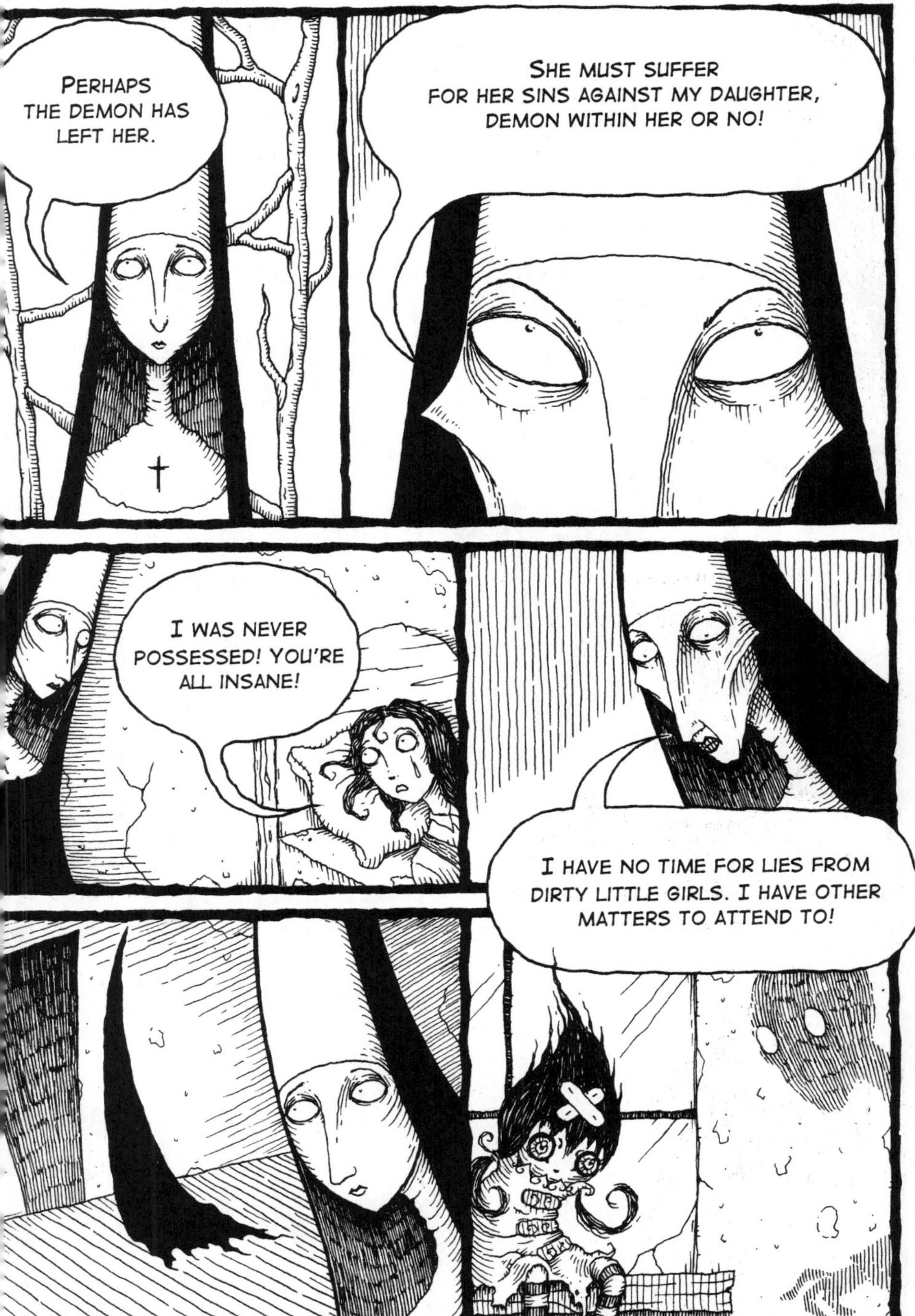
PERHAPS THE DEMON HAS LEFT HER.
SHE MUST SUFFER FOR HER SINS AGAINST MY DAUGHTER, DEMON WITHIN HER OR NO!
I WAS NEVER POSSESSED! YOU'RE ALL INSANE!
I HAVE NO TIME FOR LIES FROM DIRTY LITTLE GIRLS. I HAVE OTHER MATTERS TO ATTEND TO!

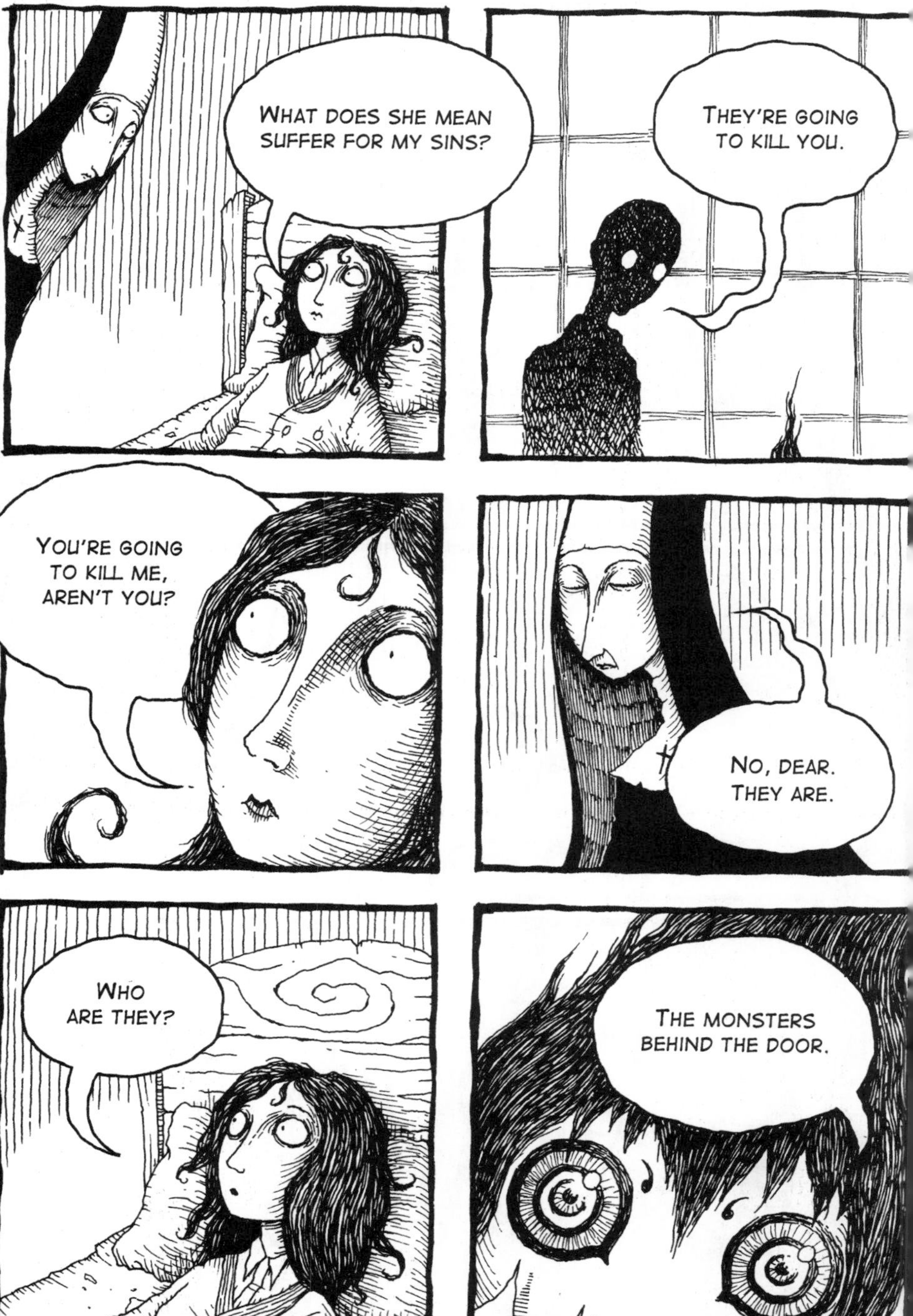
WHAT DOES SHE MEAN SUFFER FOR MY SINS?
THEY'RE GOING TO KILL YOU.
YOU'RE GOING TO KILL ME, AREN'T YOU?
NO, DEAR. THEY ARE.
WHO ARE THEY?
THE MONSTERS BEHIND THE DOOR.

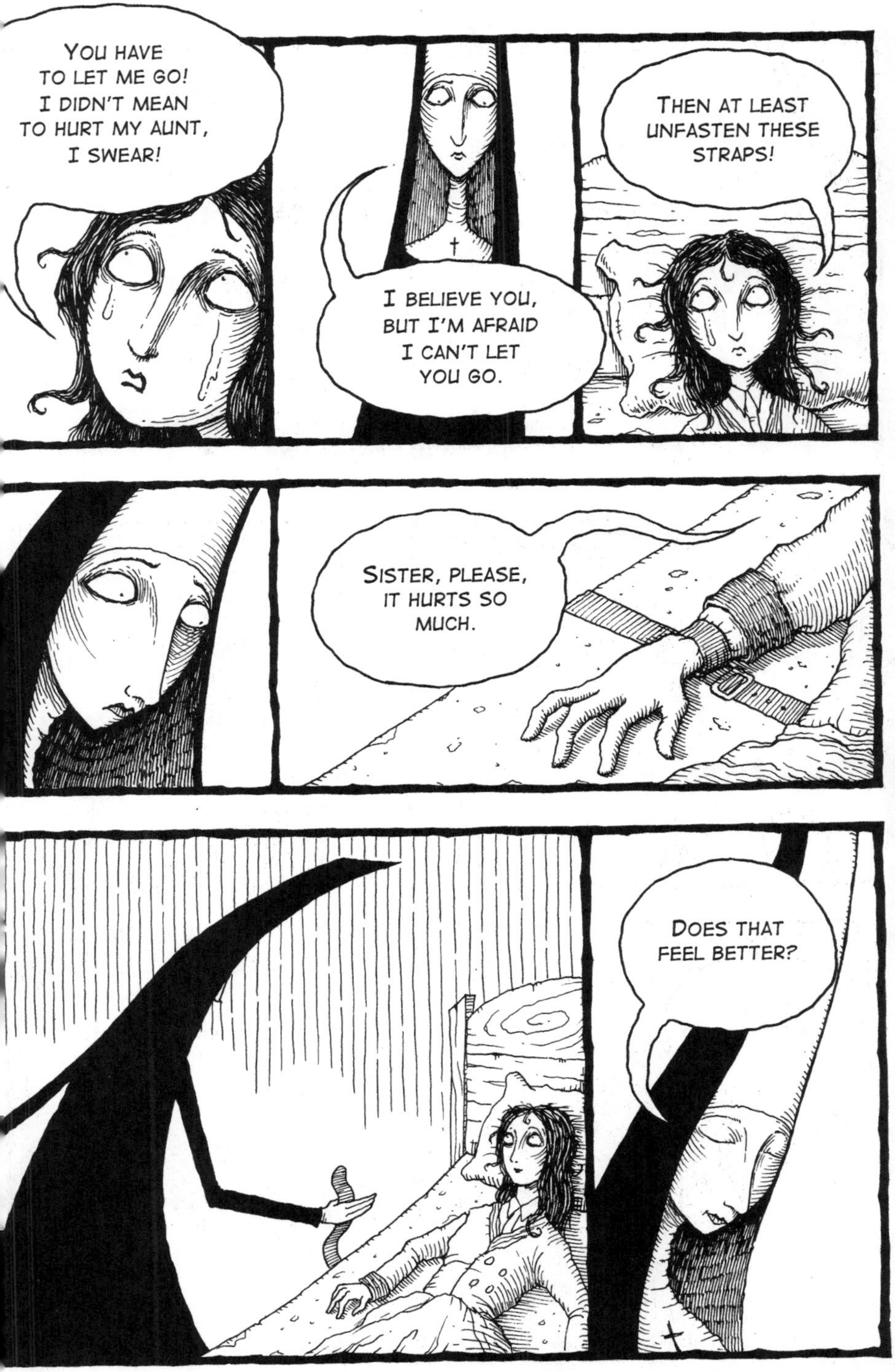
YOU HAVE TO LET ME GO! I DIDN'T MEAN TO HURT MY AUNT, I SWEAR!
I BELIEVE YOU, BUT I'M AFRAID I CAN'T LET YOU GO.
THEN AT LEAST UNFASTEN THESE STRAPS!
SISTER, PLEASE, IT HURTS SO MUCH.
DOES THAT FEEL BETTER?

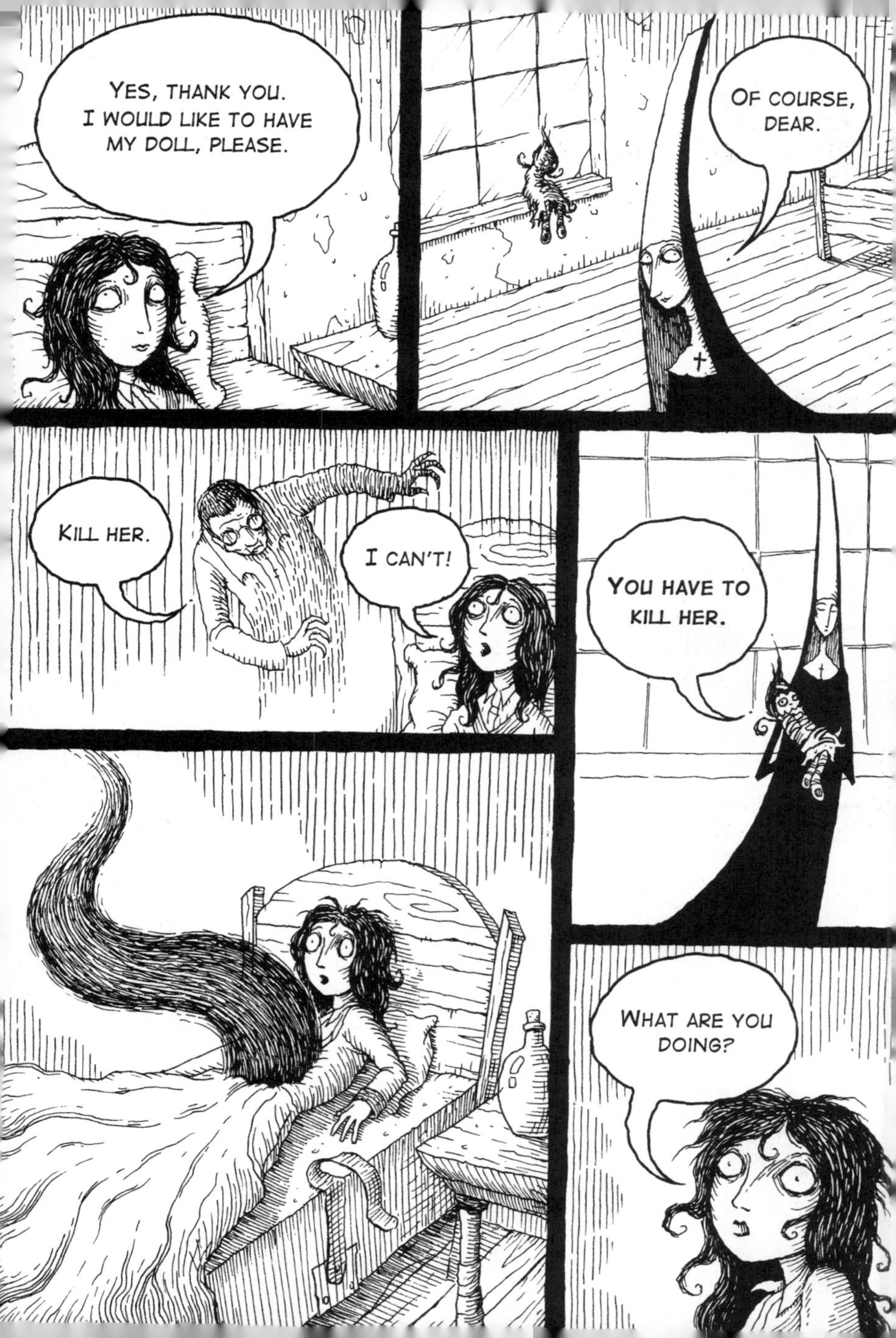
YES, THANK YOU. I WOULD LIKE TO HAVE MY DOLL, PLEASE.
OF COURSE, DEAR.
KILL HER.
I CAN'T!
YOU HAVE TO KILL HER.
WHAT ARE YOU DOING?

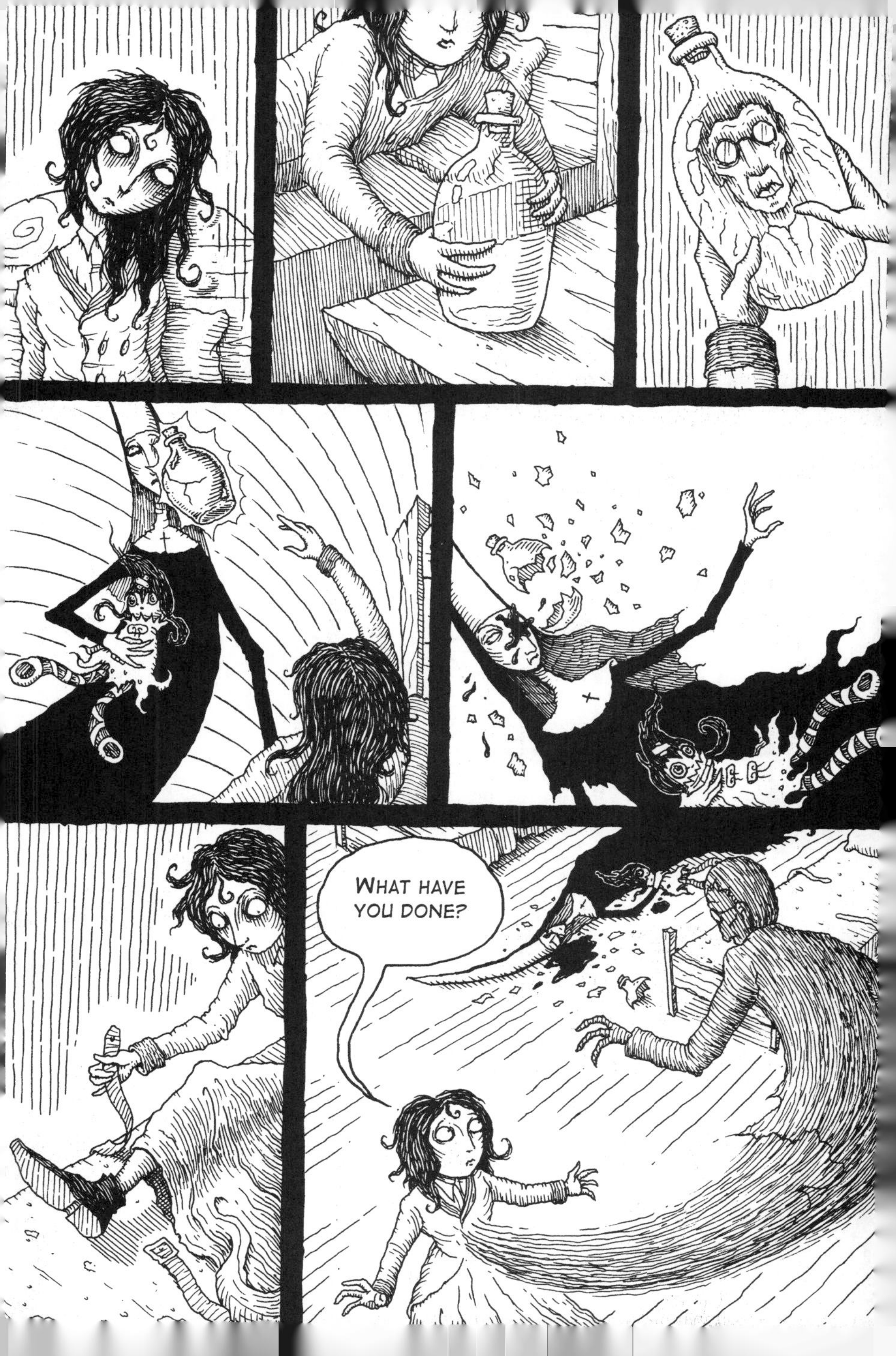
WHAT HAVE YOU DONE?

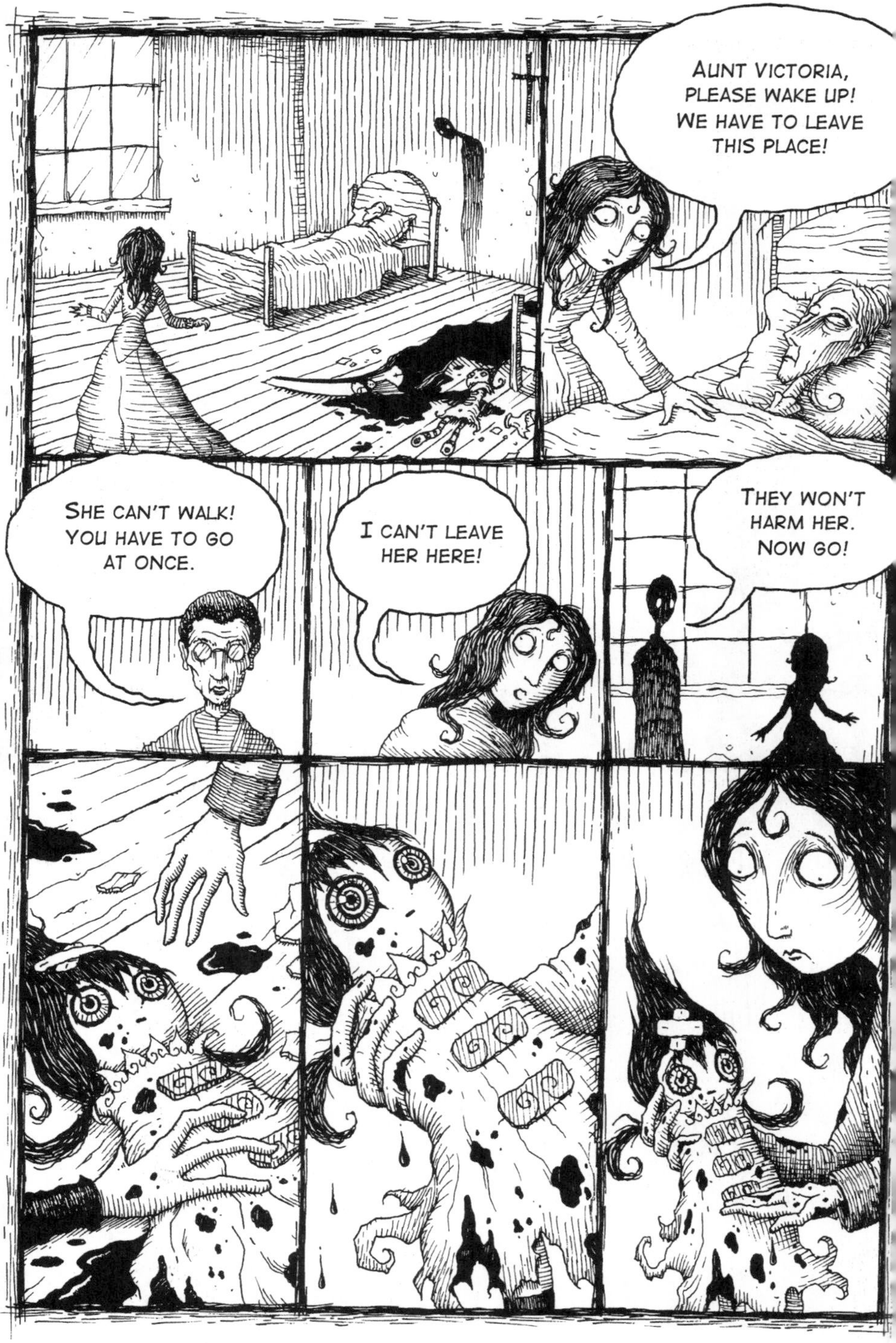

AUNT VICTORIA, PLEASE WAKE UP! WE HAVE TO LEAVE THIS PLACE!
SHE CAN'T WALK! YOU HAVE TO GO AT ONCE.
I CAN'T LEAVE HER HERE!
THEY WON'T HARM HER. NOW GO!

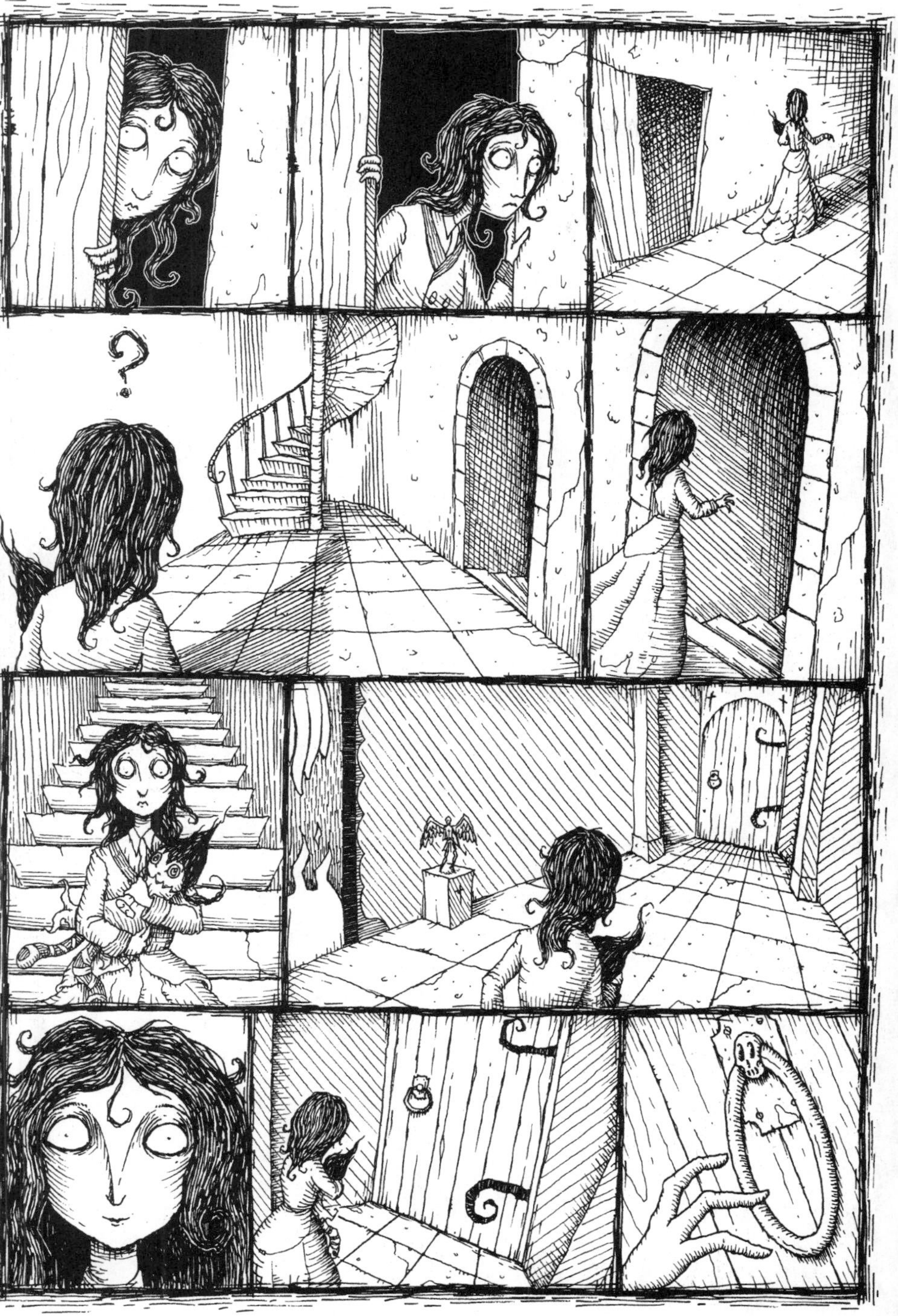
?

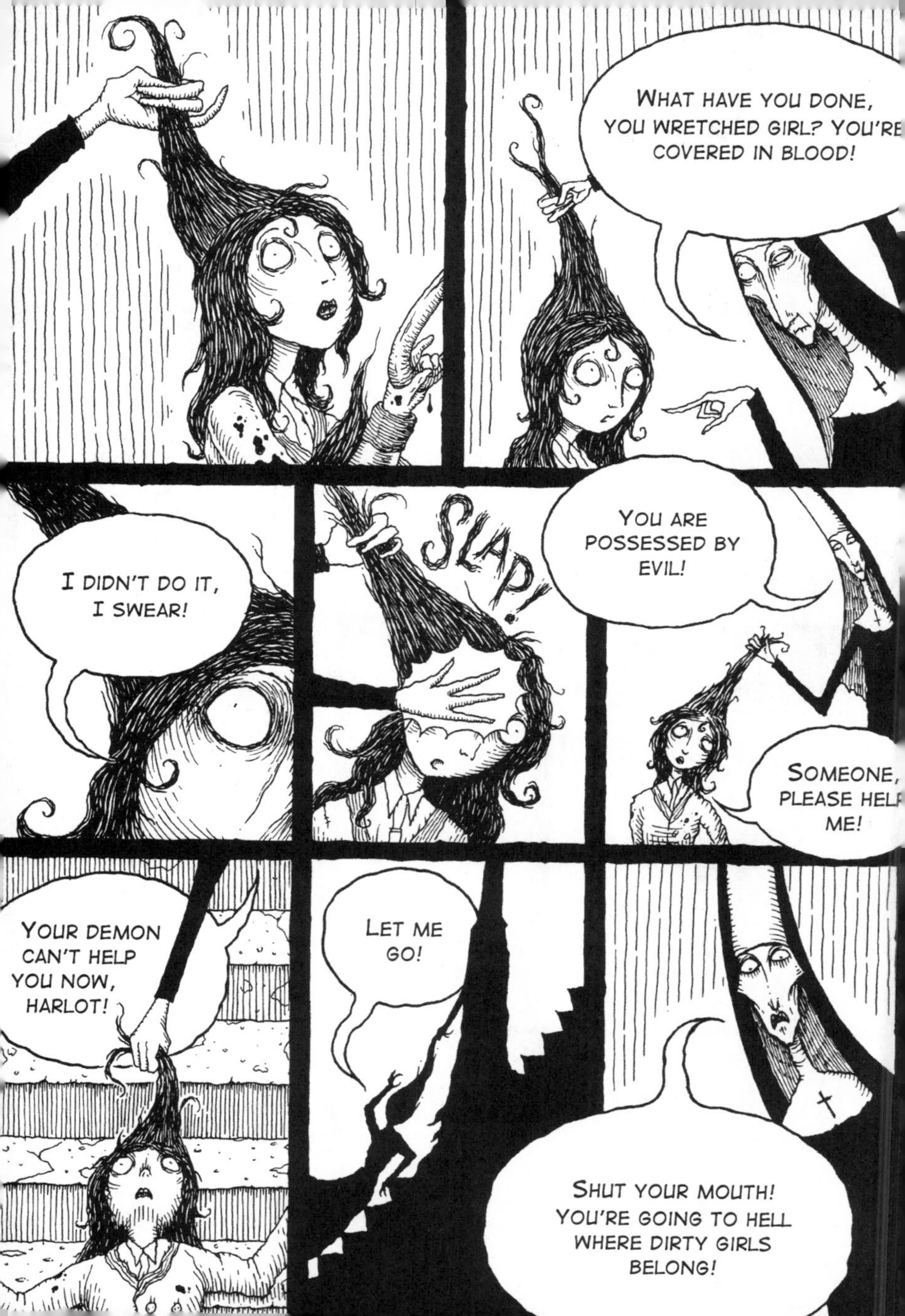

WHAT HAVE YOU DONE, YOU WRETCHED GIRL? YOU'RE COVERED IN BLOOD!
I DIDN'T DO IT, I SWEAR!
SLAP!
YOU ARE POSSESSED BY EVIL!
SOMEONE, PLEASE HELP ME!
YOUR DEMON CAN'T HELP YOU NOW, HARLOT!
LET ME GO!
SHUT YOUR MOUTH! YOU'RE GOING TO HELL WHERE DIRTY GIRLS BELONG!

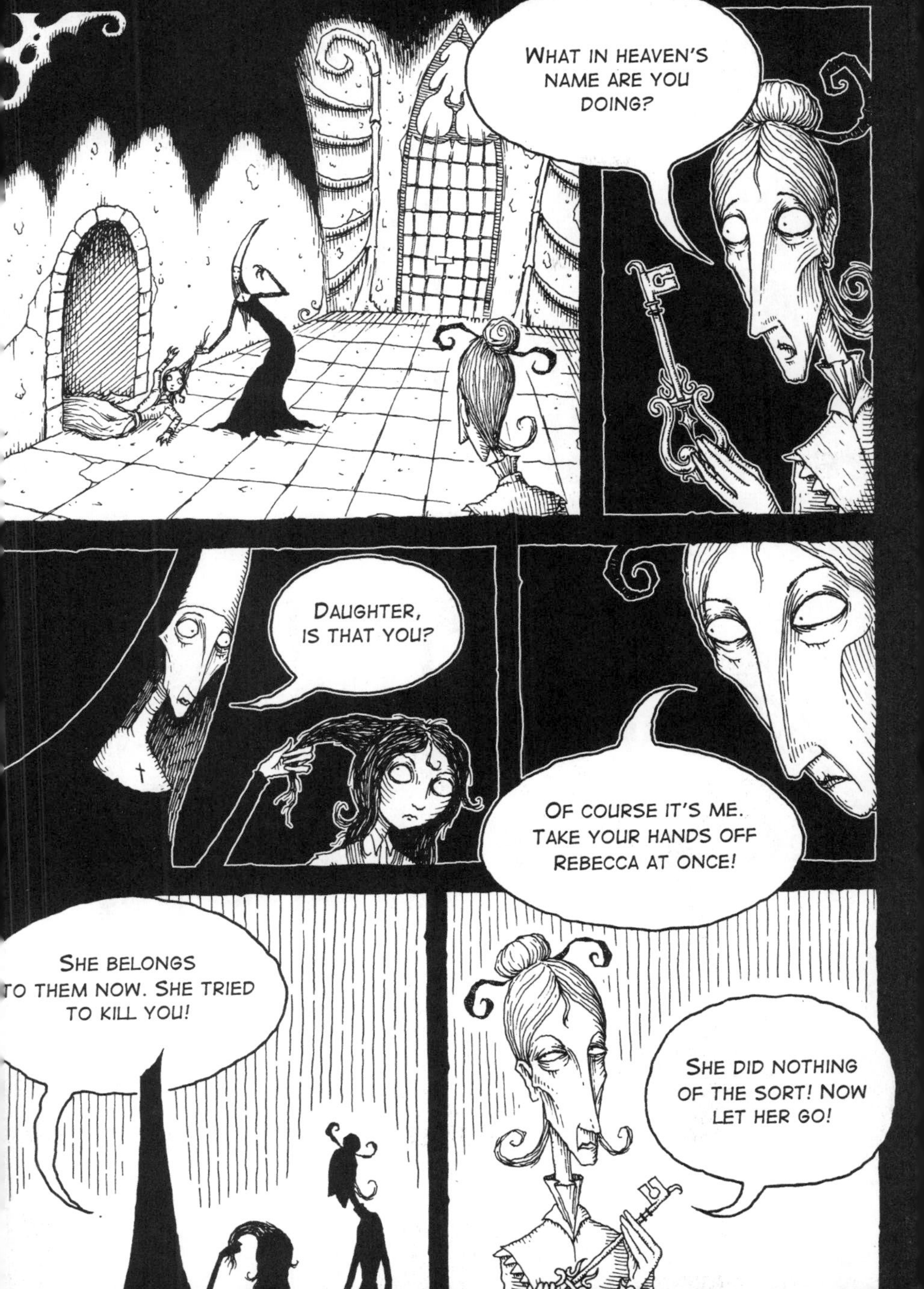
WHAT IN HEAVEN'S NAME ARE YOU DOING?
DAUGHTER, IS THAT YOU?
OF COURSE IT'S ME. TAKE YOUR HANDS OFF REBECCA AT ONCE!
SHE BELONGS TO THEM NOW. SHE TRIED TO KILL YOU!
SHE DID NOTHING OF THE SORT! NOW LET HER GO!

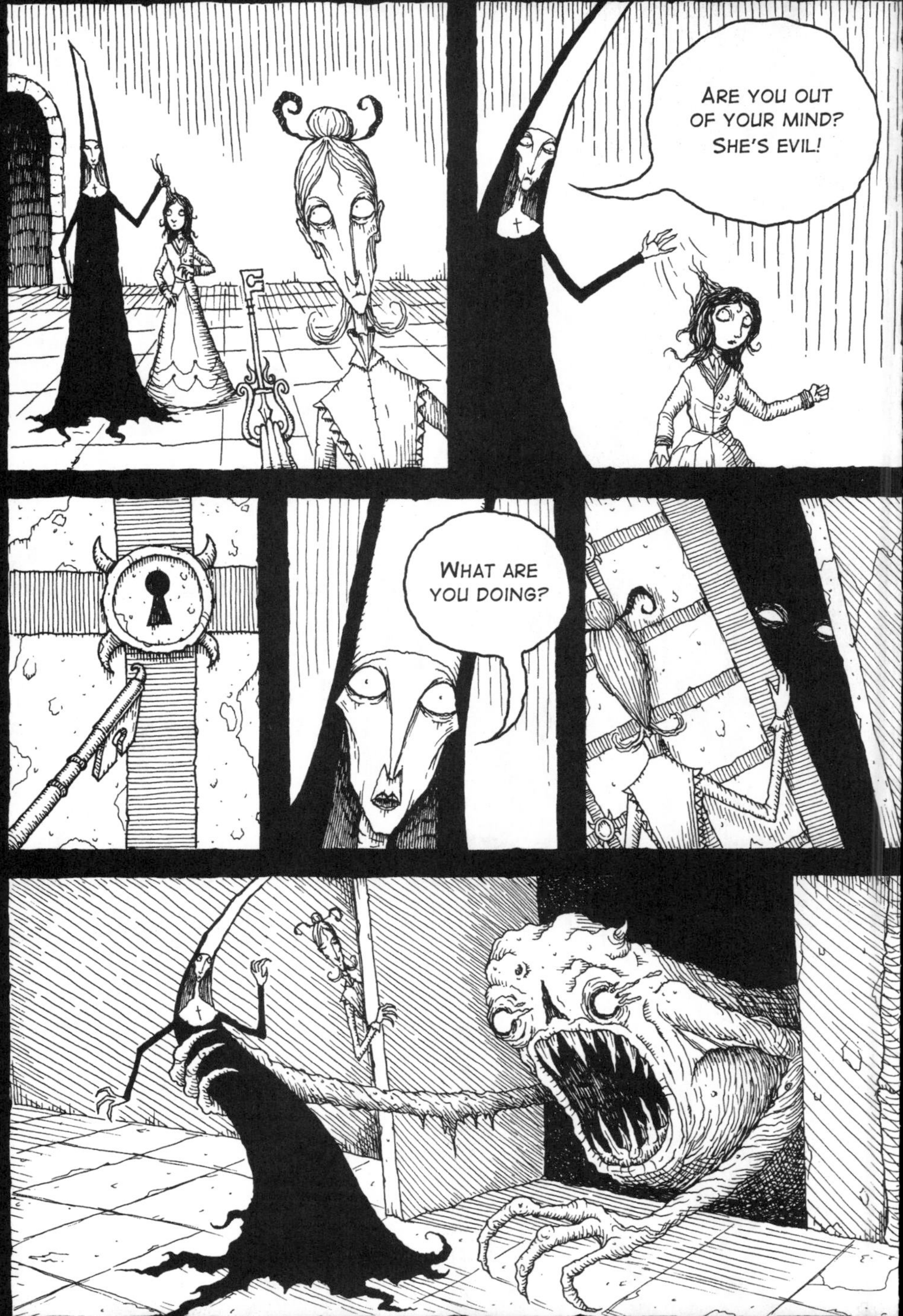
ARE YOU OUT OF YOUR MIND? SHE'S EVIL!
WHAT ARE YOU DOING?

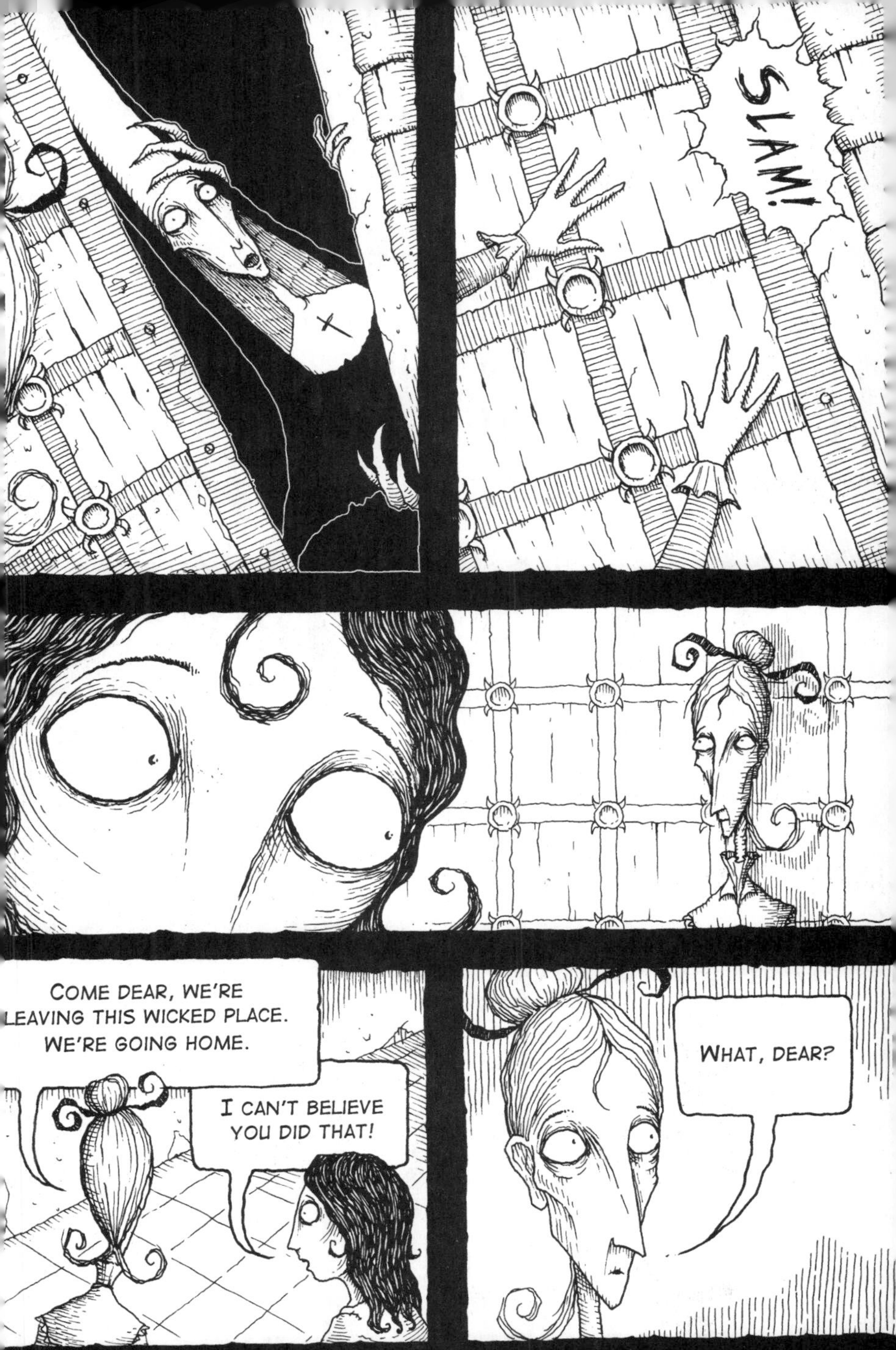
SLAM!
COME DEAR, WE'RE LEAVING THIS WICKED PLACE. WE'RE GOING HOME.
I CAN'T BELIEVE YOU DID THAT!
WHAT, DEAR?

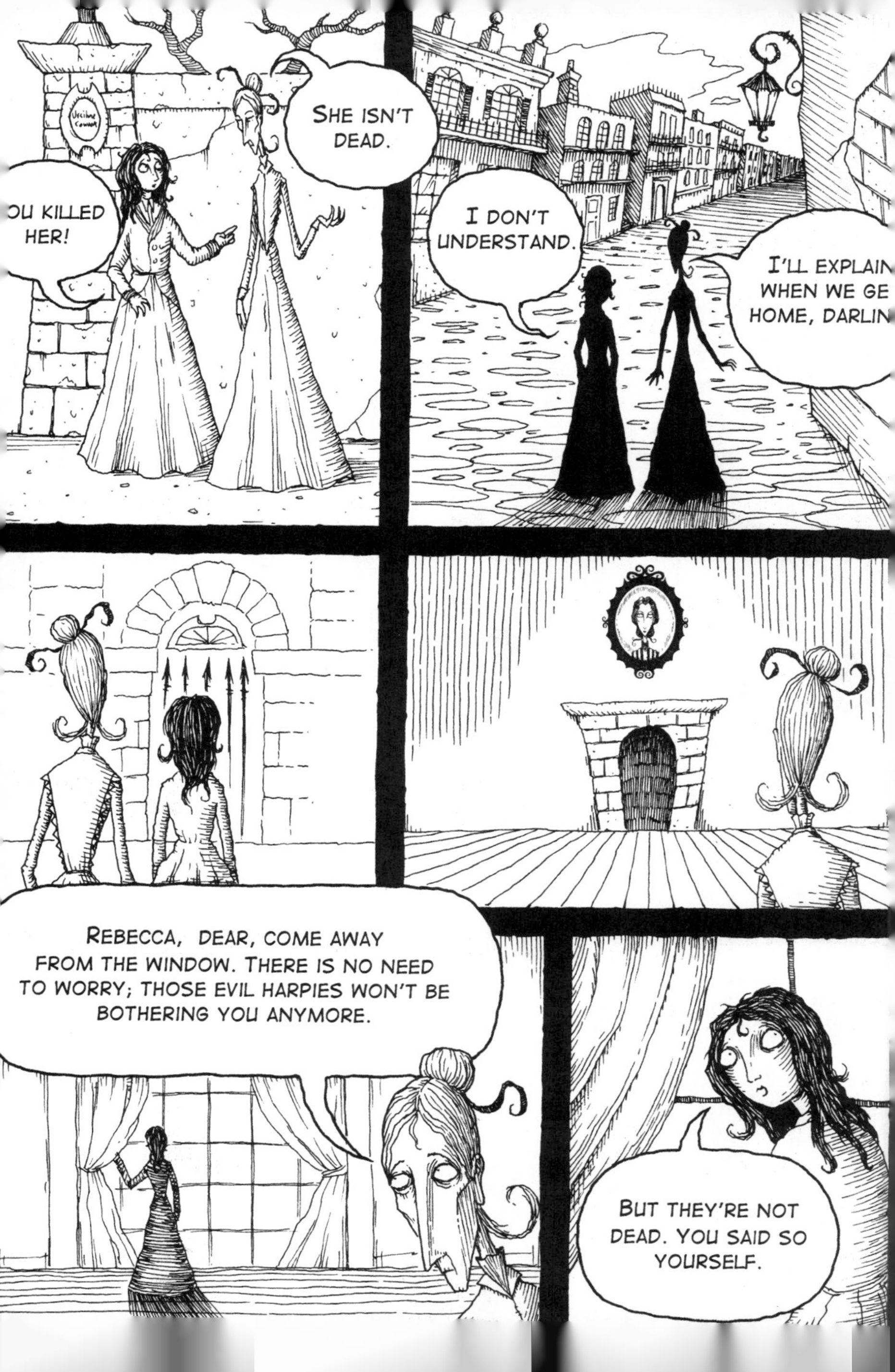
SHE ISN'T DEAD.
OU KILLED HER!
I DON'T UNDERSTAND.
I'LL EXPLAIN WHEN WE GE HOME, DARLIN
REBECCA, DEAR, COME AWAY FROM THE WINDOW. THERE IS NO NEED TO WORRY; THOSE EVIL HARPIES WON'T BE BOTHERING YOU ANYMORE.
BUT THEY'RE NOT DEAD. YOU SAID SO YOURSELF.

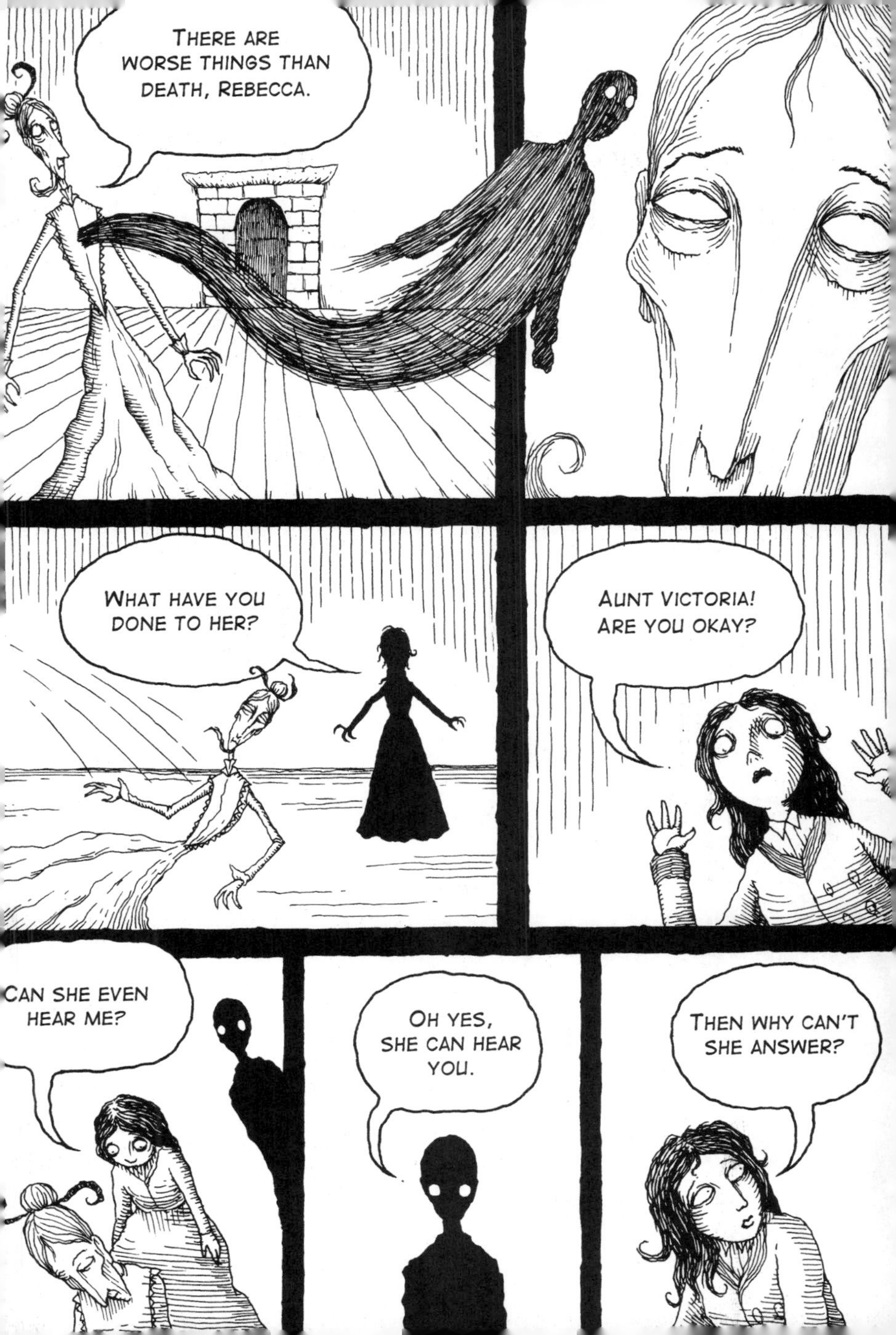
THERE ARE WORSE THINGS THAN DEATH, REBECCA.
WHAT HAVE YOU DONE TO HER?
AUNT VICTORIA! ARE YOU OKAY?
CAN SHE EVEN HEAR ME?
OH YES, SHE CAN HEAR YOU.
THEN WHY CAN'T SHE ANSWER?

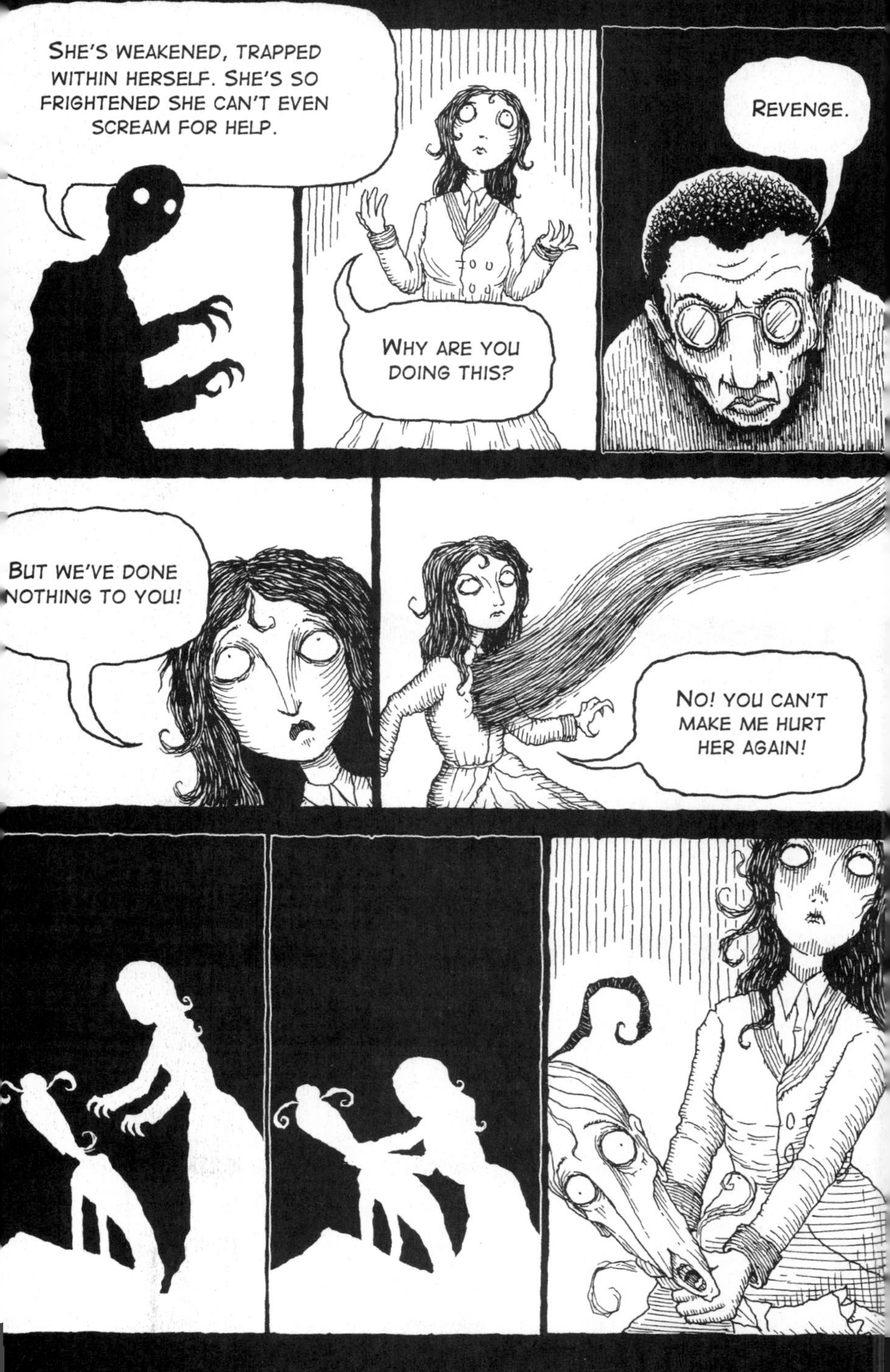
SHE'S WEAKENED, TRAPPED WITHIN HERSELF. SHE'S SO FRIGHTENED SHE CAN'T EVEN SCREAM FOR HELP.
WHY ARE YOU DOING THIS?
REVENGE.
BUT WE'VE DONE NOTHING TO YOU!
NO! YOU CAN'T MAKE ME HURT HER AGAIN!

Chapter 5

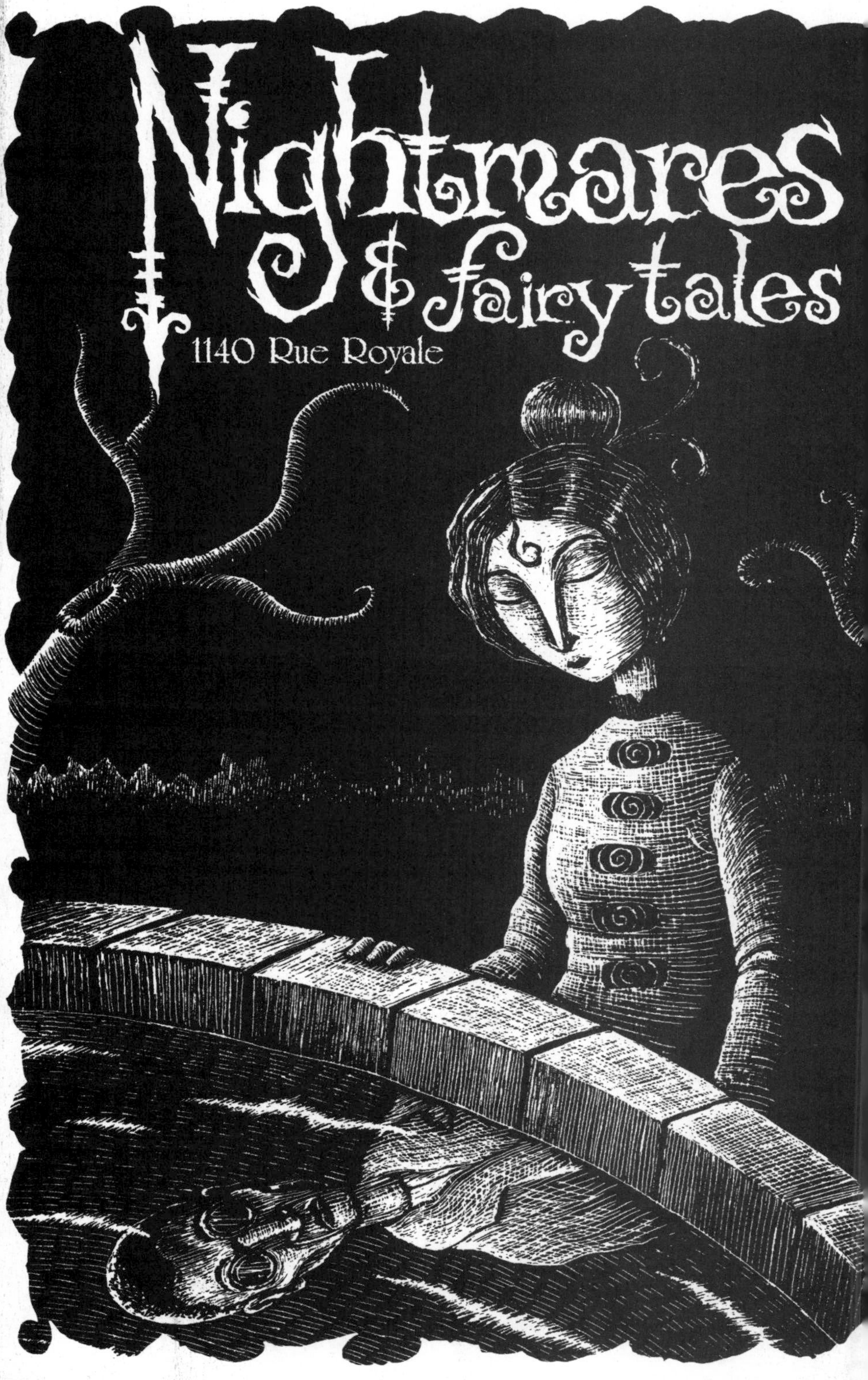
Nightmares & fairy tales
1140 Rue Royale

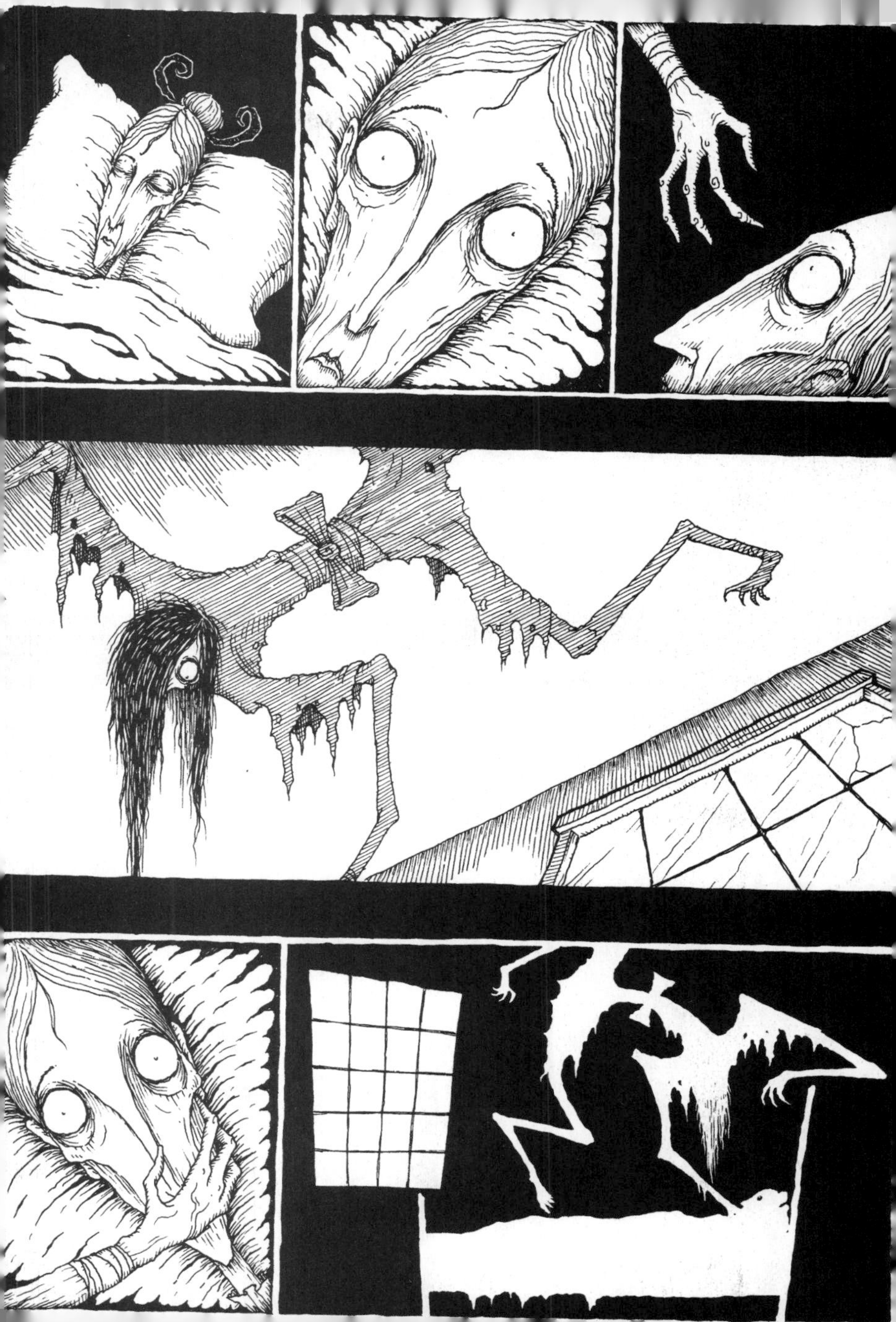

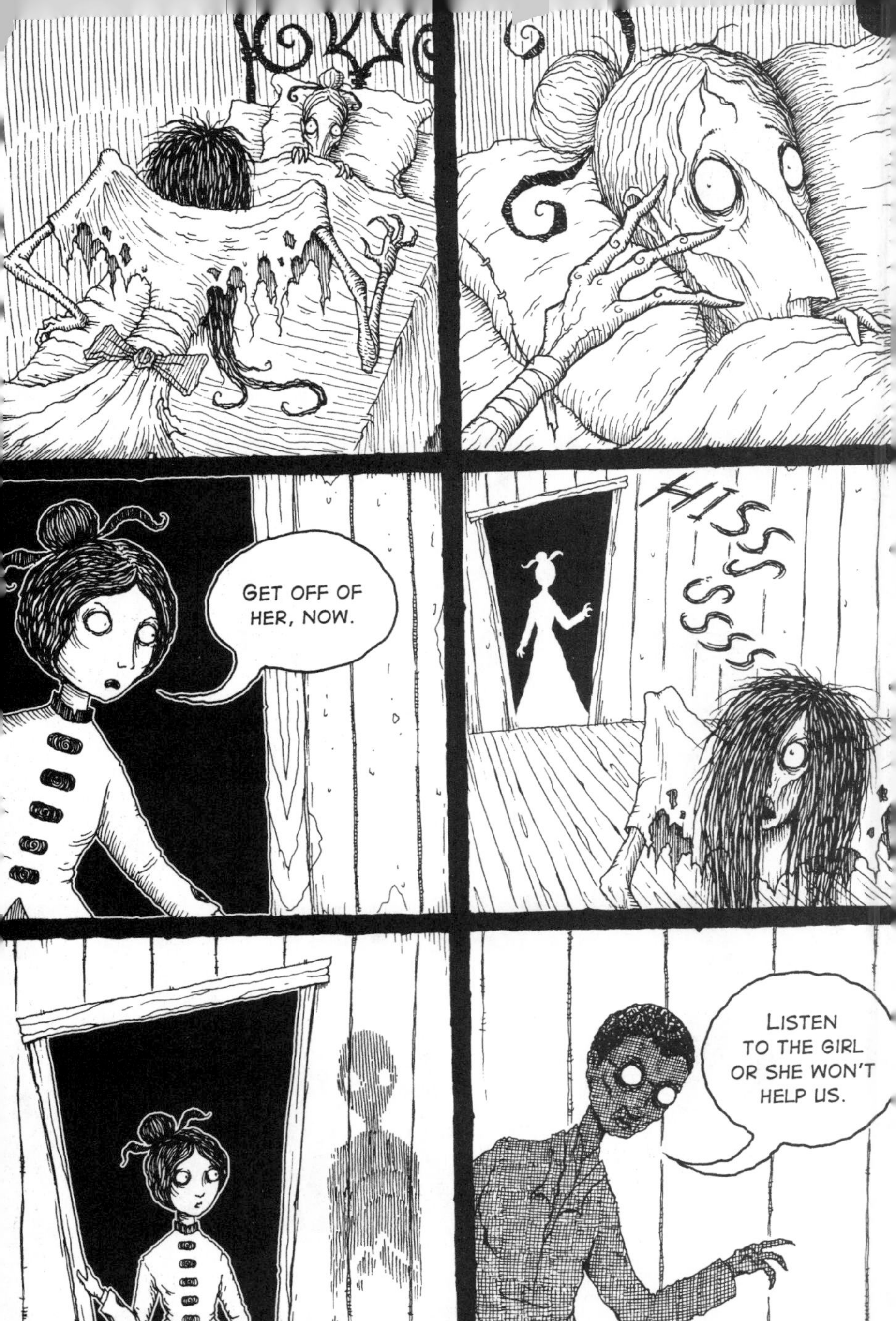
GET OFF OF HER, NOW.
HISSSSSSS
LISTEN TO THE GIRL OR SHE WON'T HELP US.

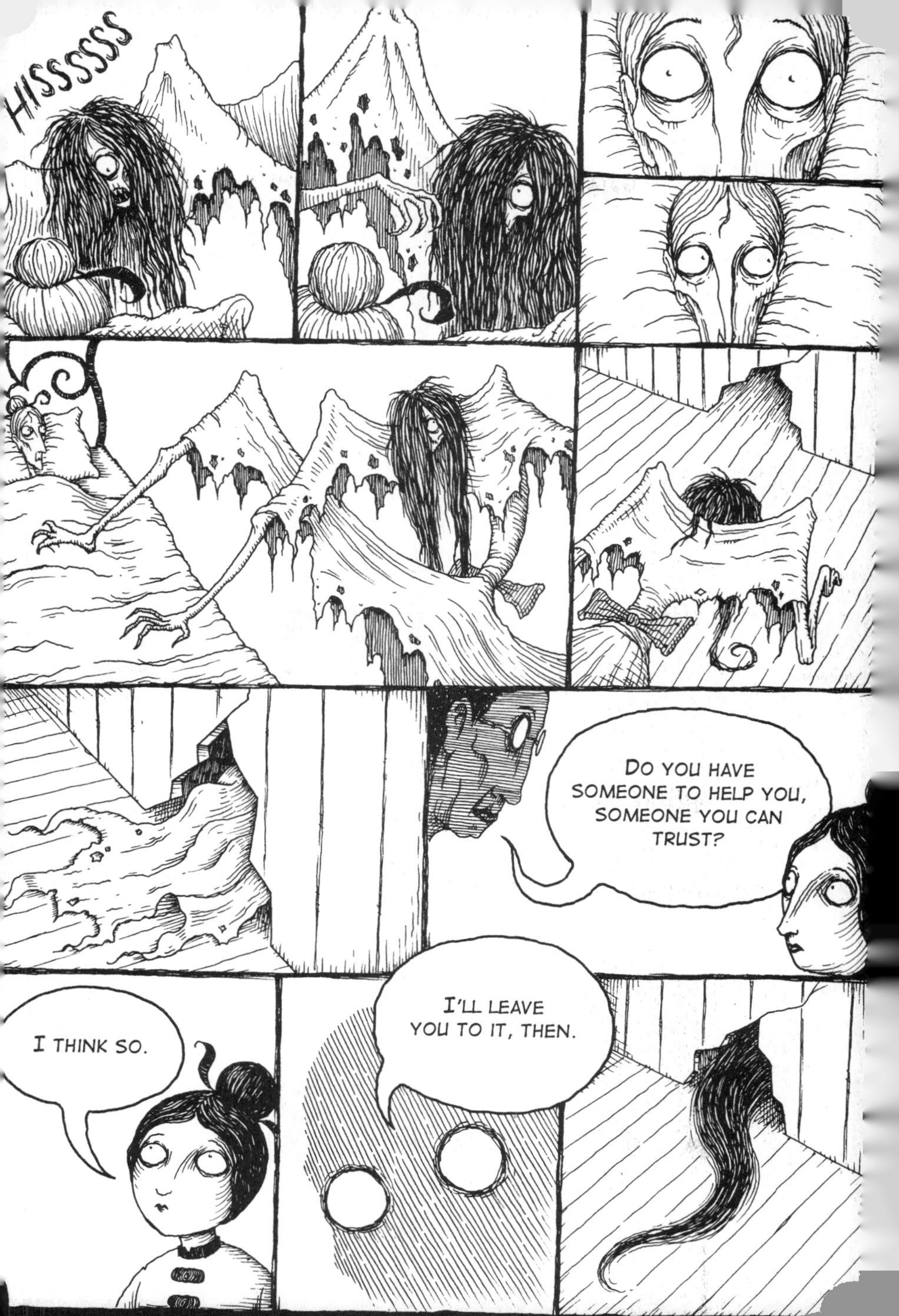
HISSSSSS
DO YOU HAVE SOMEONE TO HELP YOU, SOMEONE YOU CAN TRUST?
I THINK SO.
I'LL LEAVE YOU TO IT, THEN.

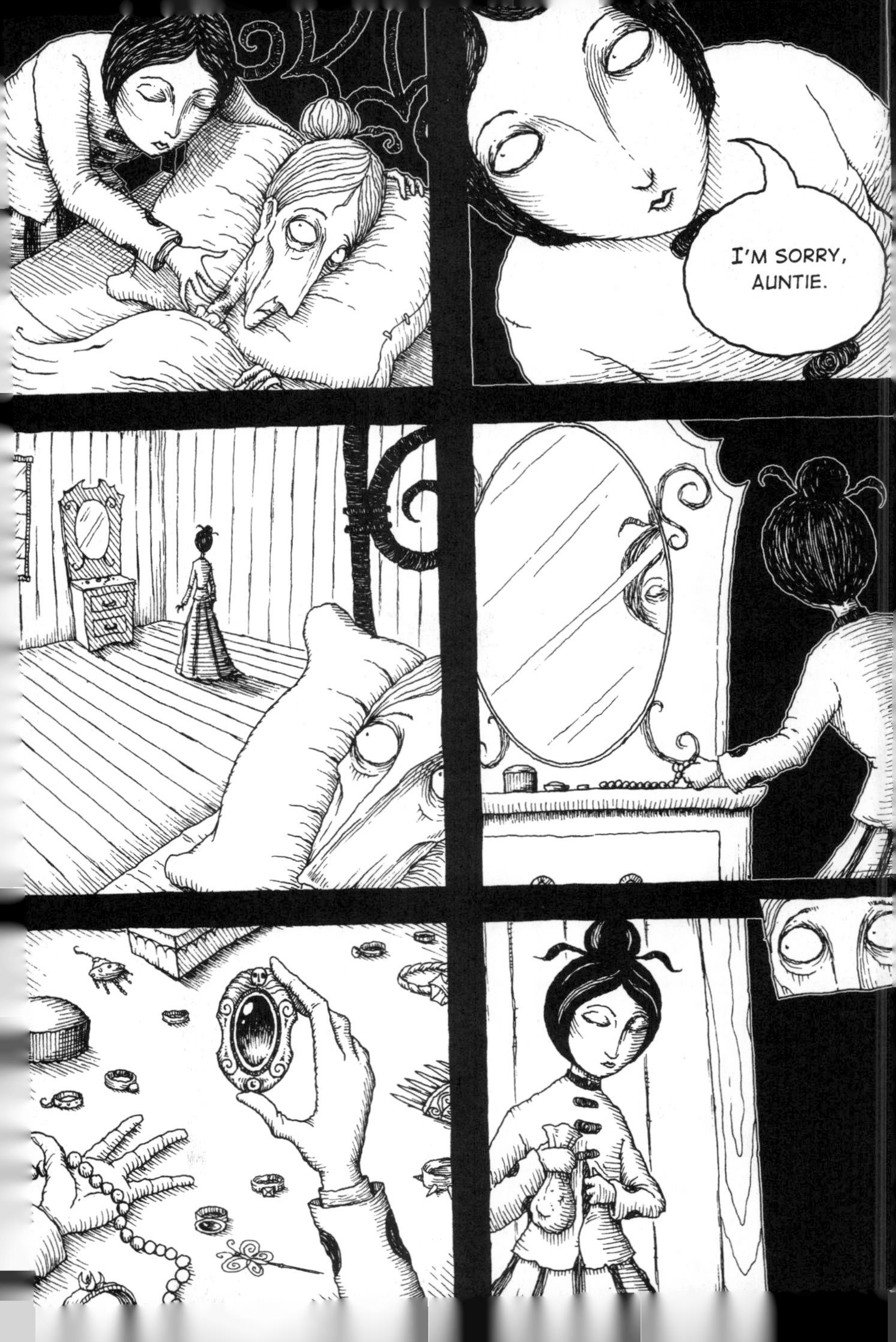
I'M SORRY, AUNTIE.

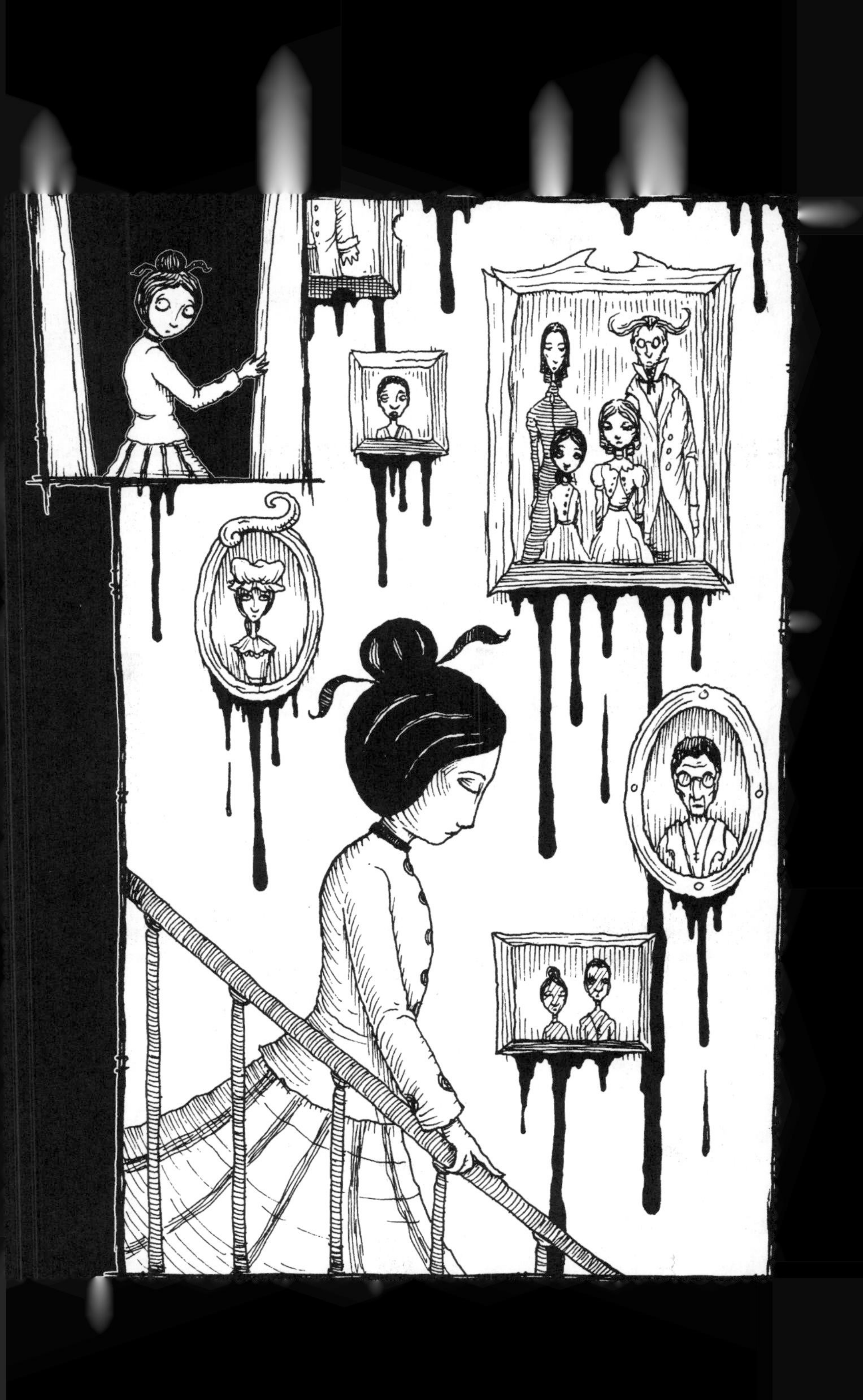

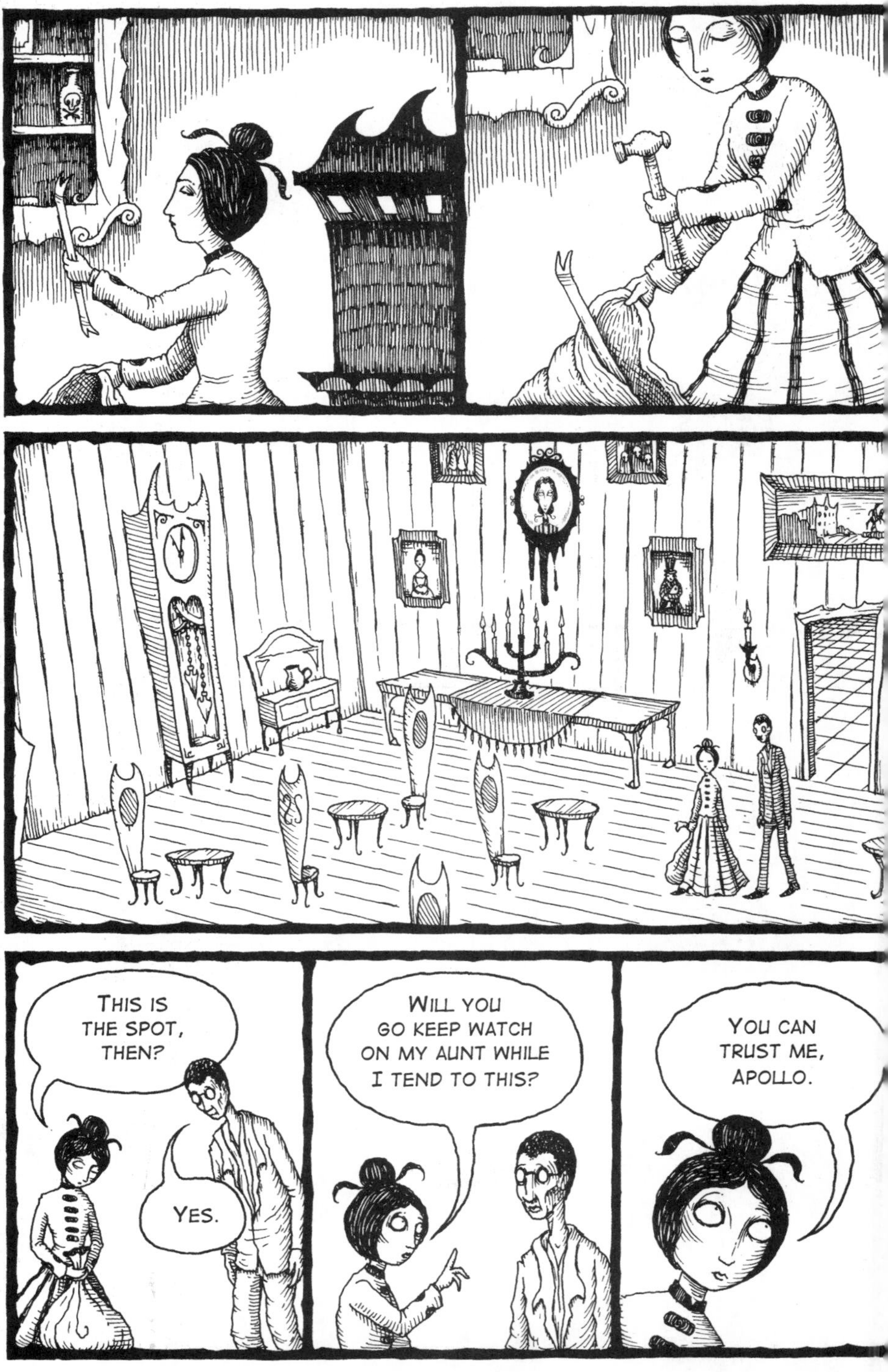
THIS IS
THE SPOT,
THEN?
YES.
WILL YOU
GO KEEP WATCH
ON MY AUNT WHILE
I TEND TO THIS?
YOU CAN
TRUST ME,
APOLLO.

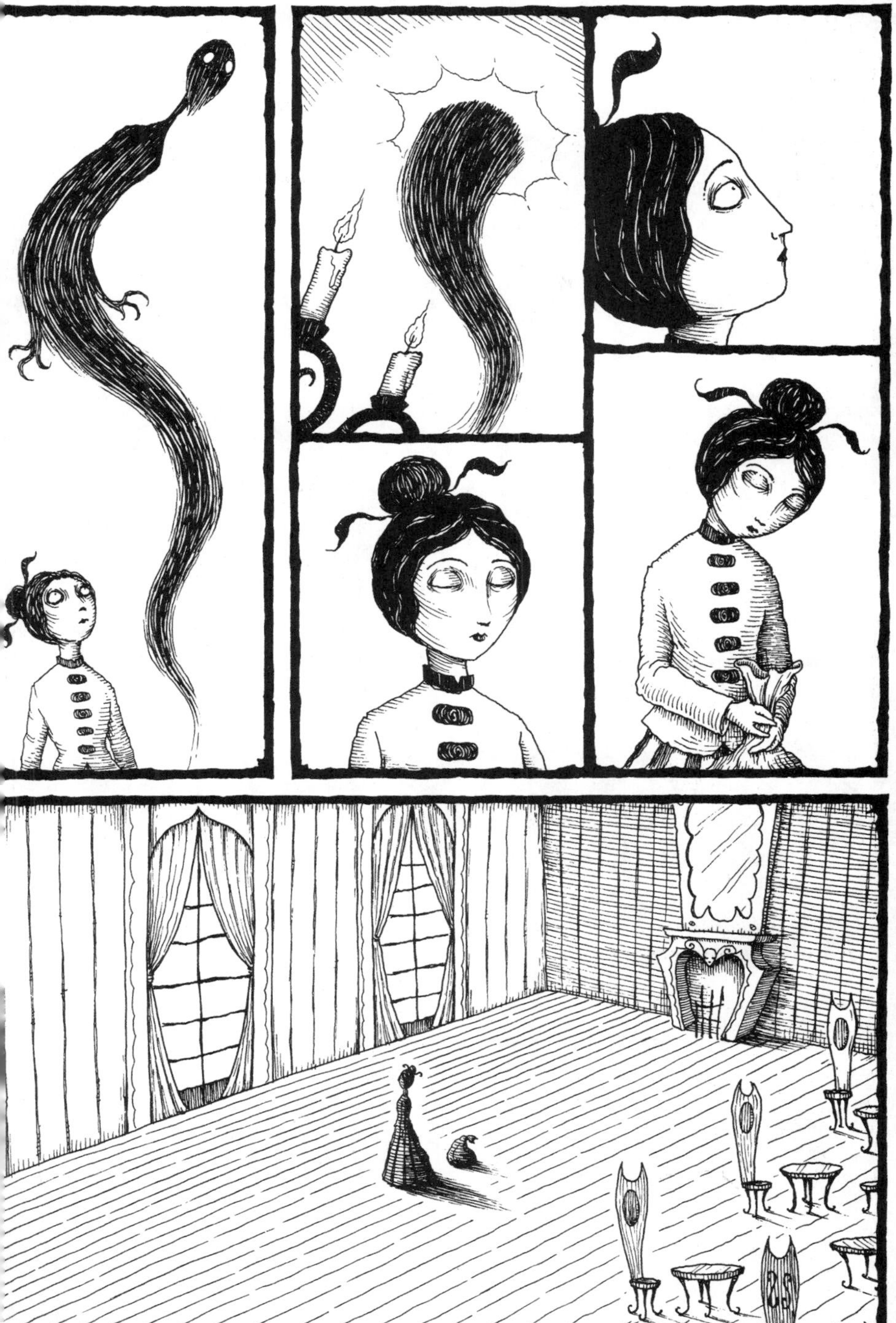

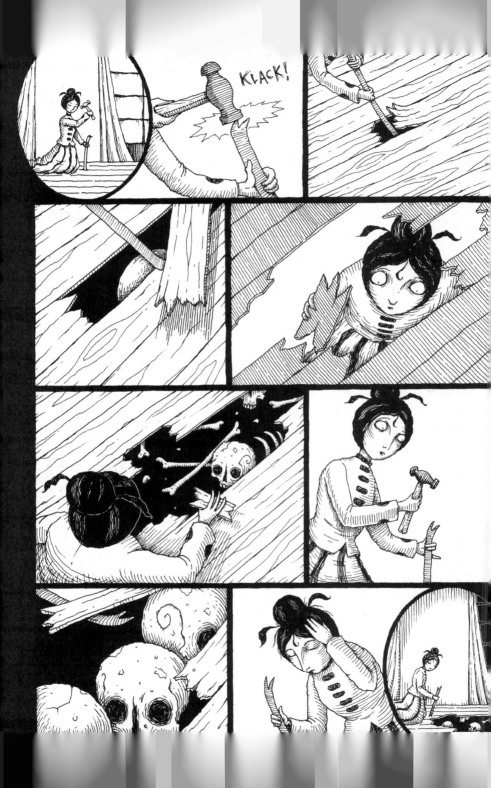

KLACK!

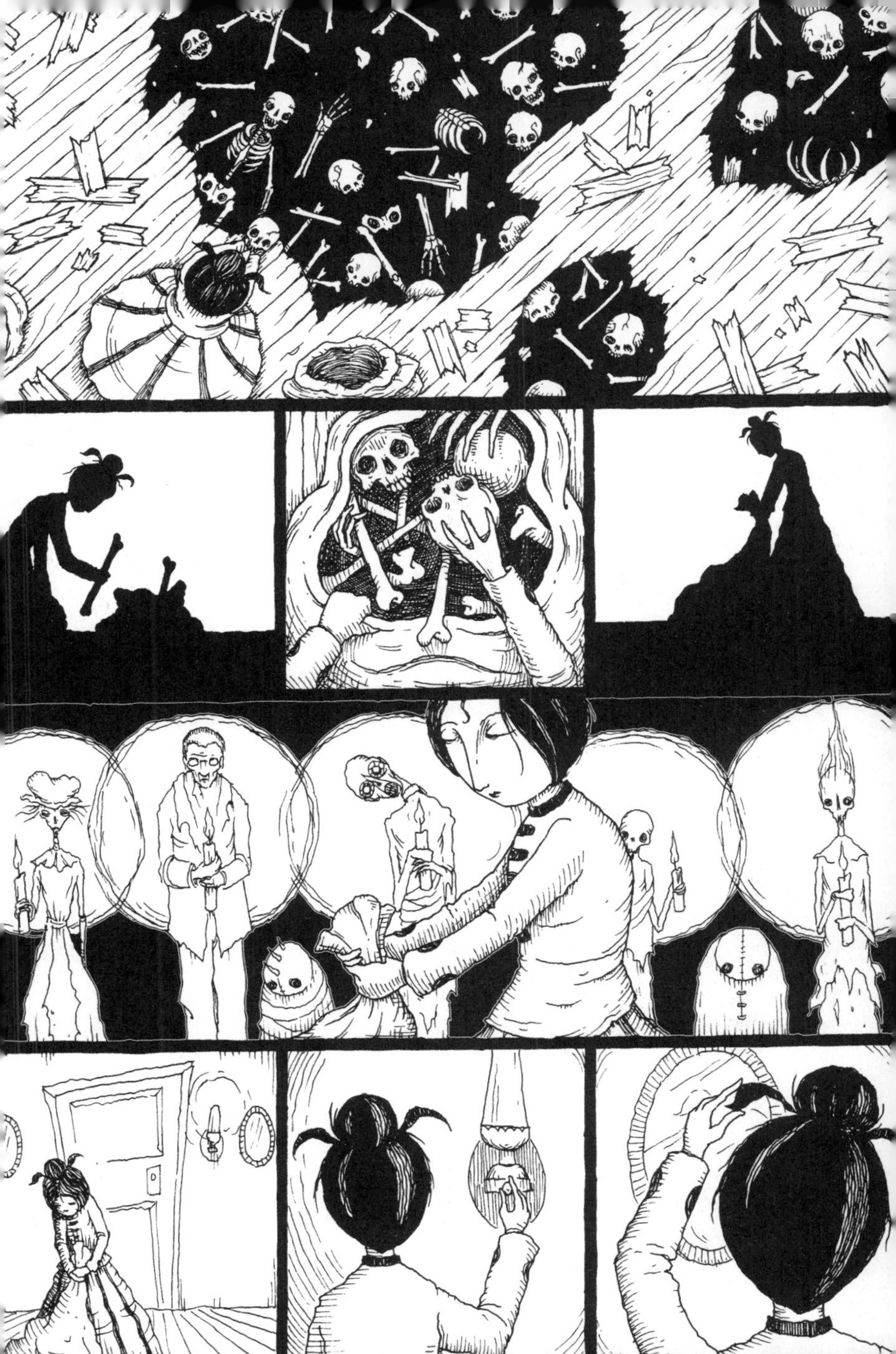

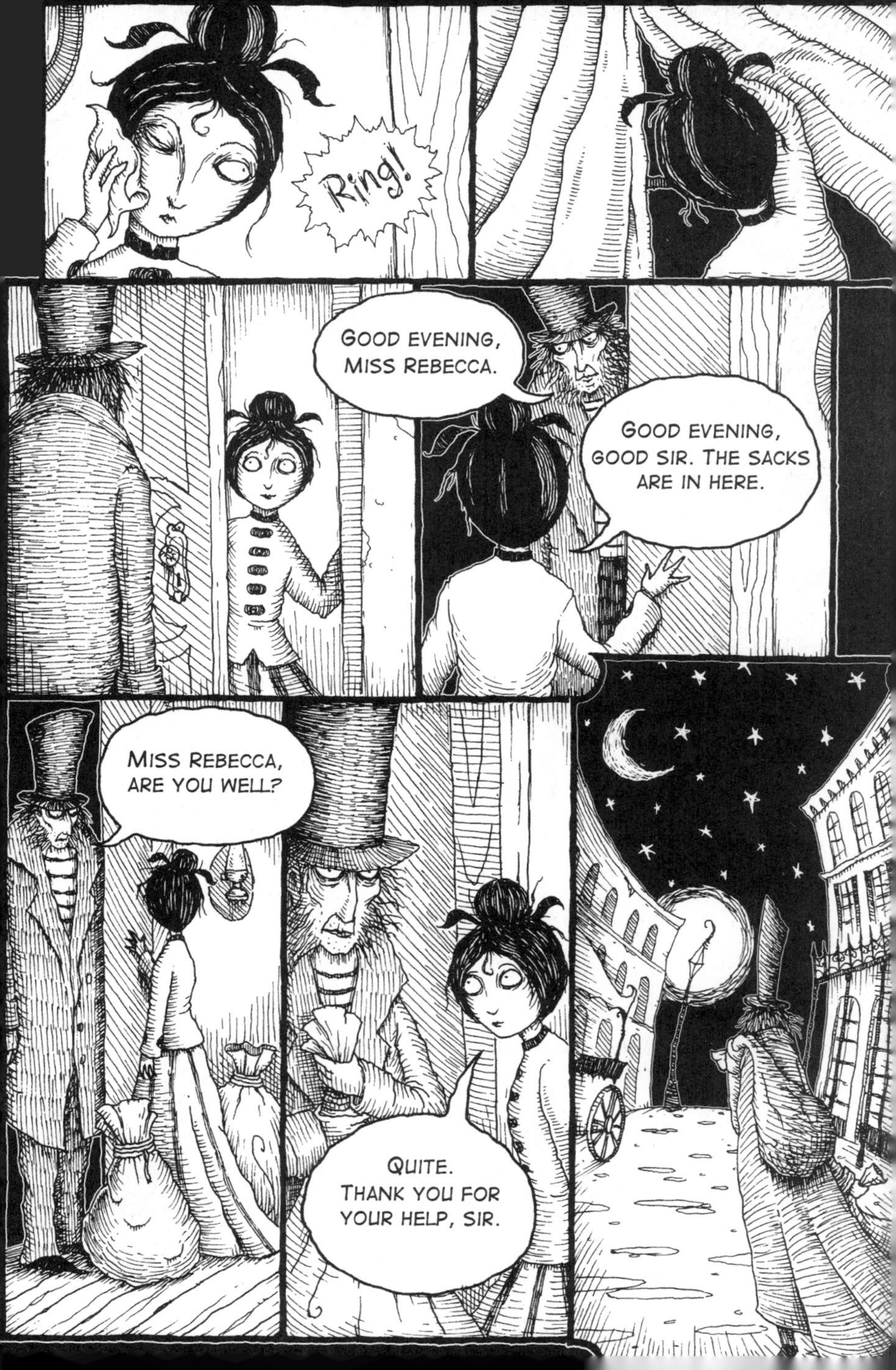
Ring!
Good evening, Miss Rebecca.
Good evening, good sir. The sacks are in here.
Miss Rebecca, are you well?
Quite. Thank you for your help, sir.

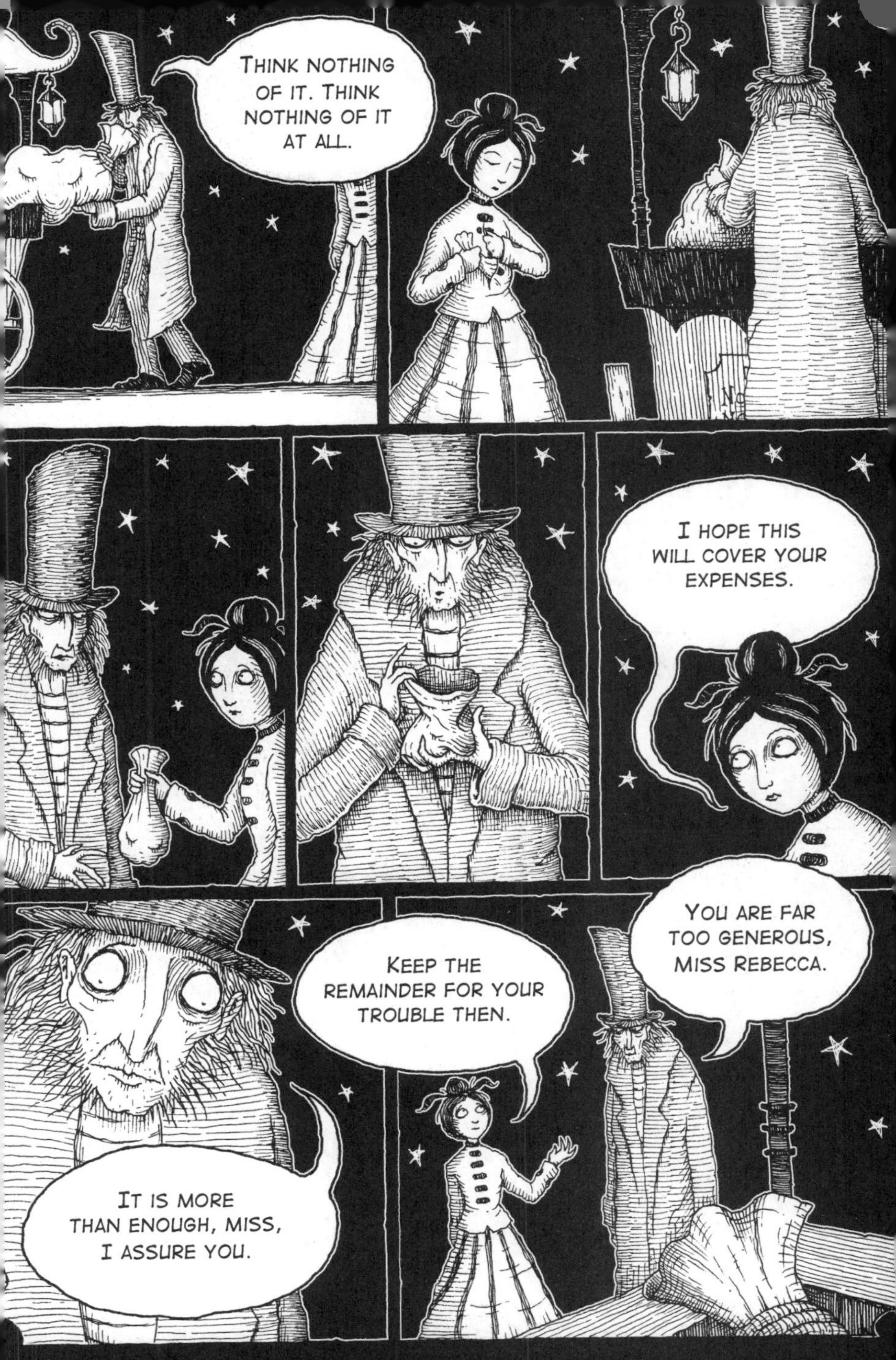
THINK NOTHING OF IT. THINK NOTHING OF IT AT ALL.
I HOPE THIS WILL COVER YOUR EXPENSES.
IT IS MORE THAN ENOUGH, MISS, I ASSURE YOU.
KEEP THE REMAINDER FOR YOUR TROUBLE THEN.
YOU ARE FAR TOO GENEROUS, MISS REBECCA.

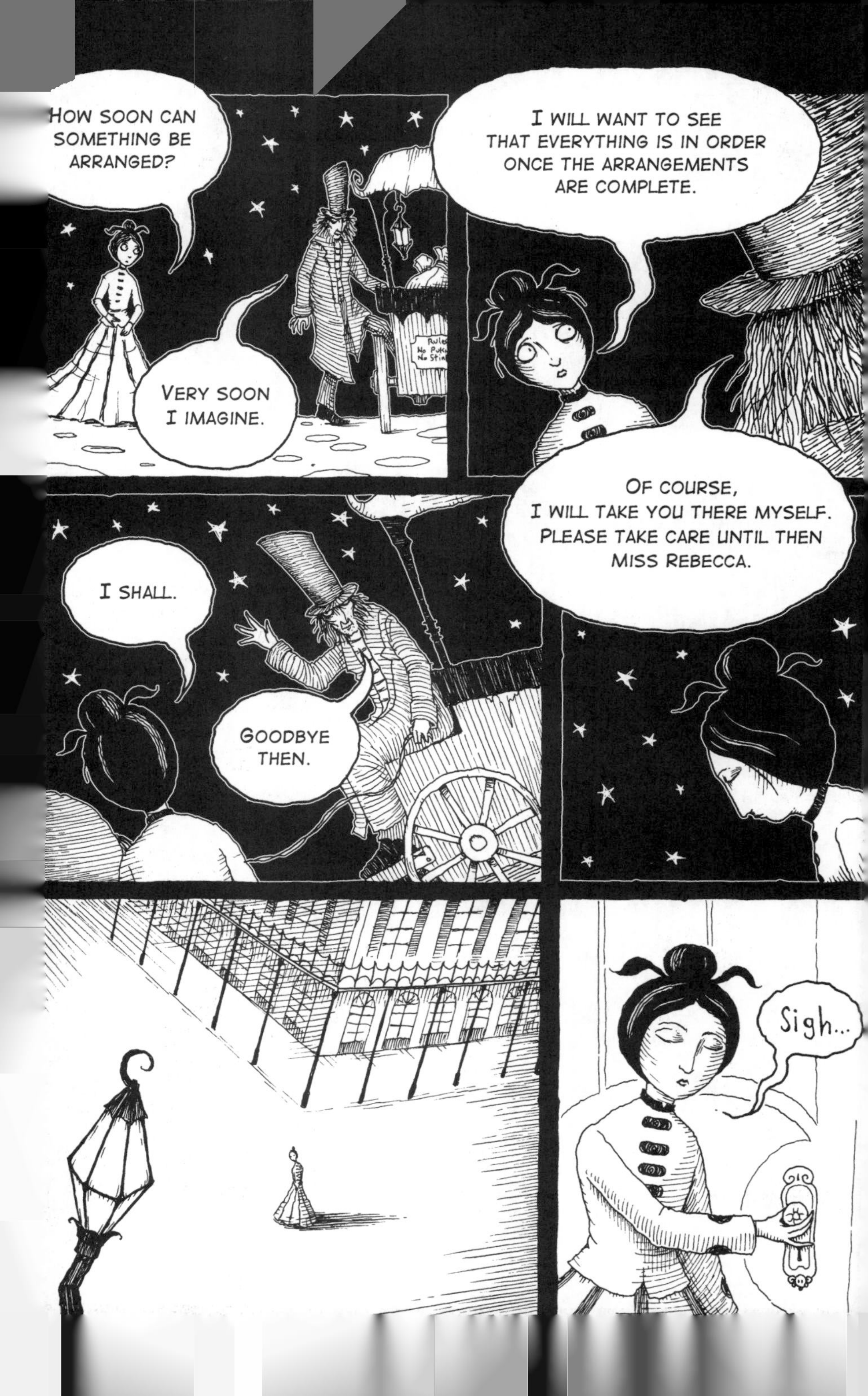
HOW SOON CAN SOMETHING BE ARRANGED?
VERY SOON I IMAGINE.
I WILL WANT TO SEE THAT EVERYTHING IS IN ORDER ONCE THE ARRANGEMENTS ARE COMPLETE.
OF COURSE, I WILL TAKE YOU THERE MYSELF. PLEASE TAKE CARE UNTIL THEN MISS REBECCA.
I SHALL.
GOODBYE THEN.
Sigh...

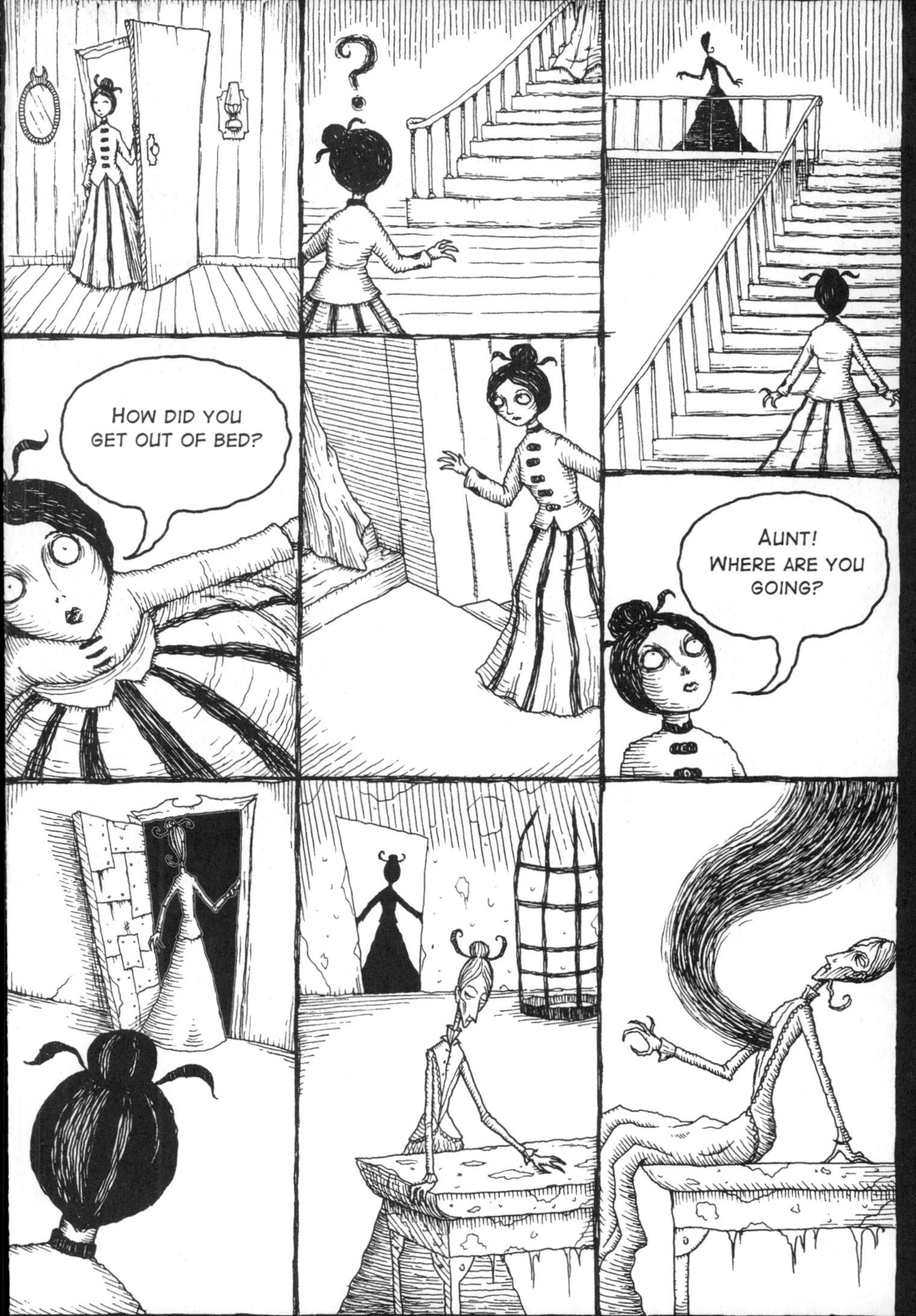
How did you get out of bed?
Aunt! Where are you going?

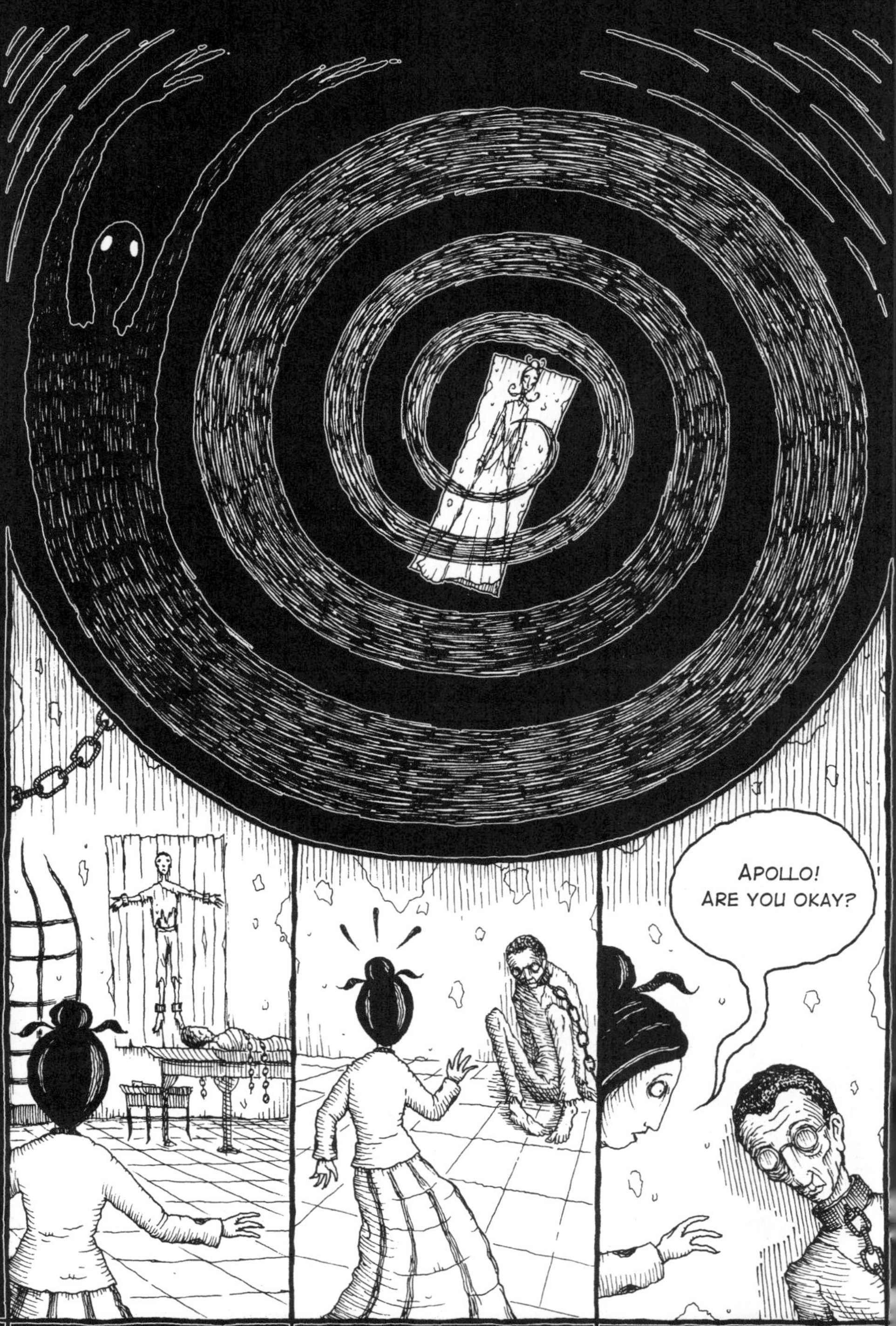
APOLLO!
ARE YOU OKAY?

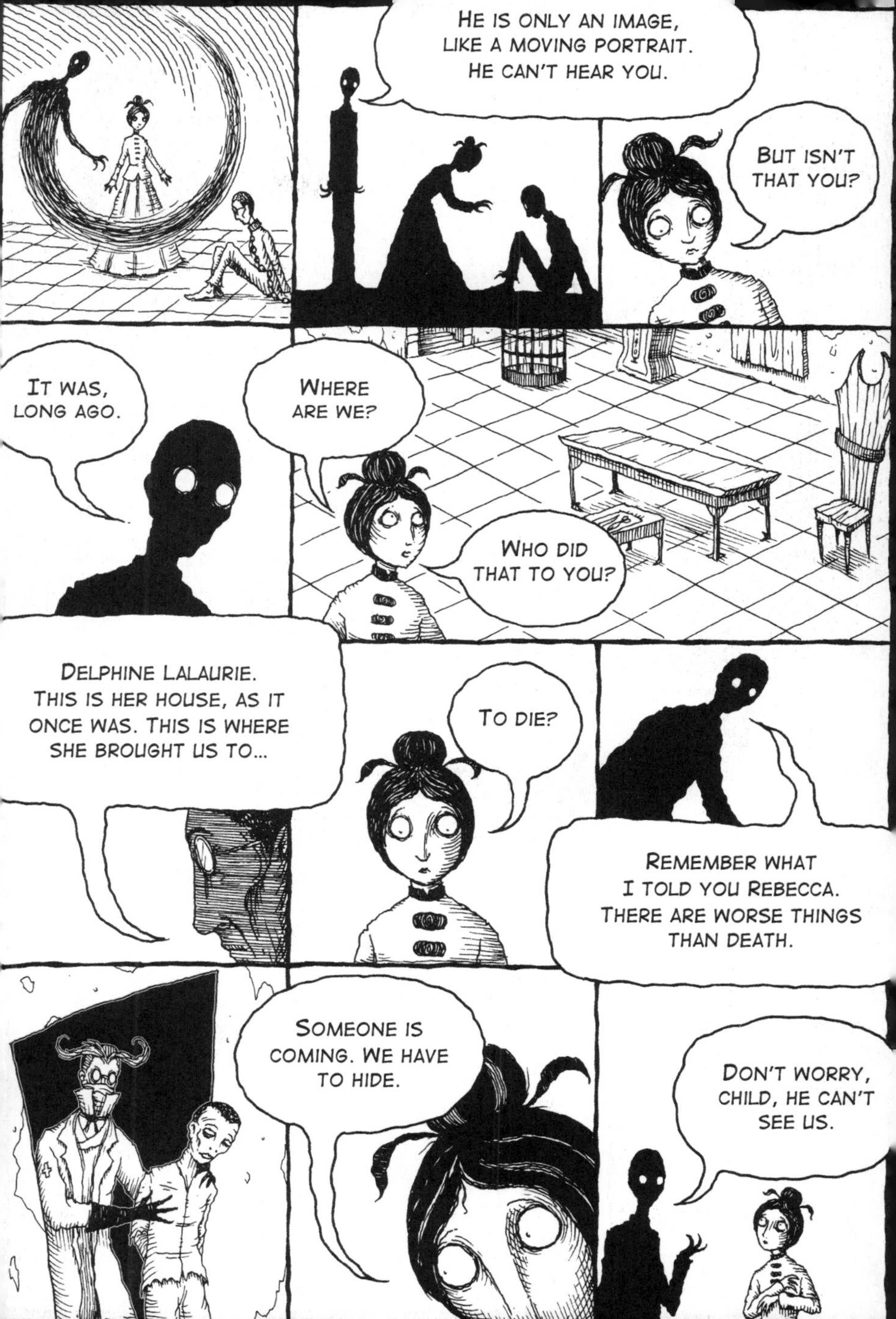
HE IS ONLY AN IMAGE, LIKE A MOVING PORTRAIT. HE CAN'T HEAR YOU.
BUT ISN'T THAT YOU?
IT WAS, LONG AGO.
WHERE ARE WE?
WHO DID THAT TO YOU?
DELPHINE LALAURIE. THIS IS HER HOUSE, AS IT ONCE WAS. THIS IS WHERE SHE BROUGHT US TO...
TO DIE?
REMEMBER WHAT I TOLD YOU REBECCA. THERE ARE WORSE THINGS THAN DEATH.
SOMEONE IS COMING. WE HAVE TO HIDE.
DON'T WORRY, CHILD, HE CAN'T SEE US.

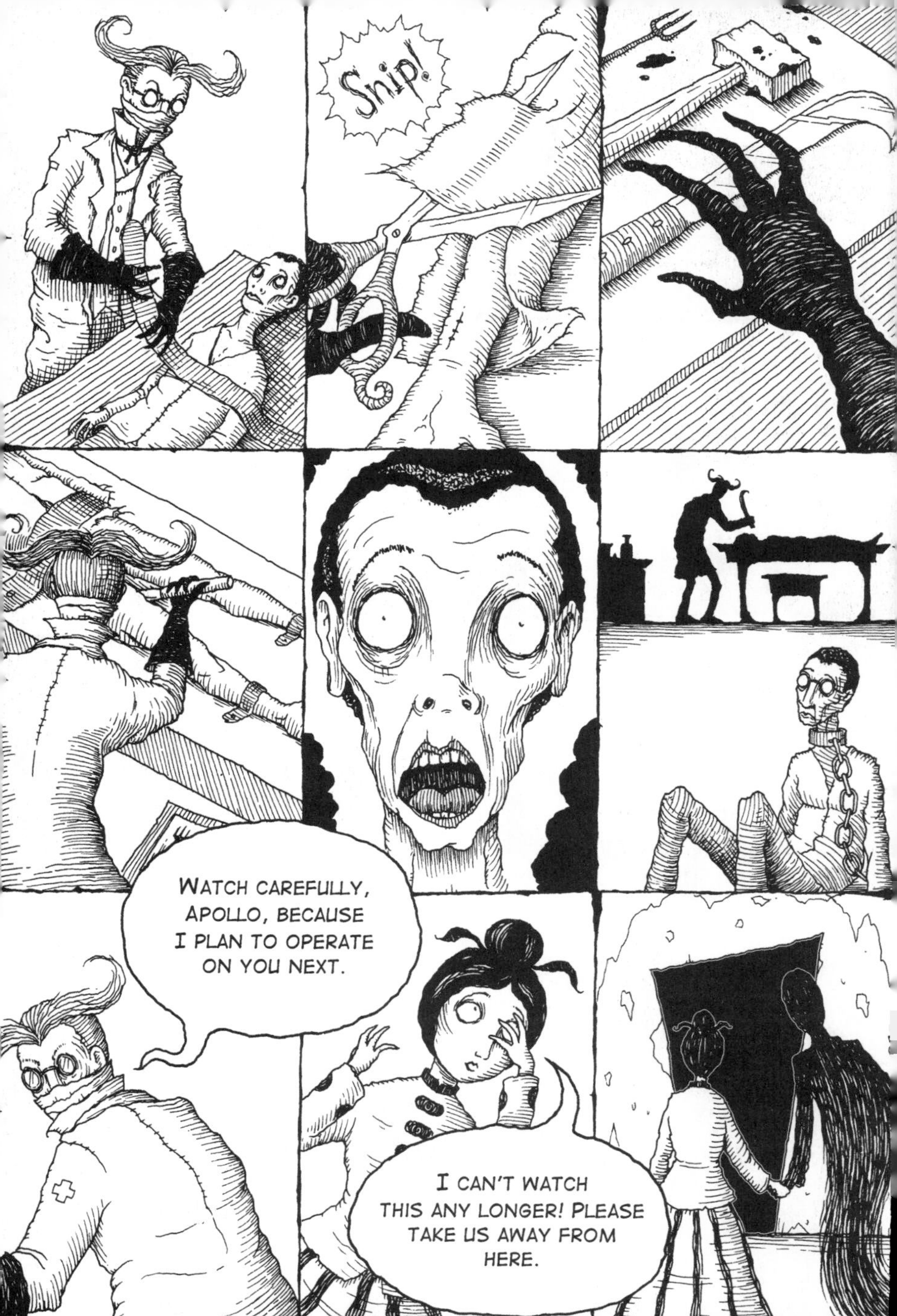
Snip!
WATCH CAREFULLY, APOLLO, BECAUSE I PLAN TO OPERATE ON YOU NEXT.
I CAN'T WATCH THIS ANY LONGER! PLEASE TAKE US AWAY FROM HERE.

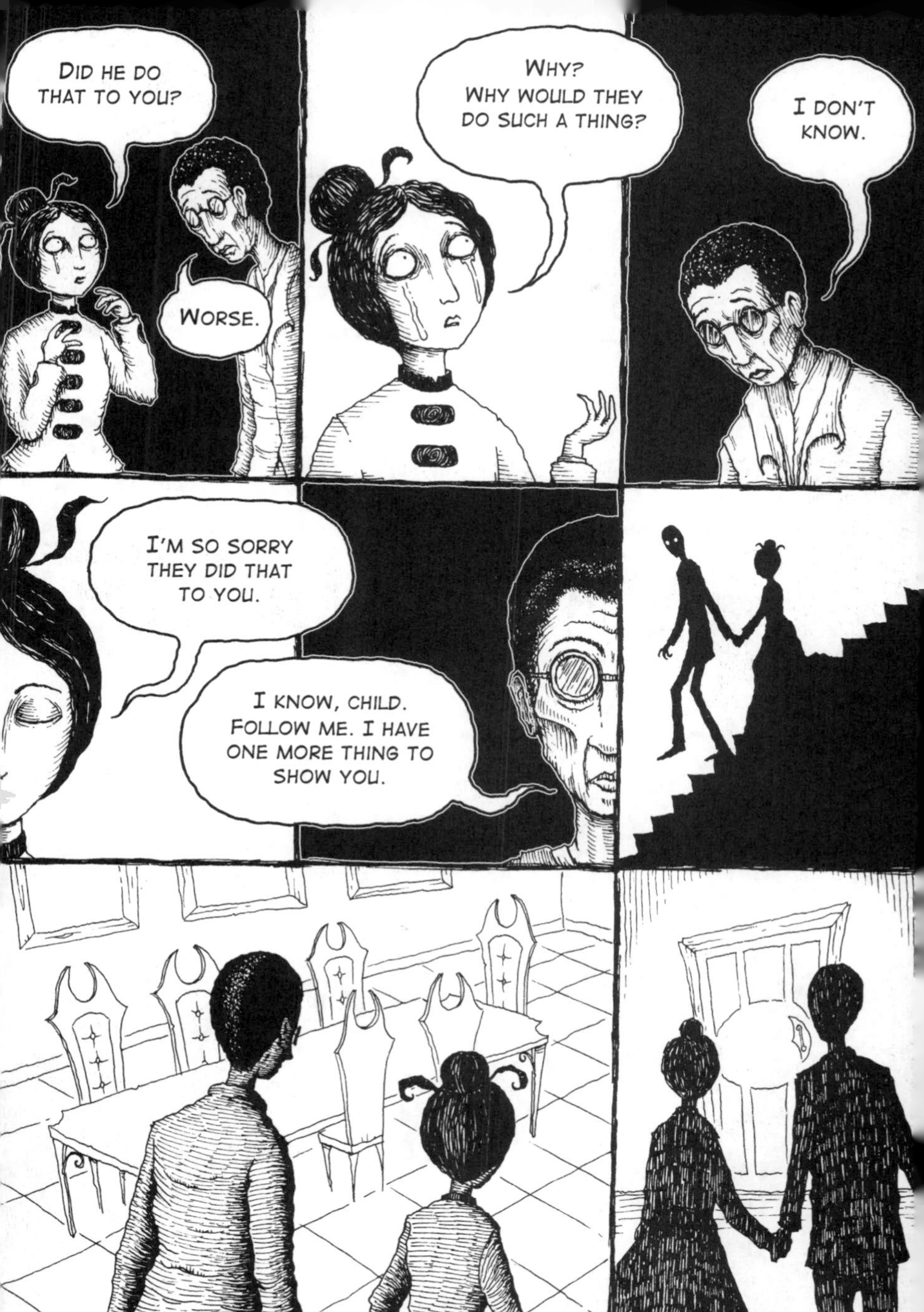
DID HE DO THAT TO YOU?
WORSE.
WHY? WHY WOULD THEY DO SUCH A THING?
I DON'T KNOW.
I'M SO SORRY THEY DID THAT TO YOU.
I KNOW, CHILD. FOLLOW ME. I HAVE ONE MORE THING TO SHOW YOU.

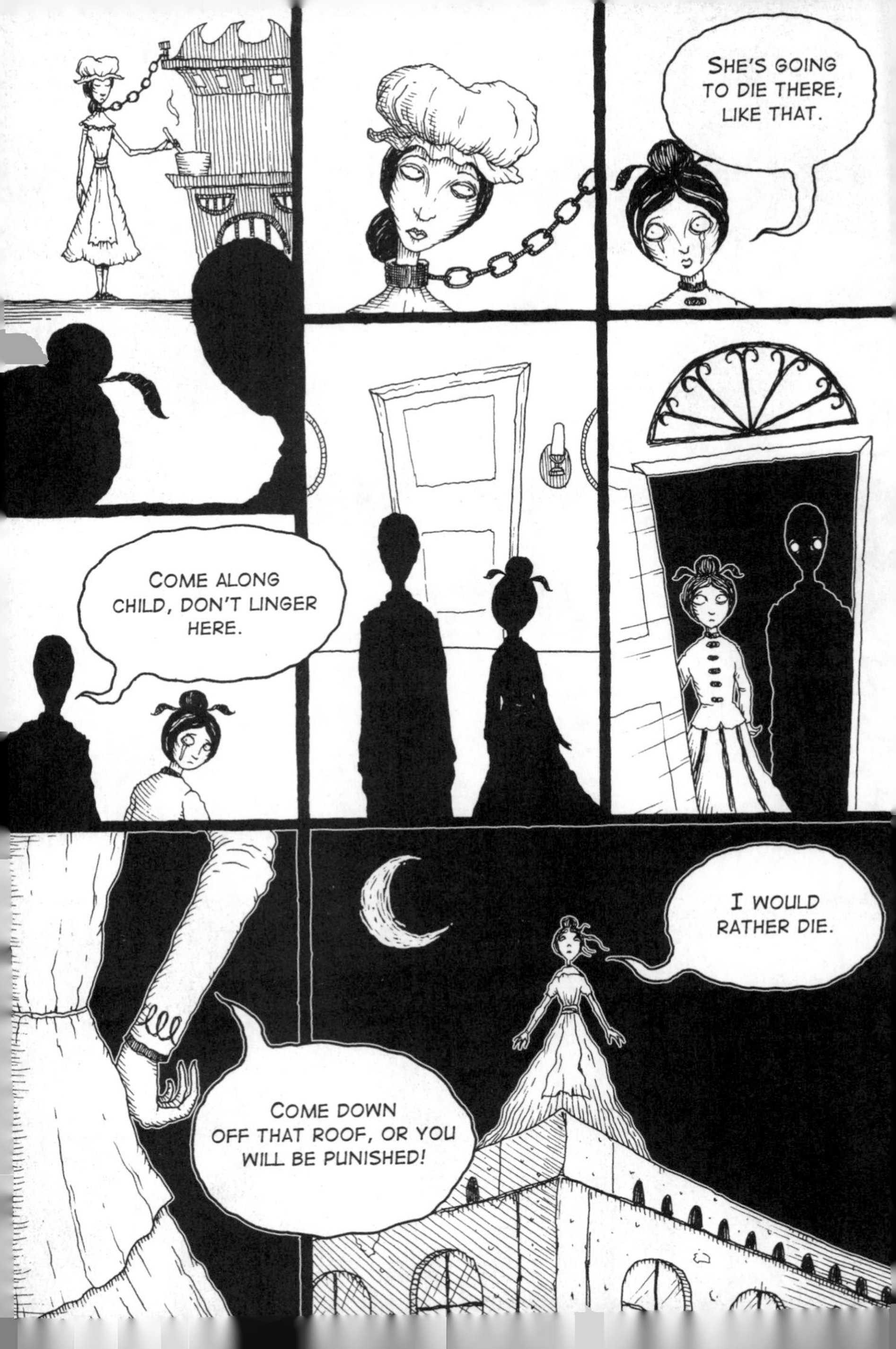
SHE'S GOING TO DIE THERE, LIKE THAT.
COME ALONG CHILD, DON'T LINGER HERE.
COME DOWN OFF THAT ROOF, OR YOU WILL BE PUNISHED!
I WOULD RATHER DIE.

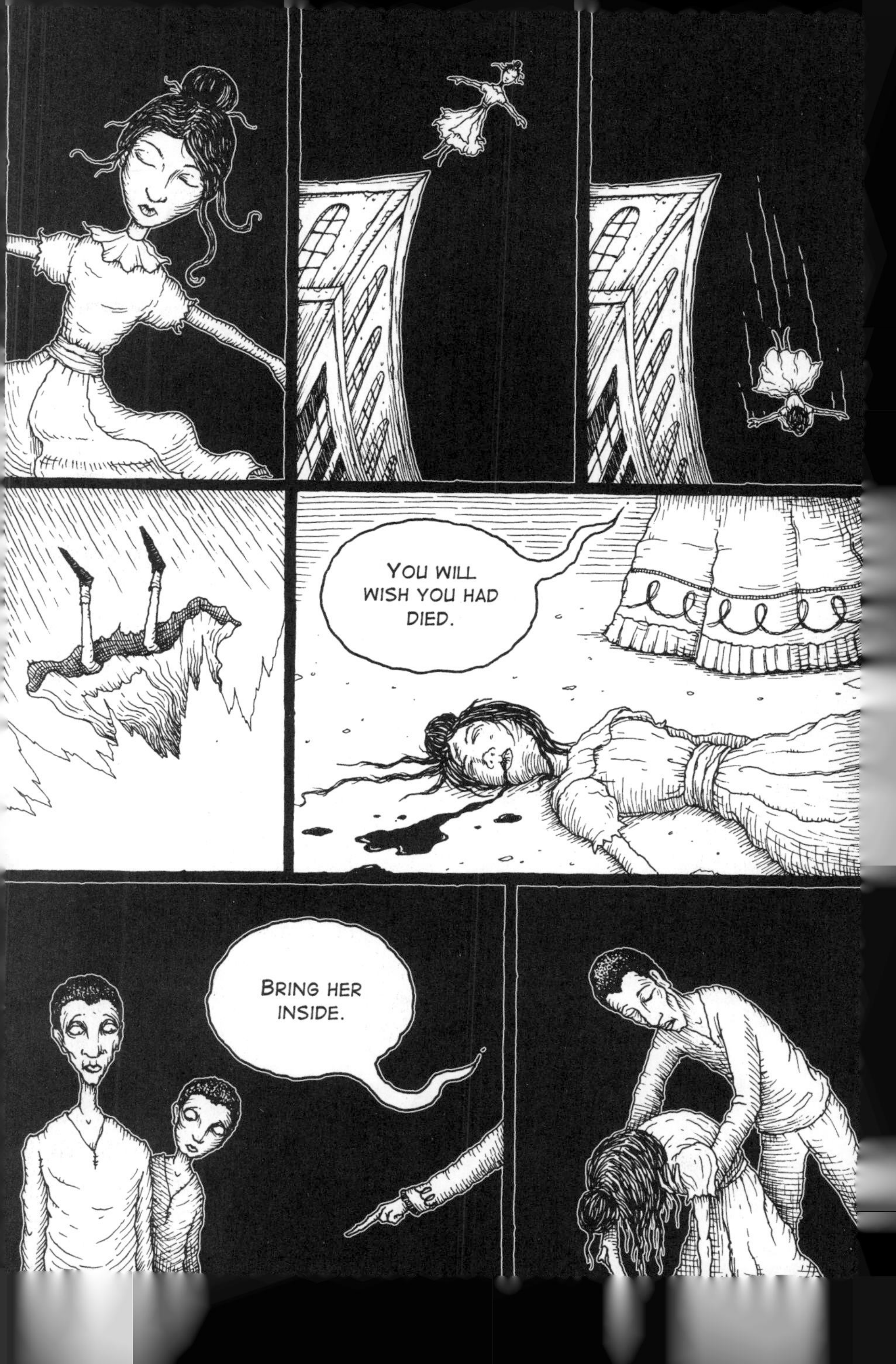
YOU WILL WISH YOU HAD DIED.
BRING HER INSIDE.

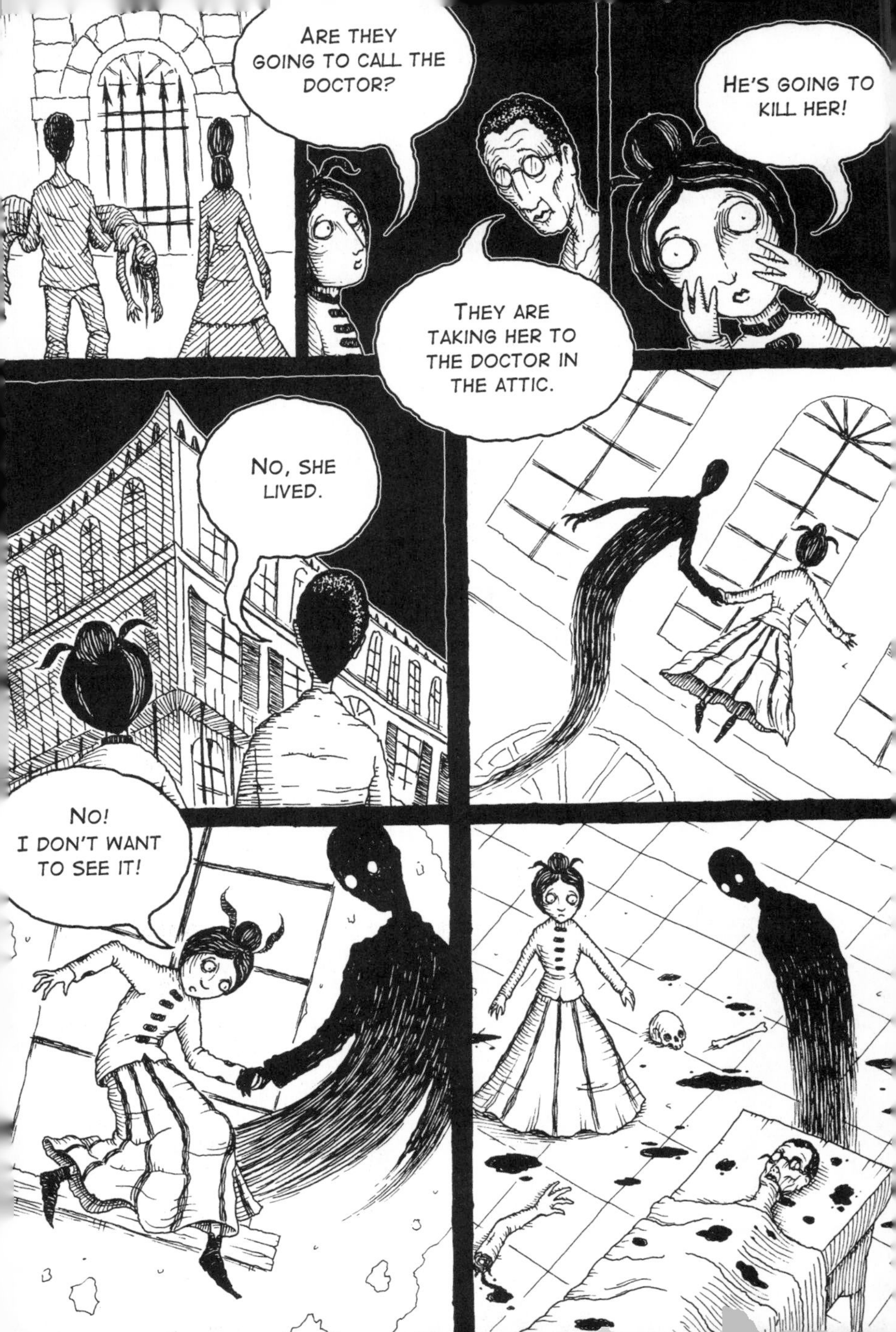
ARE THEY GOING TO CALL THE DOCTOR?
THEY ARE TAKING HER TO THE DOCTOR IN THE ATTIC.
HE'S GOING TO KILL HER!
NO, SHE LIVED.
NO! I DON'T WANT TO SEE IT!

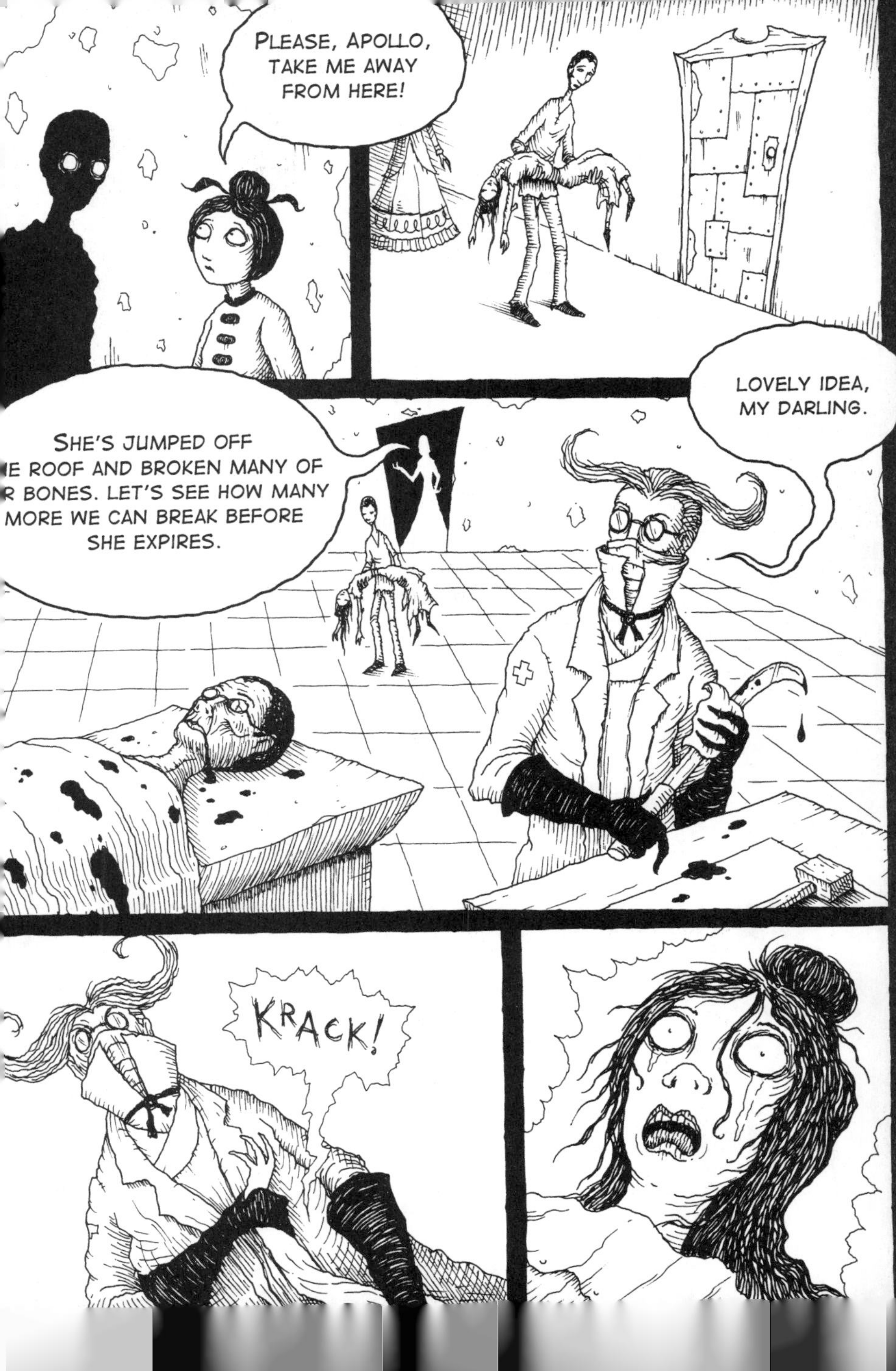
PLEASE, APOLLO, TAKE ME AWAY FROM HERE!
SHE'S JUMPED OFF E ROOF AND BROKEN MANY OF R BONES. LET'S SEE HOW MANY MORE WE CAN BREAK BEFORE SHE EXPIRES.
LOVELY IDEA, MY DARLING.
KRACK!

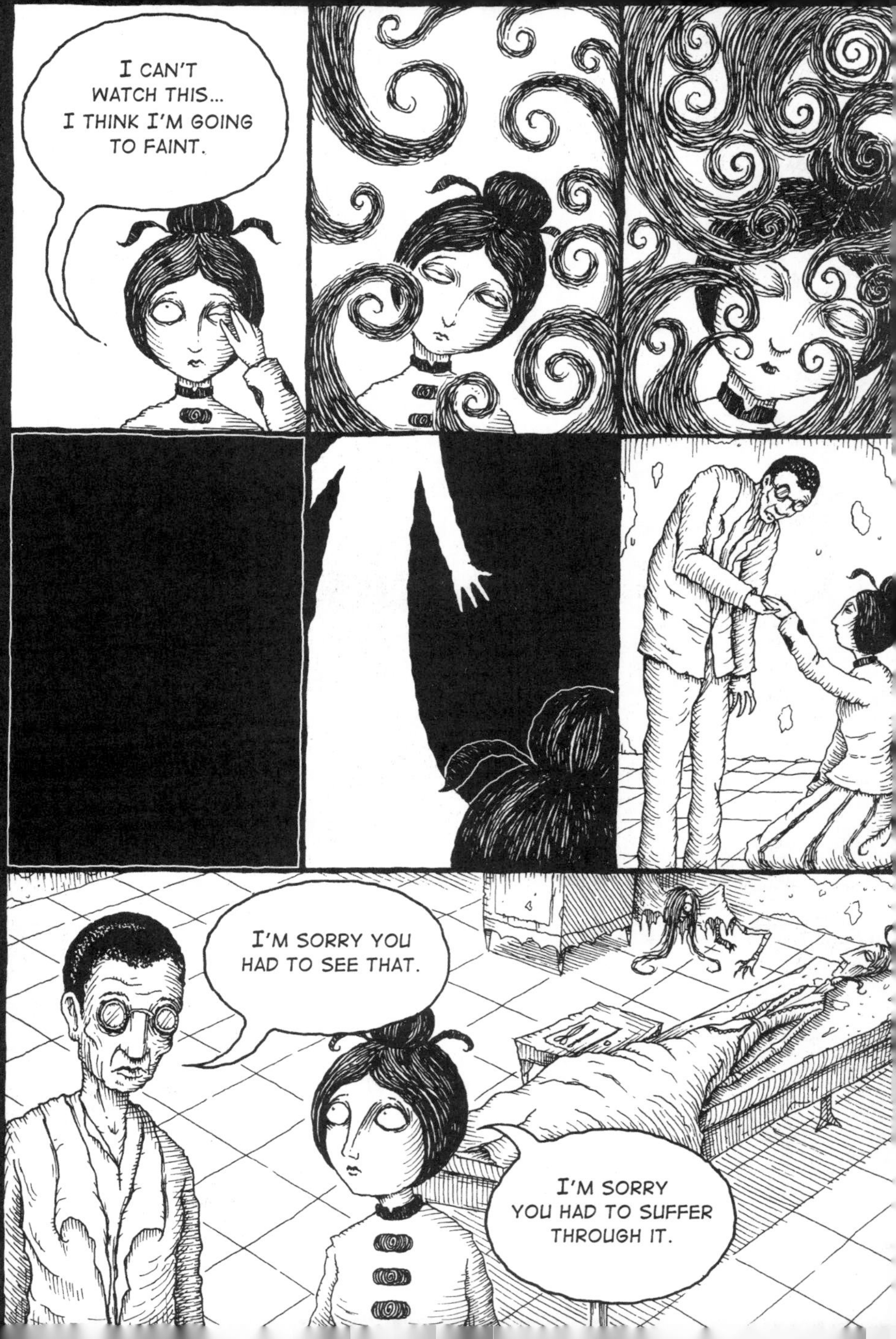
I CAN'T WATCH THIS... I THINK I'M GOING TO FAINT.
I'M SORRY YOU HAD TO SEE THAT.
I'M SORRY YOU HAD TO SUFFER THROUGH IT.

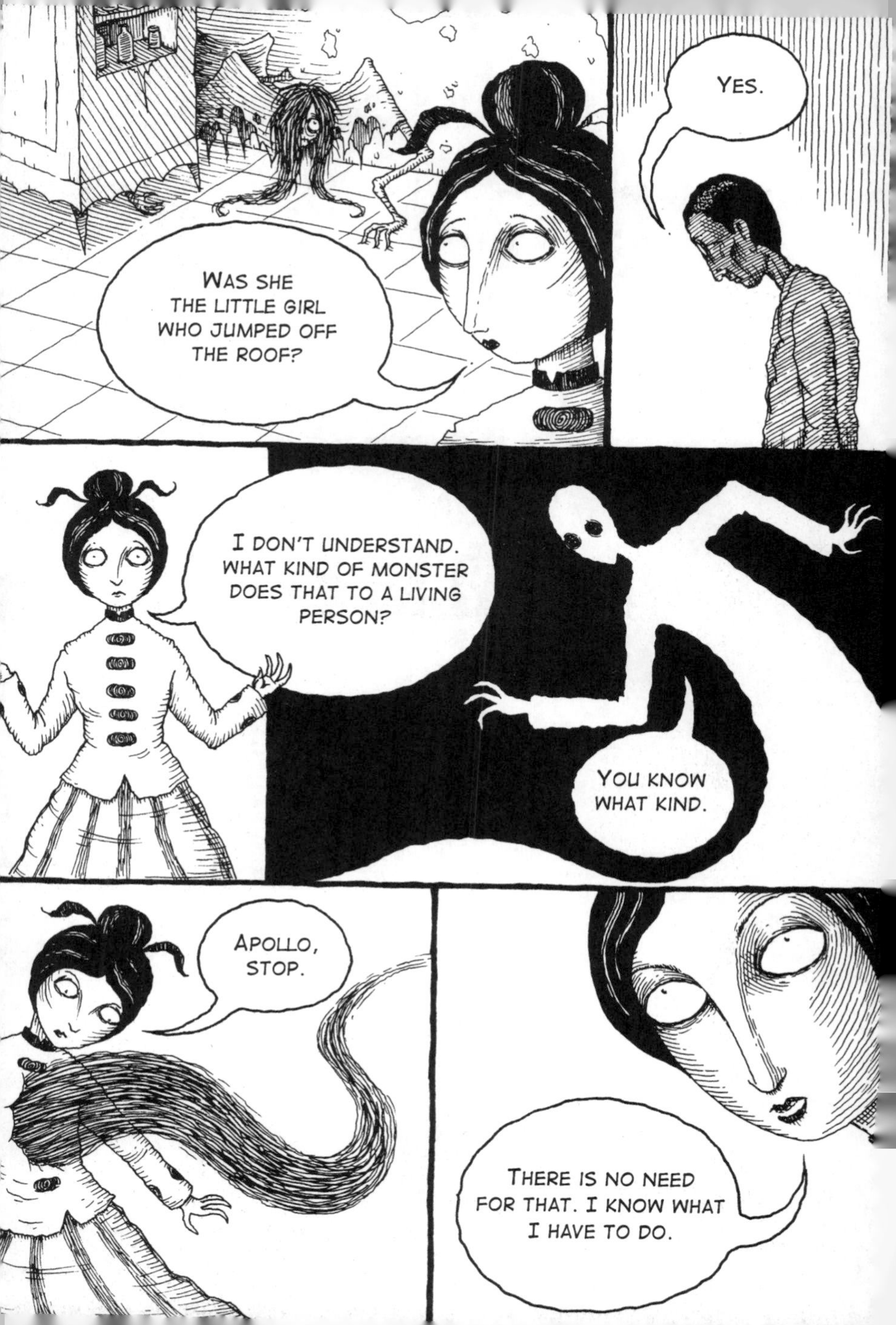
WAS SHE THE LITTLE GIRL WHO JUMPED OFF THE ROOF?
YES.
I DON'T UNDERSTAND. WHAT KIND OF MONSTER DOES THAT TO A LIVING PERSON?
YOU KNOW WHAT KIND.
APOLLO, STOP.
THERE IS NO NEED FOR THAT. I KNOW WHAT I HAVE TO DO.

Chapter 6

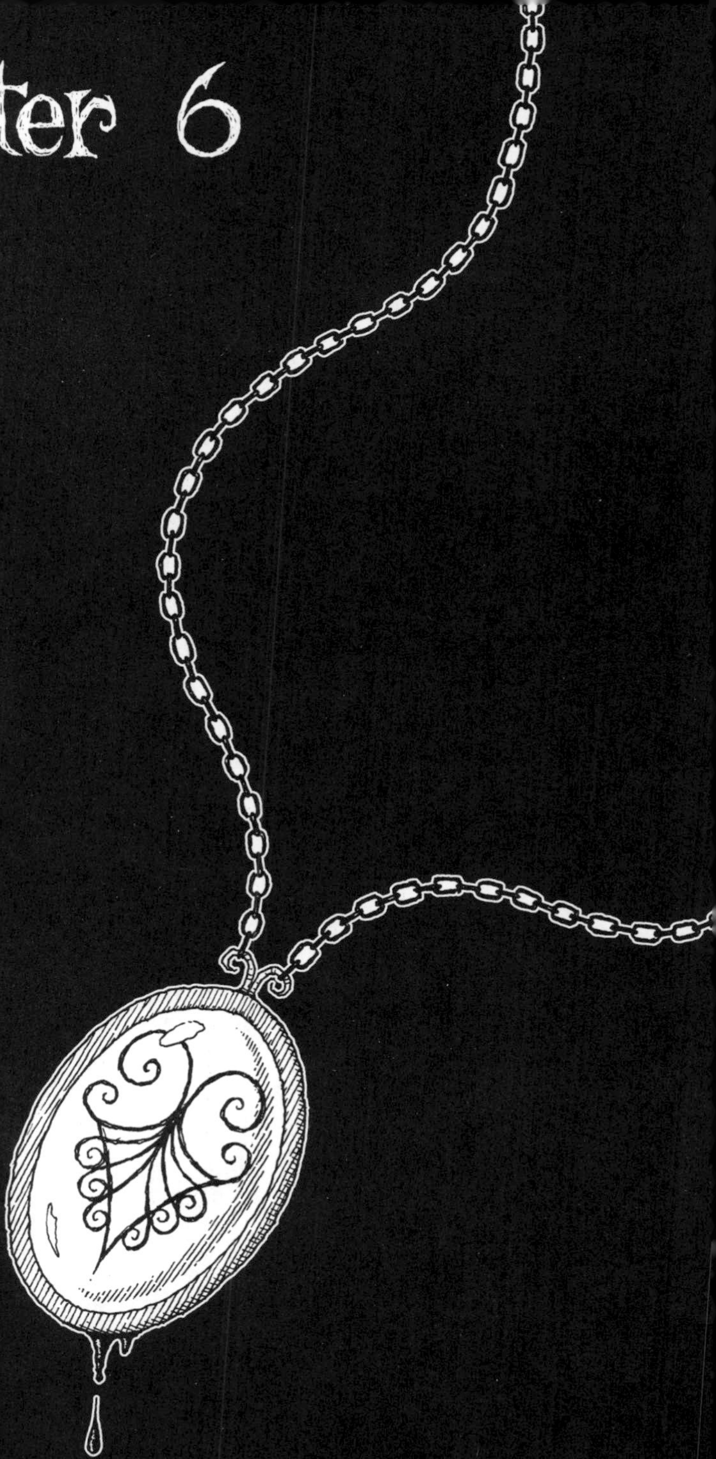

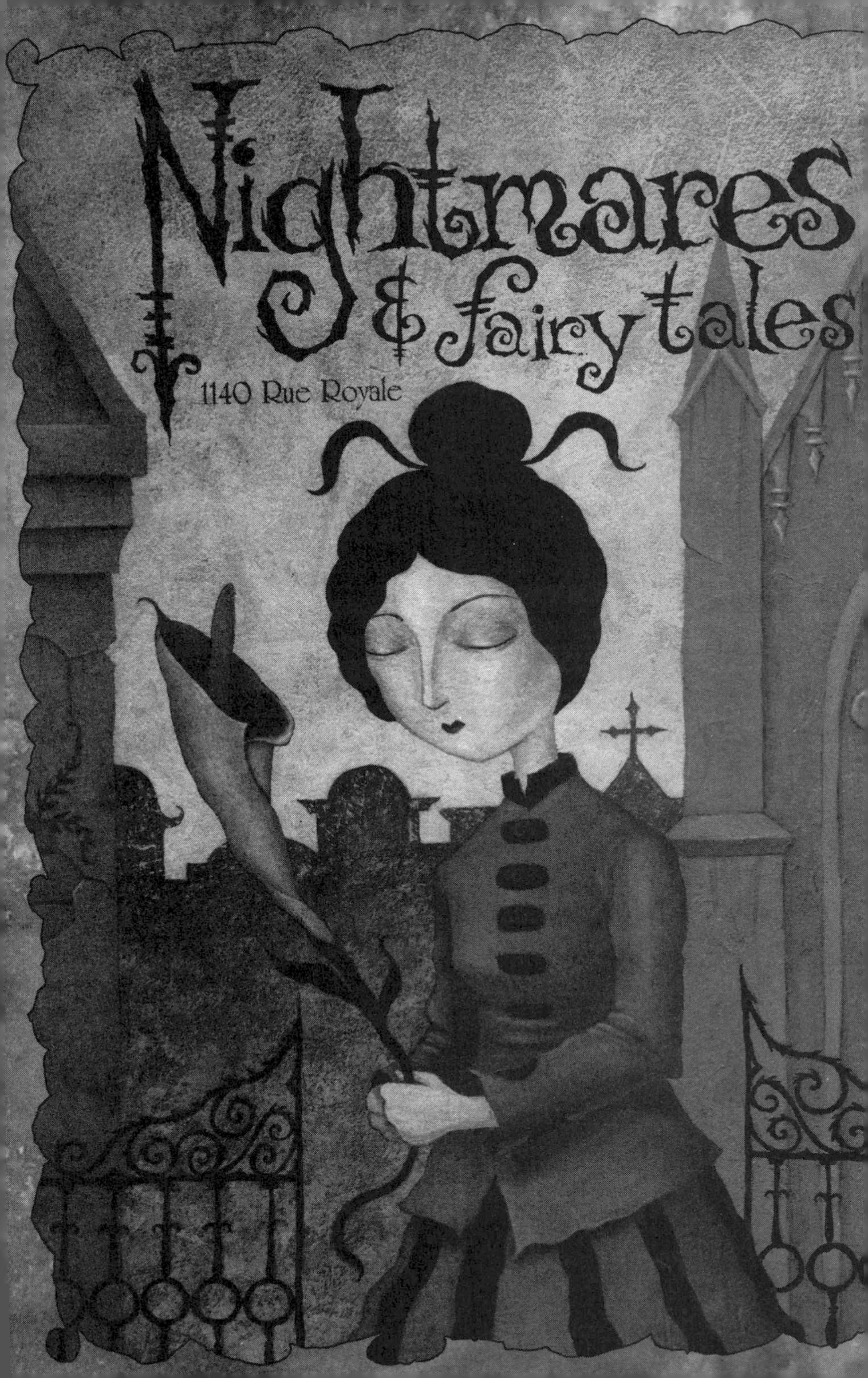
Nightmares & fairy tales
1140 Rue Royale

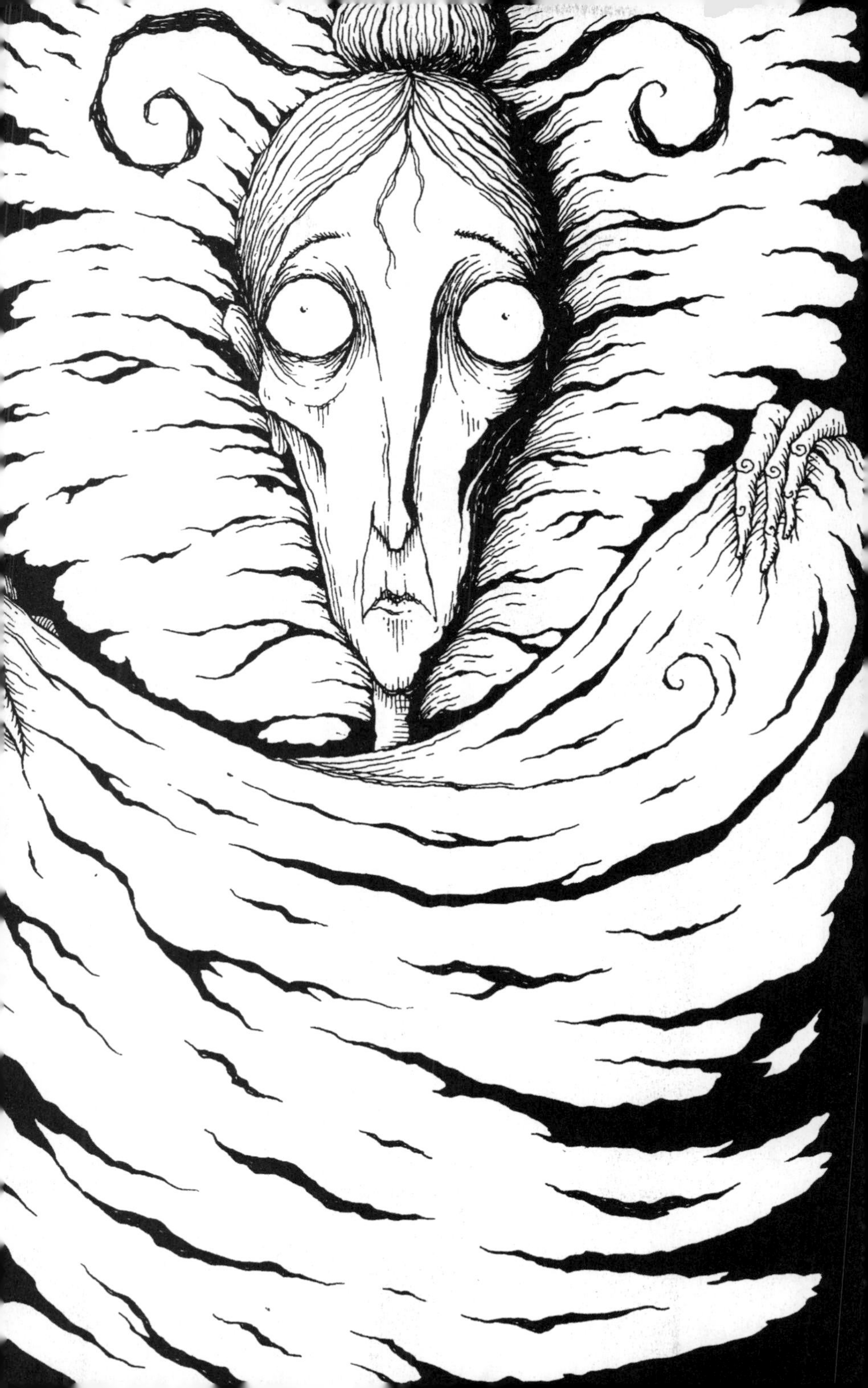

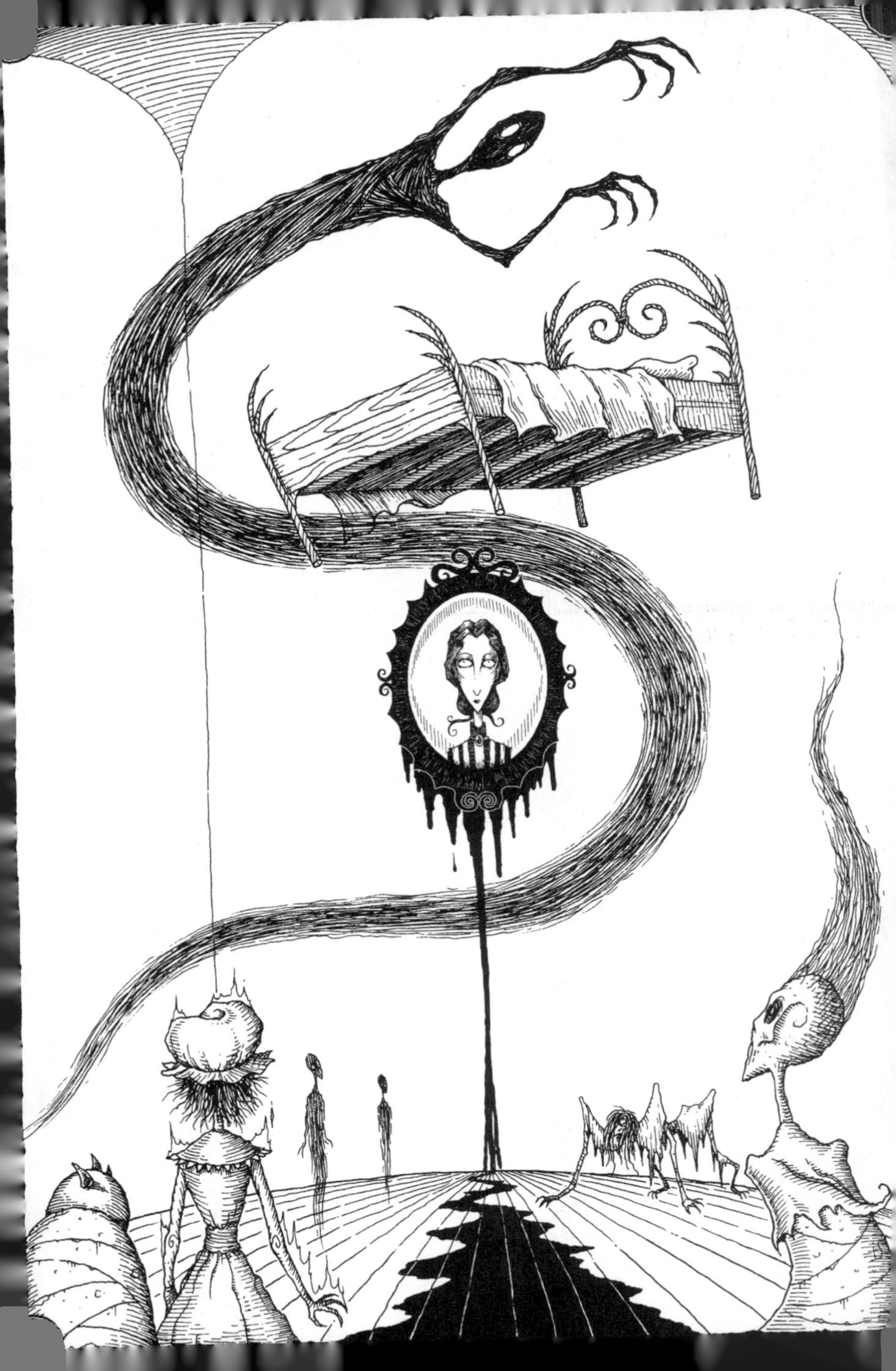

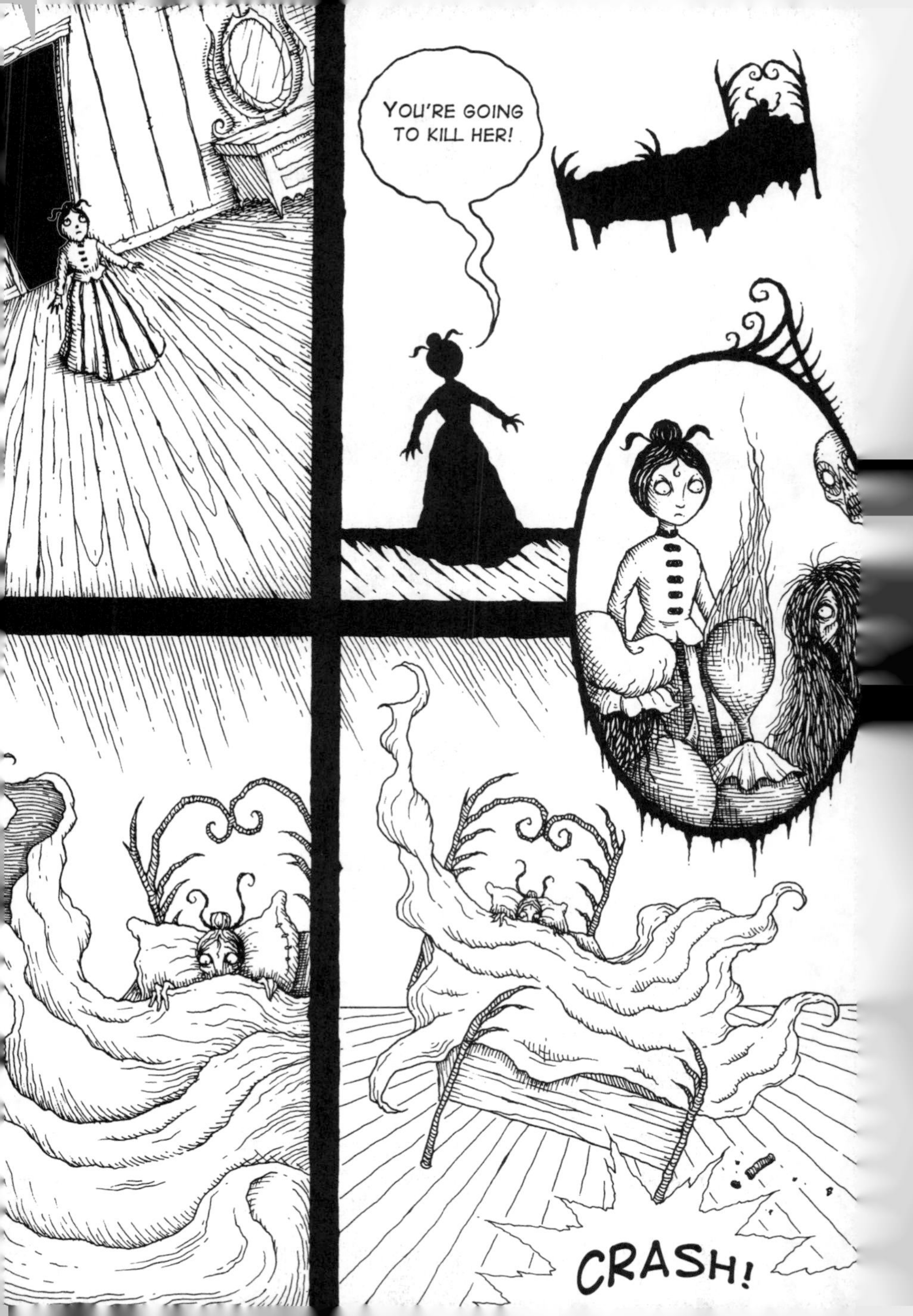
YOU'RE GOING TO KILL HER!
CRASH!

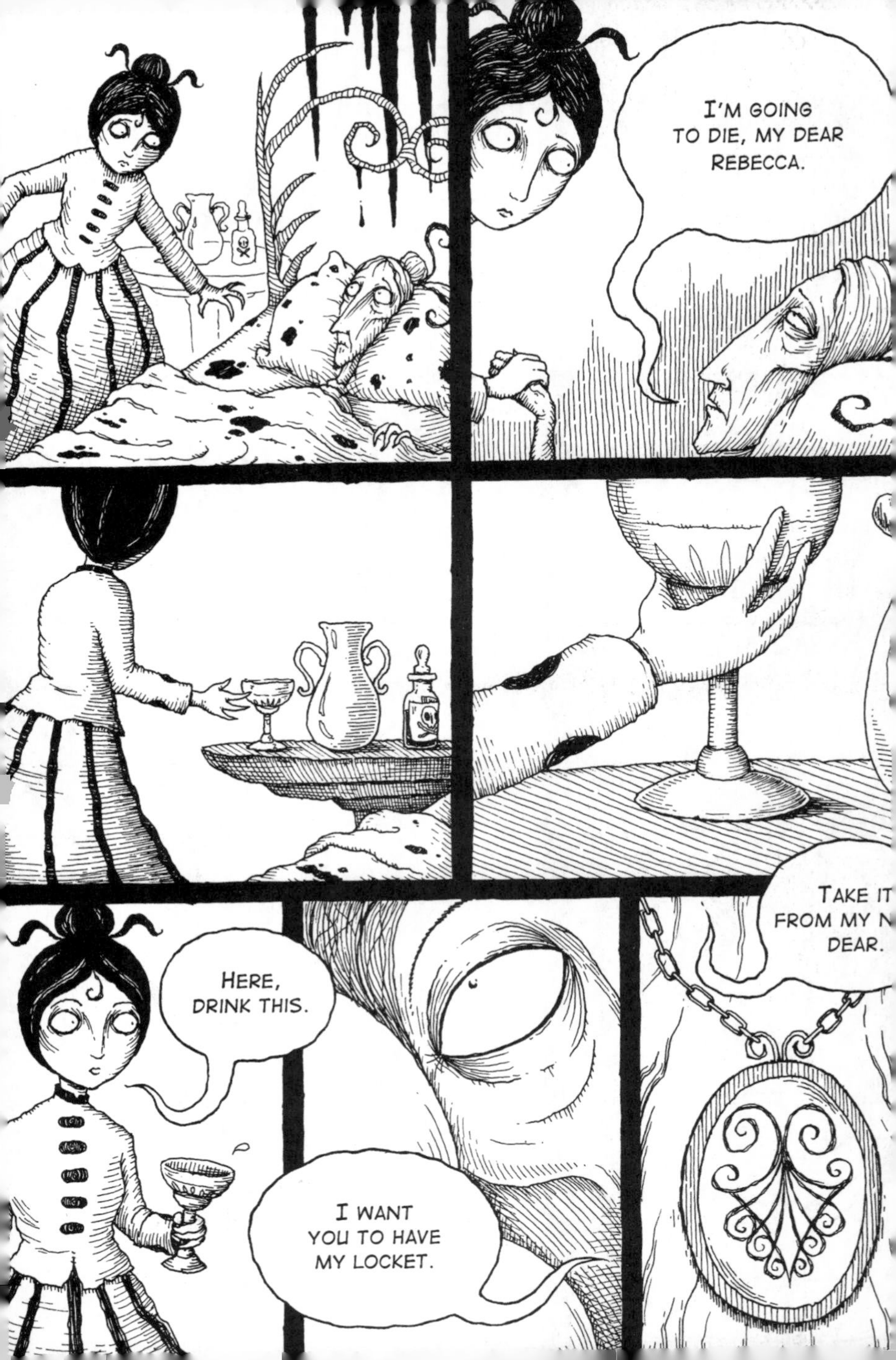
I'M GOING TO DIE, MY DEAR REBECCA.
HERE, DRINK THIS.
I WANT YOU TO HAVE MY LOCKET.
TAKE IT FROM MY N DEAR.

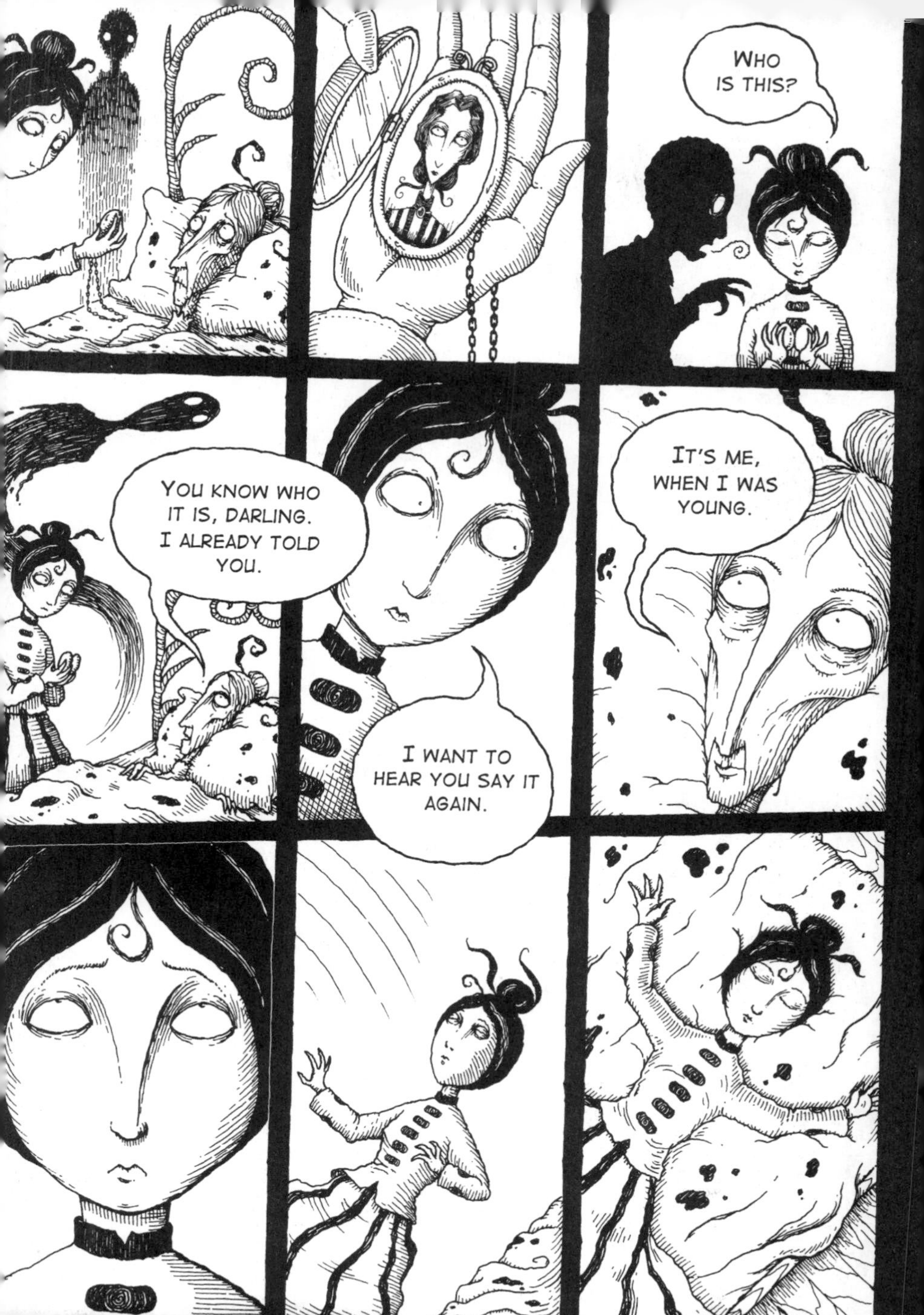
WHO IS THIS?
YOU KNOW WHO IT IS, DARLING. I ALREADY TOLD YOU.
IT'S ME, WHEN I WAS YOUNG.
I WANT TO HEAR YOU SAY IT AGAIN.

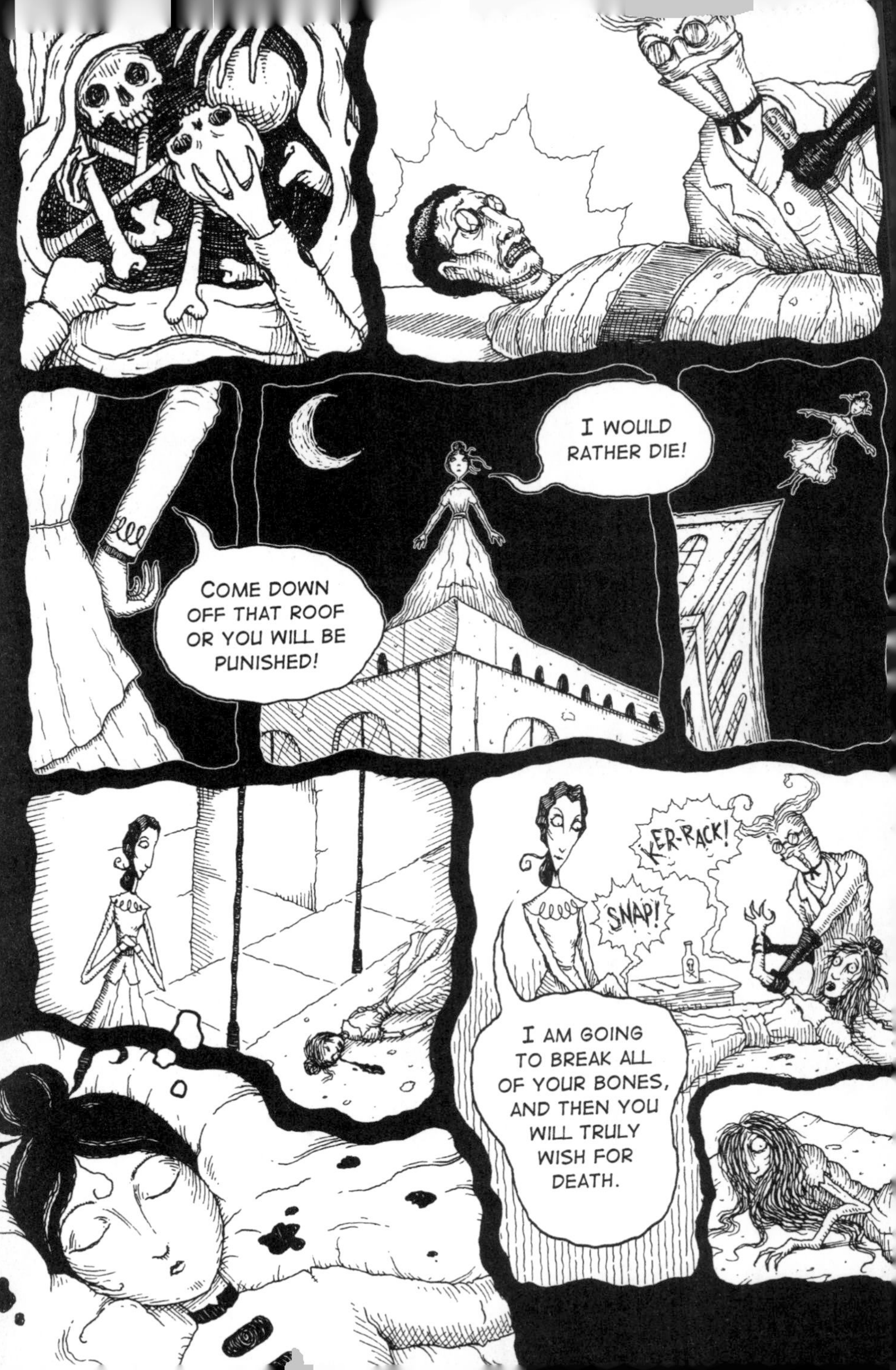
I WOULD RATHER DIE!
COME DOWN OFF THAT ROOF OR YOU WILL BE PUNISHED!
KER-RACK!
SNAP!
I AM GOING TO BREAK ALL OF YOUR BONES, AND THEN YOU WILL TRULY WISH FOR DEATH.

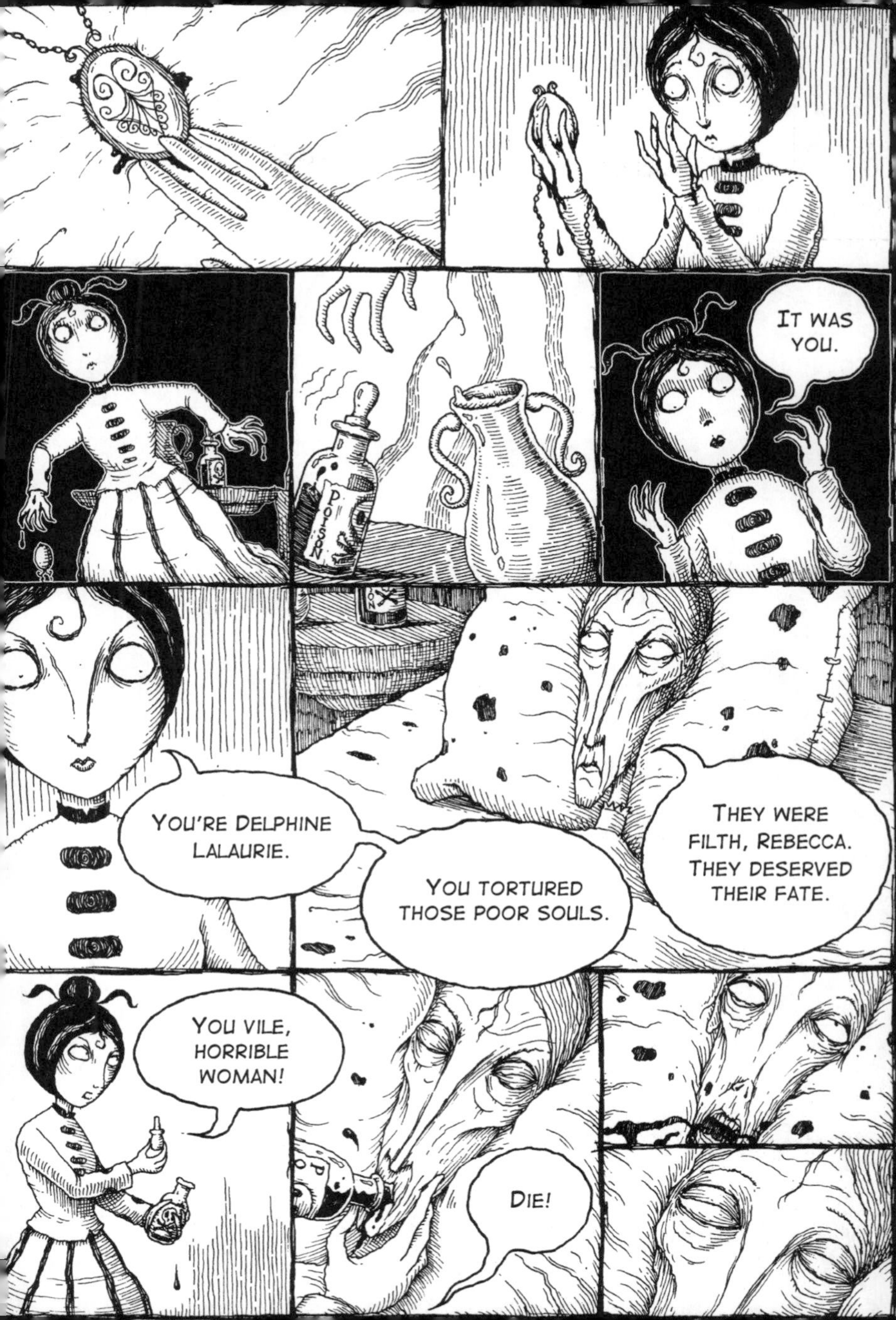

It was you.
You're Delphine Lalaurie.
You tortured those poor souls.
They were filth, Rebecca. They deserved their fate.
You vile, horrible woman!
Die!

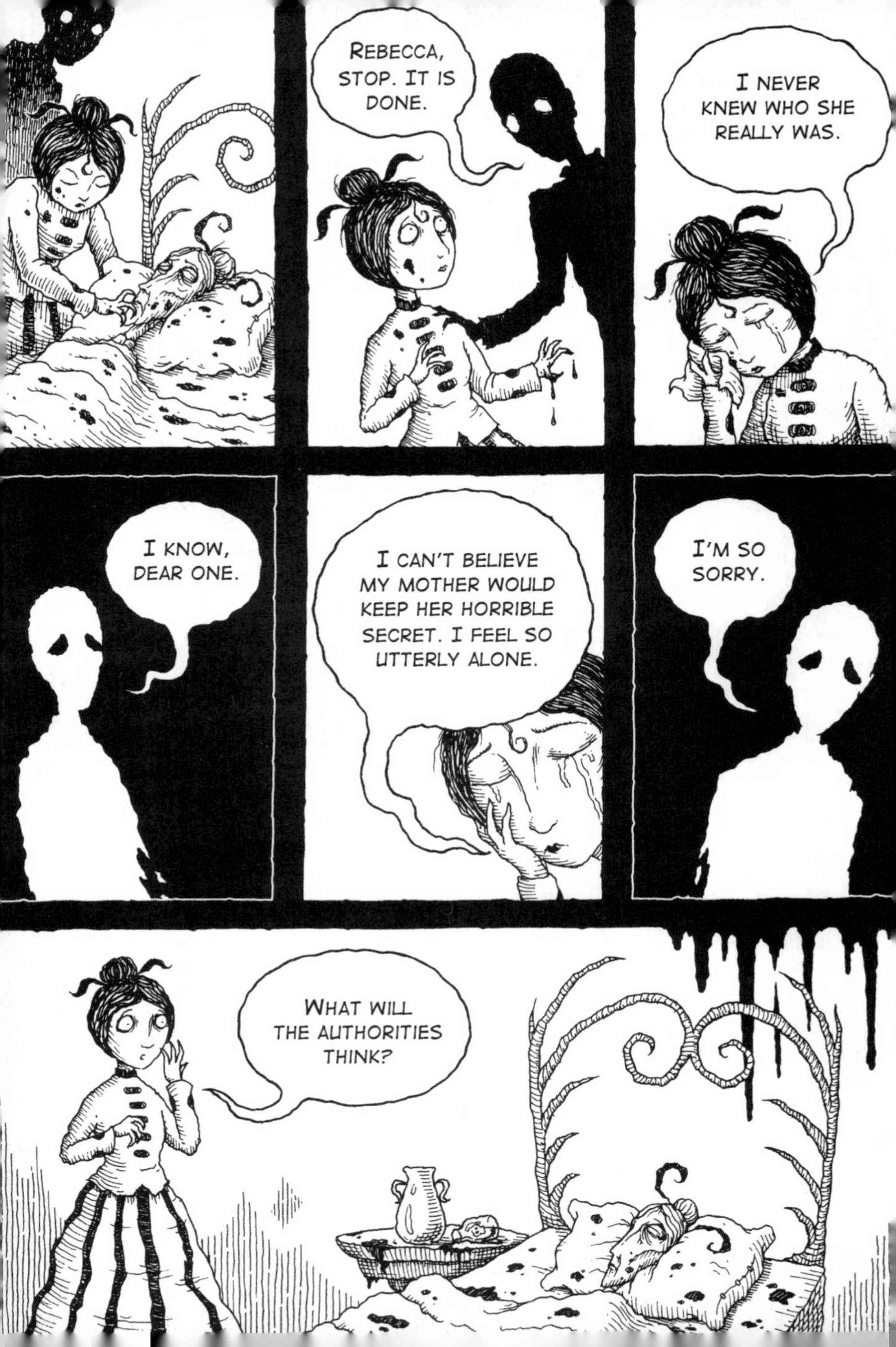
REBECCA, STOP. IT IS DONE.
I NEVER KNEW WHO SHE REALLY WAS.
I KNOW, DEAR ONE.
I CAN'T BELIEVE MY MOTHER WOULD KEEP HER HORRIBLE SECRET. I FEEL SO UTTERLY ALONE.
I'M SO SORRY.
WHAT WILL THE AUTHORITIES THINK?

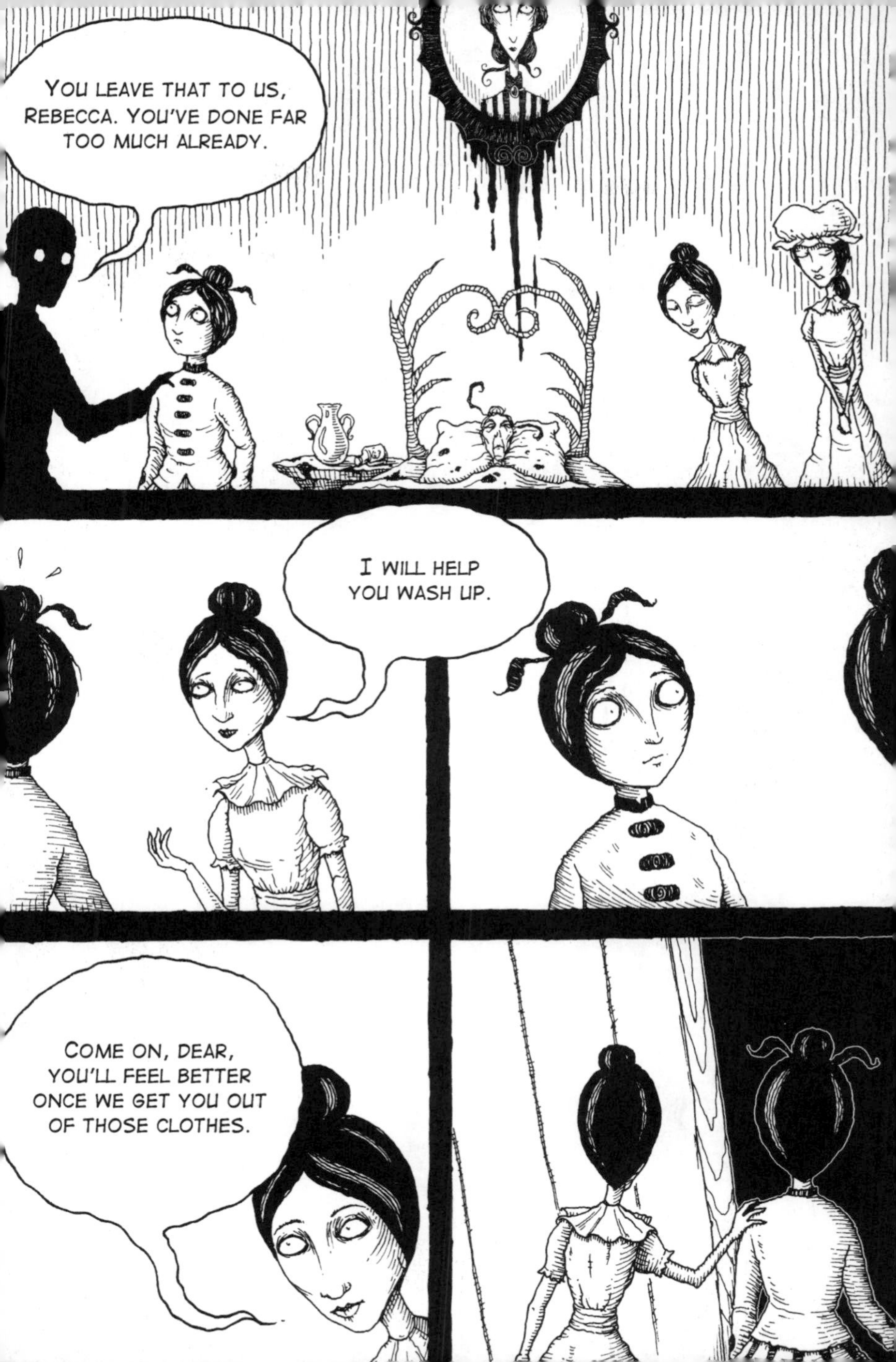
YOU LEAVE THAT TO US, REBECCA. YOU'VE DONE FAR TOO MUCH ALREADY.
I WILL HELP YOU WASH UP.
COME ON, DEAR, YOU'LL FEEL BETTER ONCE WE GET YOU OUT OF THOSE CLOTHES.

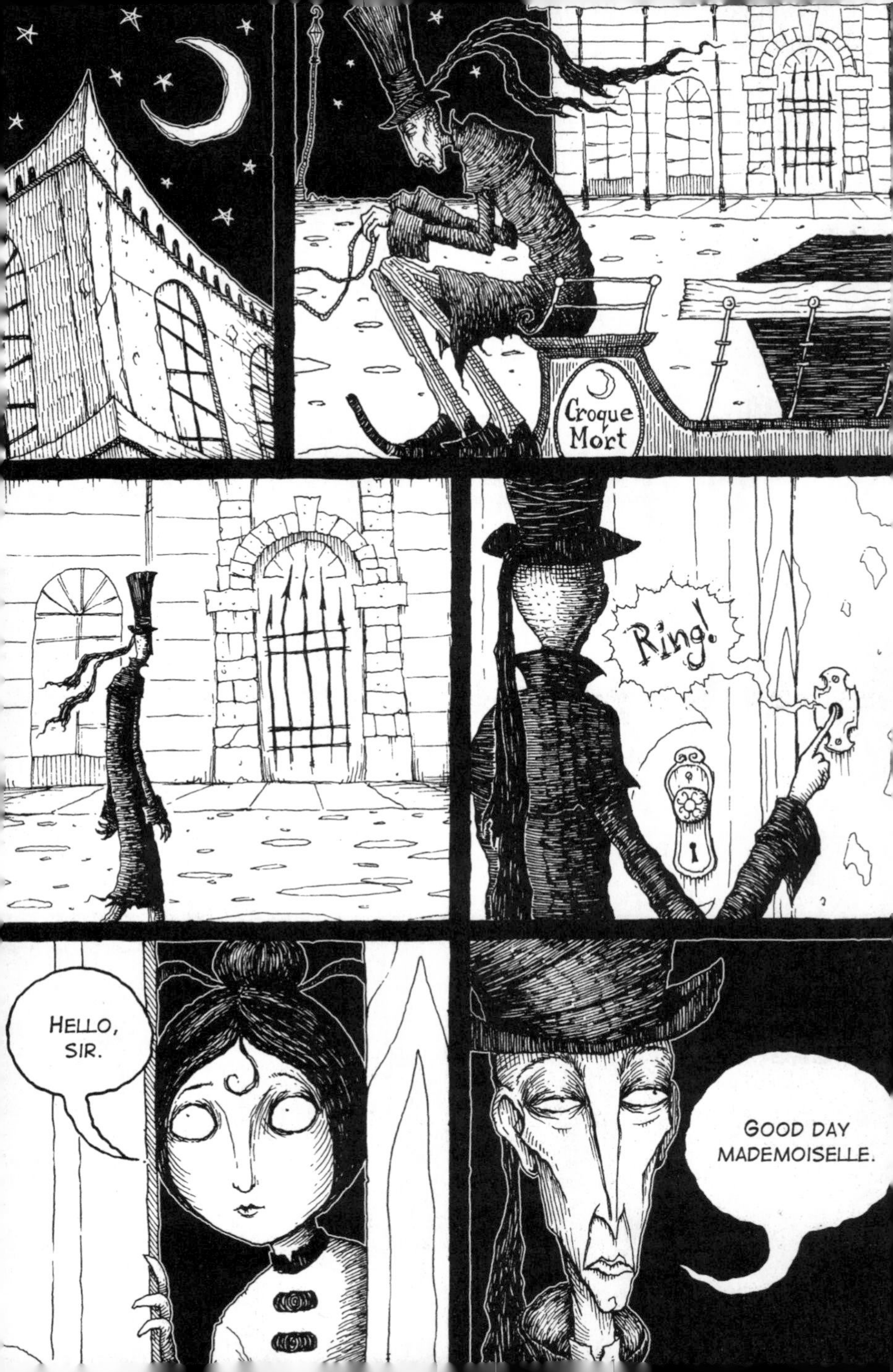
Croque Mort
Ring!
HELLO, SIR.
GOOD DAY MADEMOISELLE.

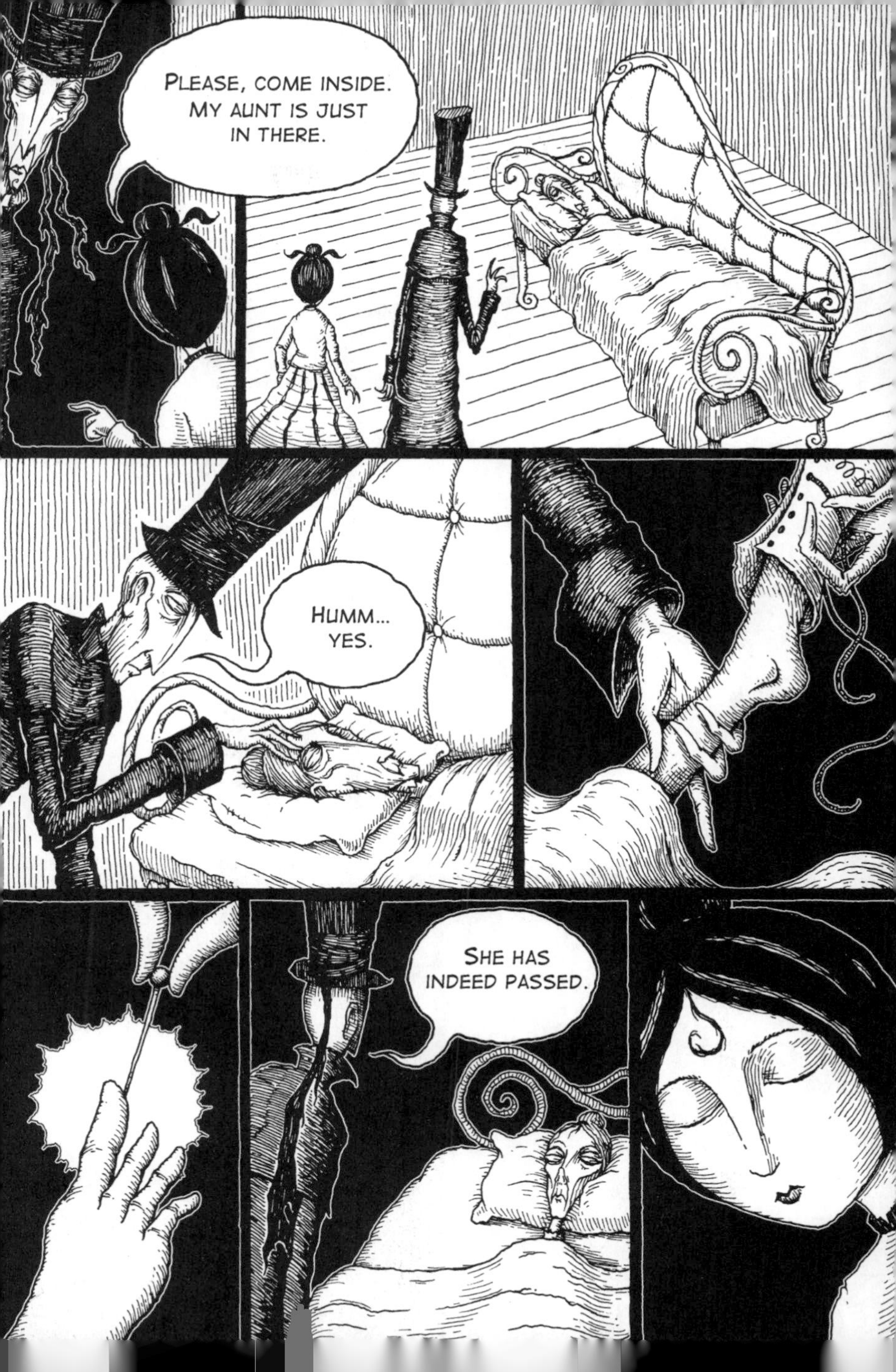
PLEASE, COME INSIDE. MY AUNT IS JUST IN THERE.
HUMM... YES.
SHE HAS INDEED PASSED.

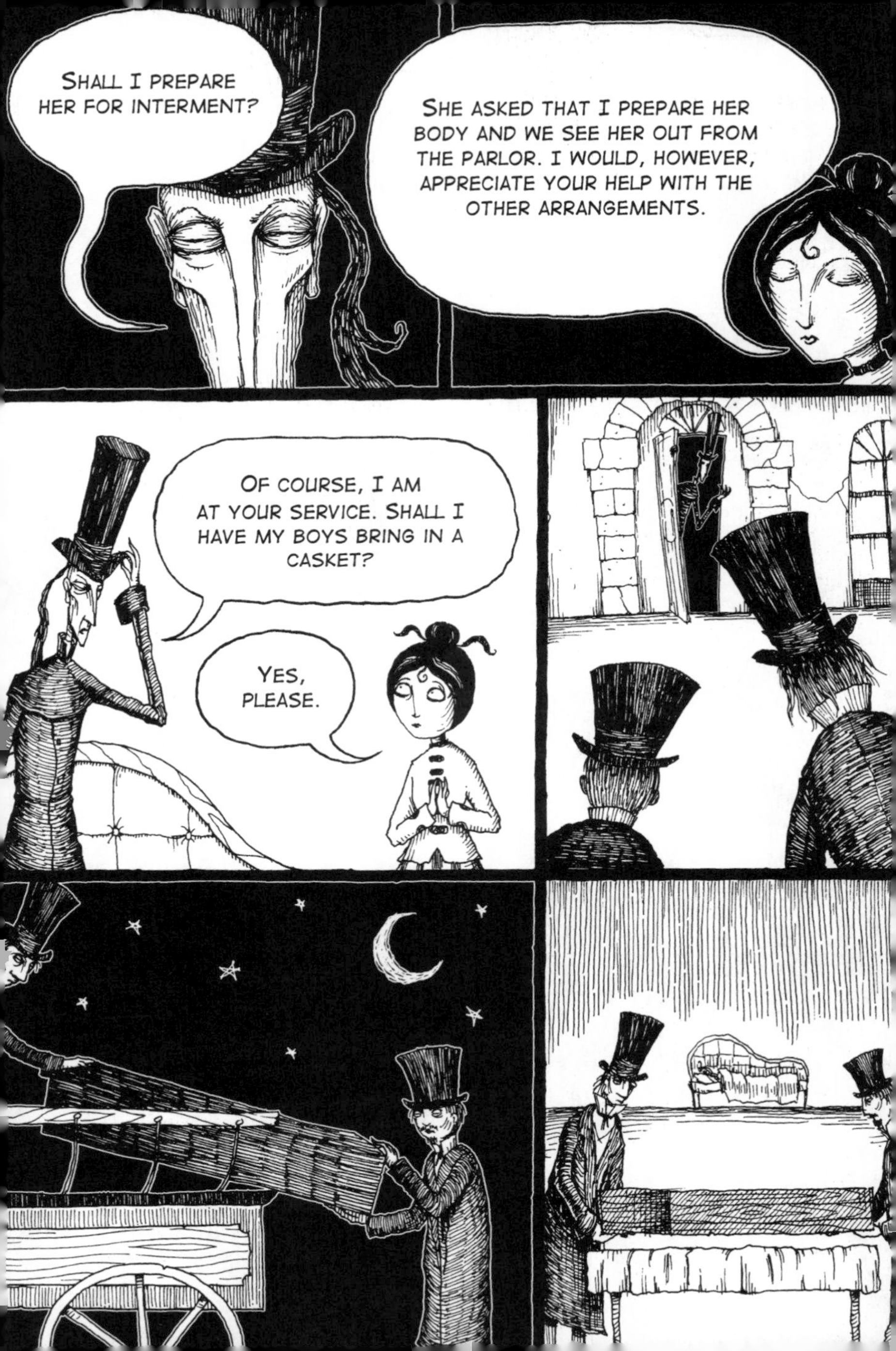
SHALL I PREPARE HER FOR INTERMENT?
SHE ASKED THAT I PREPARE HER BODY AND WE SEE HER OUT FROM THE PARLOR. I WOULD, HOWEVER, APPRECIATE YOUR HELP WITH THE OTHER ARRANGEMENTS.
OF COURSE, I AM AT YOUR SERVICE. SHALL I HAVE MY BOYS BRING IN A CASKET?
YES, PLEASE.

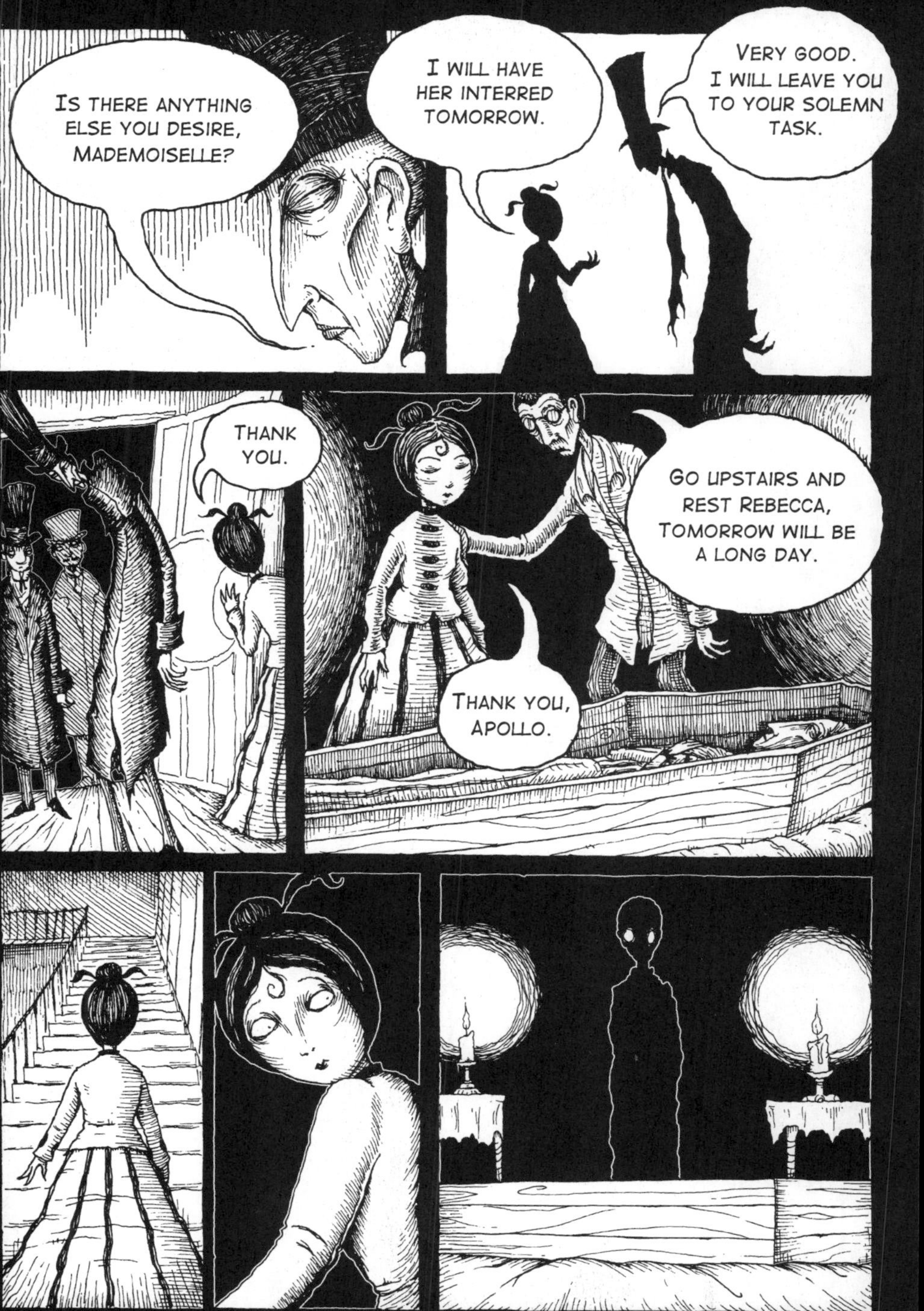
IS THERE ANYTHING ELSE YOU DESIRE, MADEMOISELLE?
I WILL HAVE HER INTERRED TOMORROW.
VERY GOOD. I WILL LEAVE YOU TO YOUR SOLEMN TASK.
THANK YOU.
GO UPSTAIRS AND REST REBECCA, TOMORROW WILL BE A LONG DAY.
THANK YOU, APOLLO.

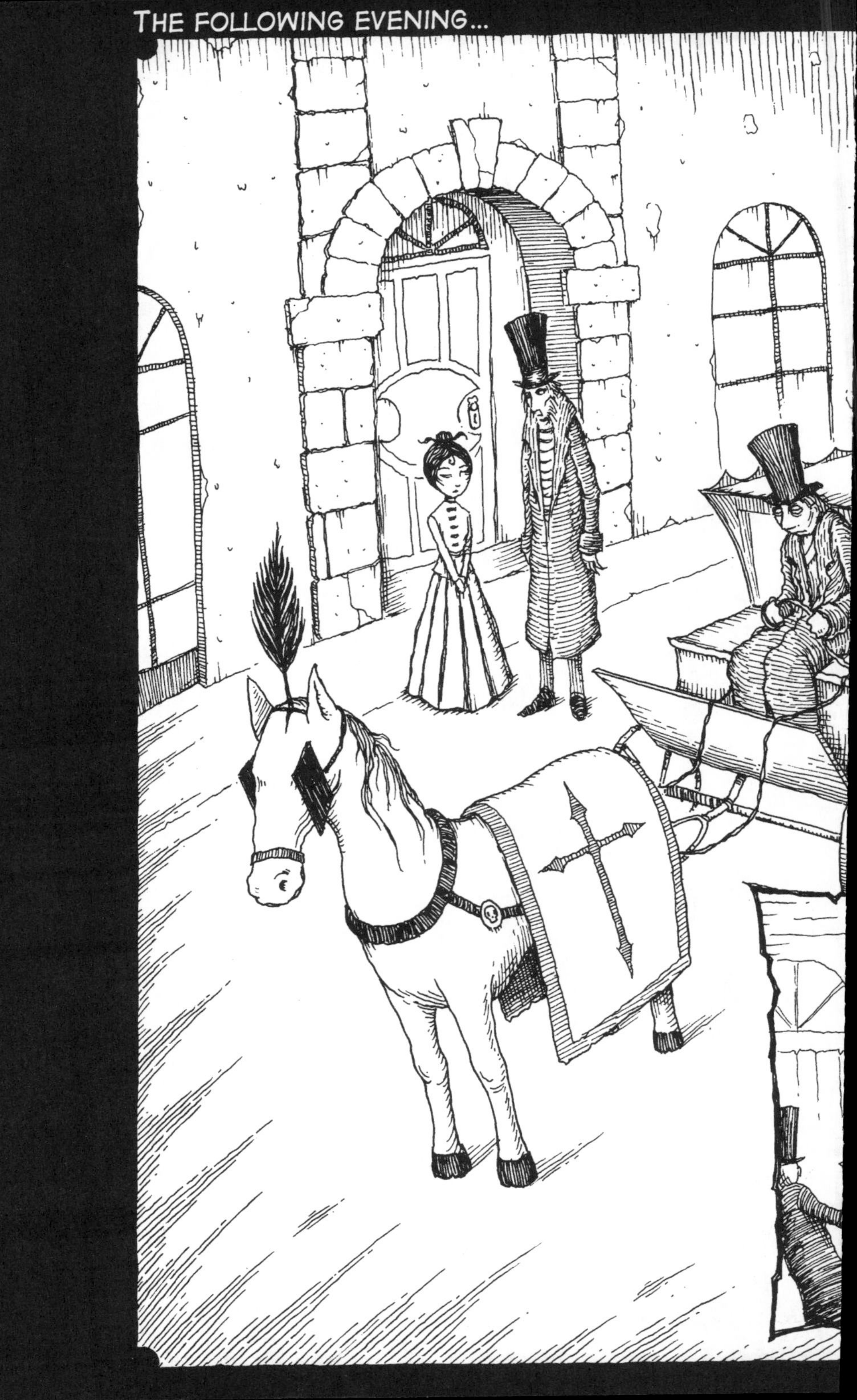
THE FOLLOWING EVENING...

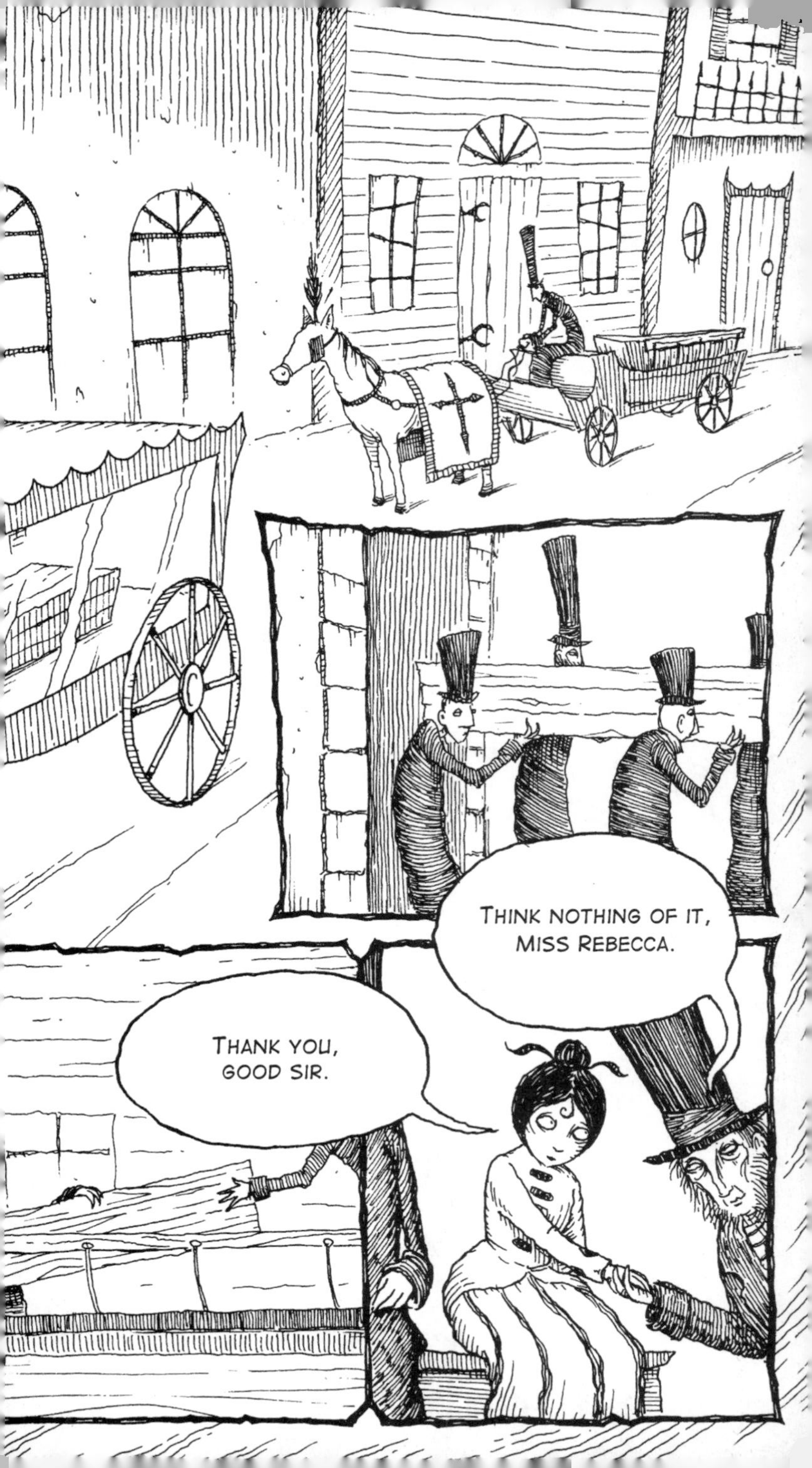
THINK NOTHING OF IT, MISS REBECCA.
THANK YOU, GOOD SIR.

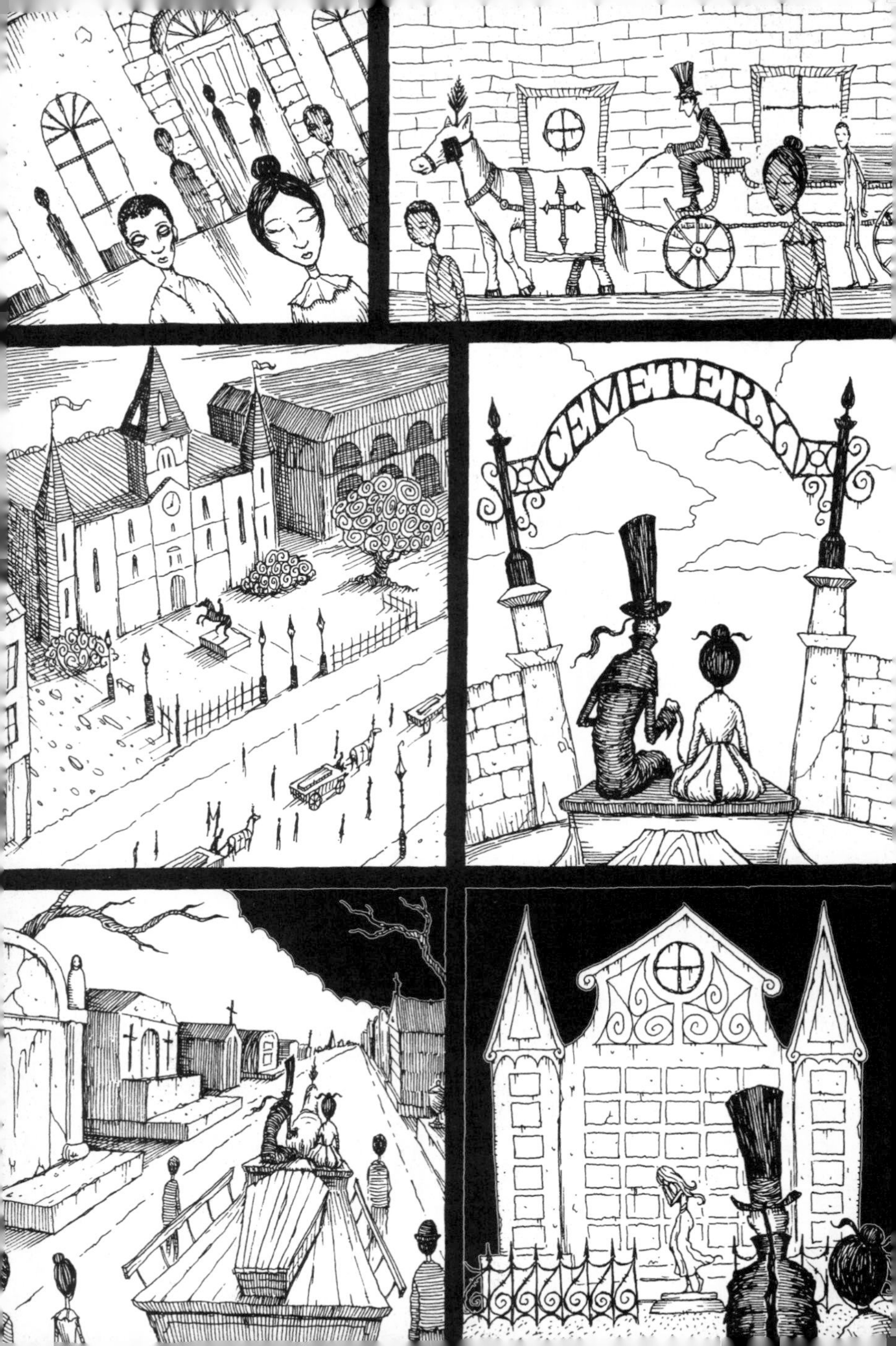
CEMETERY

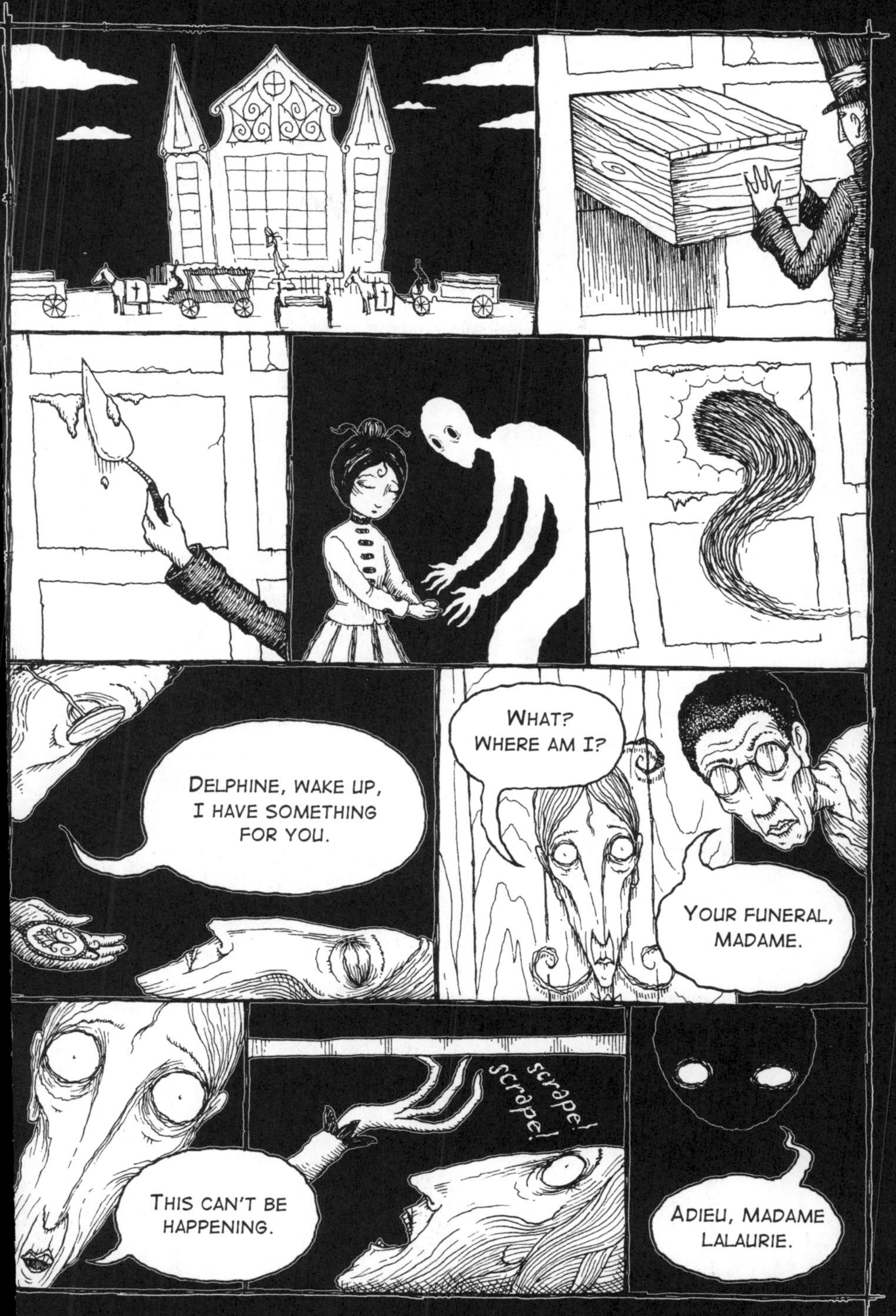
DELPHINE, WAKE UP, I HAVE SOMETHING FOR YOU.
WHAT? WHERE AM I?
YOUR FUNERAL, MADAME.
THIS CAN'T BE HAPPENING.
scrape! scrape!
ADIEU, MADAME LALAURIE.

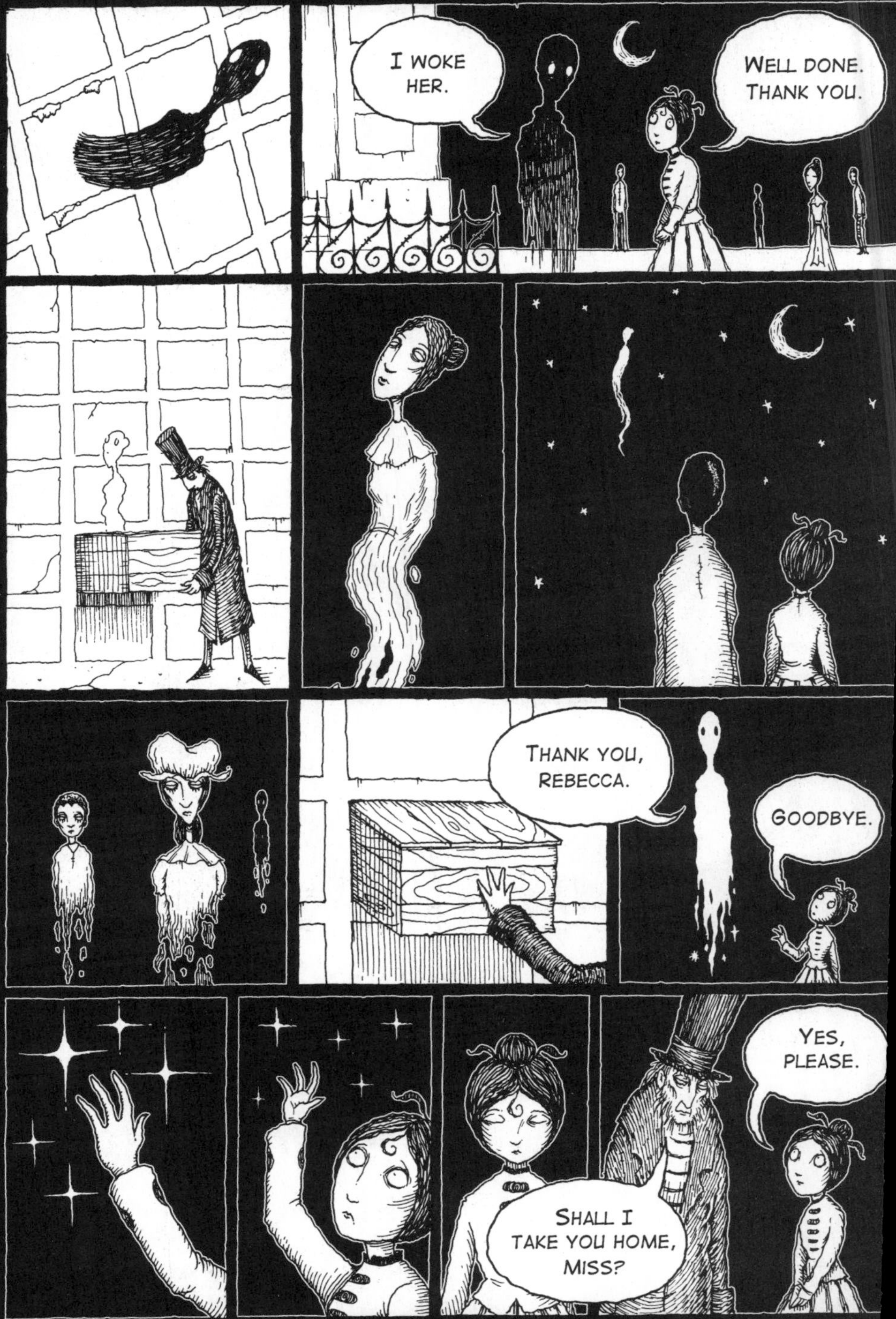
I WOKE HER.
WELL DONE. THANK YOU.
THANK YOU, REBECCA.
GOODBYE.
SHALL I TAKE YOU HOME, MISS?
YES, PLEASE.

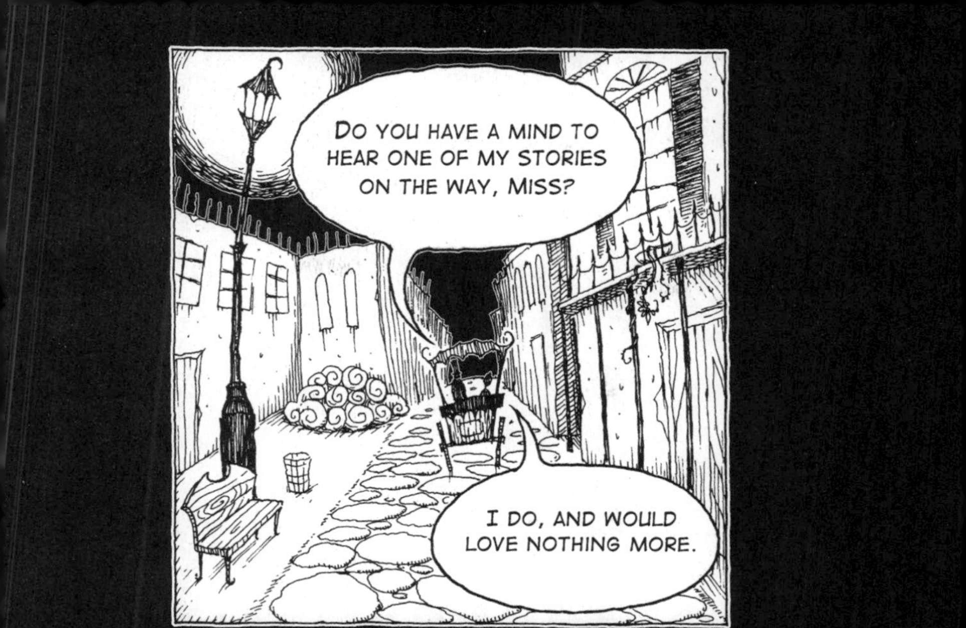
DO YOU HAVE A MIND TO HEAR ONE OF MY STORIES ON THE WAY, MISS?
I DO, AND WOULD LOVE NOTHING MORE.

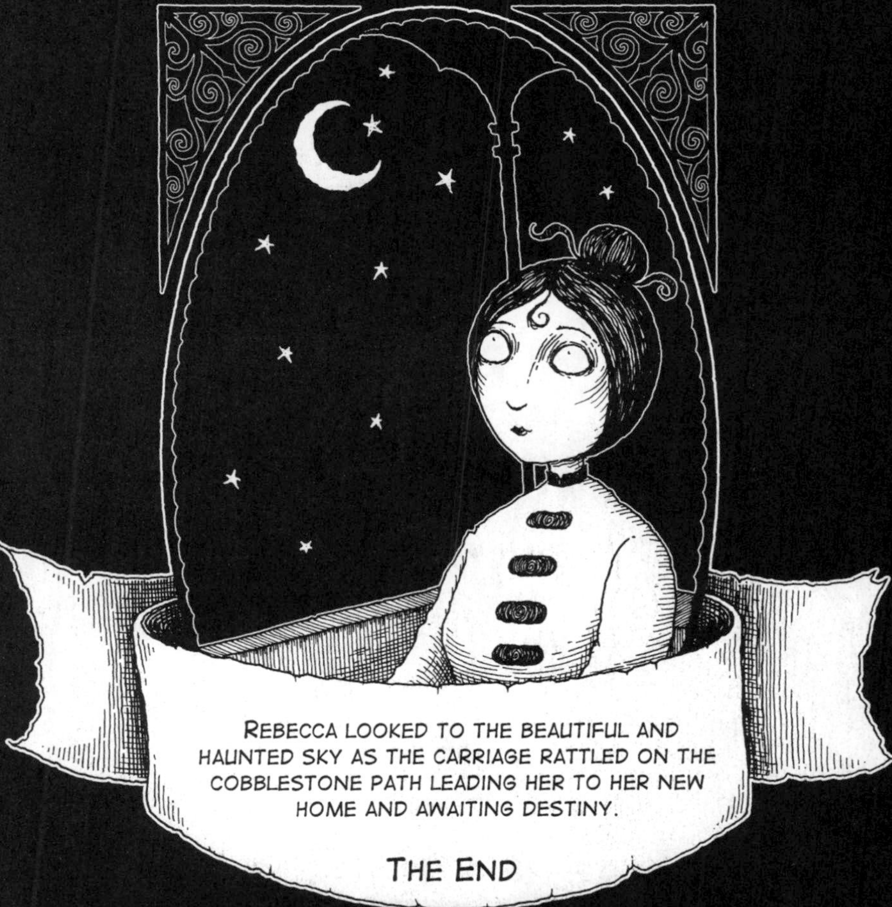
REBECCA LOOKED TO THE BEAUTIFUL AND HAUNTED SKY AS THE CARRIAGE RATTLED ON THE COBBLESTONE PATH LEADING HER TO HER NEW HOME AND AWAITING DESTINY.
THE END

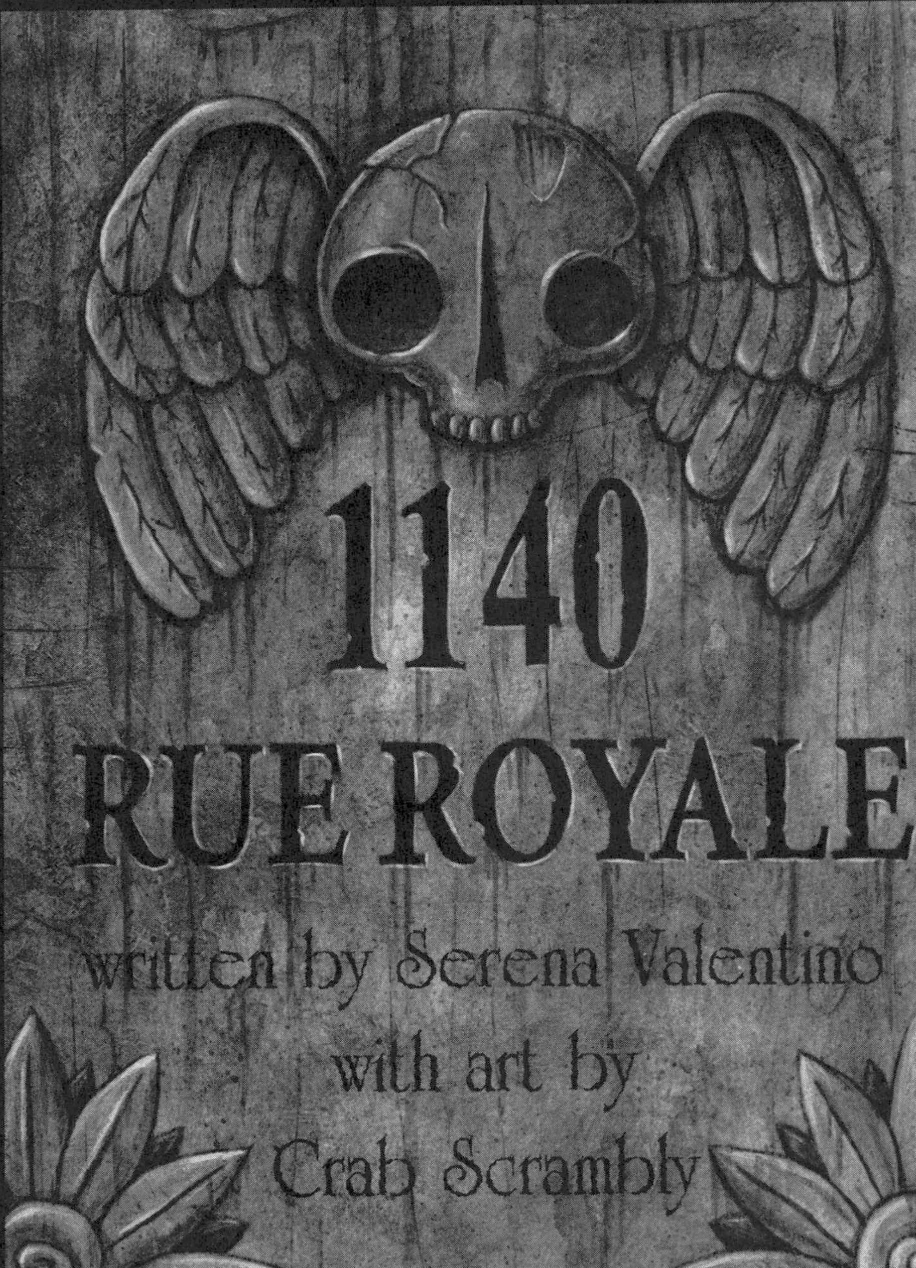
1140
RUE ROYALE
written by Serena Valentino
with art by
Crab Scrambly

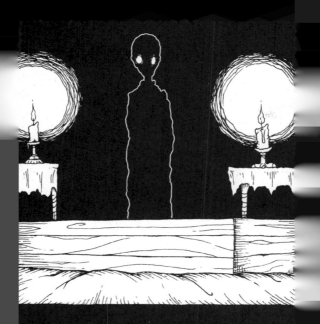

A VALENTINO'S ACKNOWLEDG

stis: for her love, inspiration and enc
ns: I wrote this book for you. Eric Russ
upport. Jim Fitzmorris: for inspiring m
Renewal of Purpose. Crab Scrambly: yo
pect and appreciation. Jhonen Vasque
s and the use of your scanner. Dan Vado,
eb Moskyok, Eleanor Lawson, Joe Naka
like Moss and Joshua Archer: for being s
th. My friends & family: for your love a
rs: I appreciate you more than you co

B SCRAMBLY'S ACKNOWLEDGEN

r use of his giant mechanical thing, Mik
tly shot the first cover, and the Goldber
support.